JESUS'
DOCTRINE
—— OF ——
MARRIAGE

PUBLISHING

ISBN: 978-1-966954-65-1 (paperback)
ISBN: 978-1-966954-66-8 (hardcover)
ISBN: 978-1-966954-67-5 (epub)

Library of Congress Control Number: 2025915404

JESUS'
DOCTRINE
of
MARRIAGE

JOHN D. KELLER

DEDICATION

To the children of broken families, and especially to that little Amy and little Tommy, who long to live with their creation-marriage biological father or mother; and by all of God's love and righteousness deserve and have the absolute right to have it so; also, to the memory of the brave little ten year old girl, Zahra Baker; we will never forget your beautiful smiling face with those cute freckles. Also, to all the creation-marriage husbands and wives who have been betrayed by a spouse, some who have been divorced by the unfaithful spouse, and are being faithful to our Lord and Savior Jesus Christ by remaining alone, praying and waiting with great long-suffering for the full repentance, restoration, and salvation of their departed beloved spouse.

What therefore

God hath joined

together,

let not man put asunder.

Mark 10:9

CONTENTS

ABBREVIATIONS

AJA - American Journal of Archaeology
ANET - Ancient Near East Texts
AV - Authorized Version
CU - Code of Ur Nammu
CE - Code of Eshnunna
CL - Code of Lipit-Ishtar
CH - Code of Hammurabi
ISBE - International Standard Bible Encyclopedia
JJS - Journal of Jewish Studies
JPS - Jewish Publication Society
KJV - King James Version
KDOTC - Keil and Delitzsch, OT Commentary
LXX - Septuagint
MDR - Marriage Divorce Remarriage
MS - Manuscript
NIBC - New International Bible Commentary
NICNT - New International Commentary NT
NSRB - New Scofield Reference Bible 1967
NT - New Testament
NTC - New Testament Commentary
OT - Old Testament

SRB - Scofield Reference Bible 1909

INTRODUCTION

God is not the author of confusion, but of peace. As men are at peace with their understanding of God's Law of Gravity, so they should be at peace with God's Doctrine of Marriage. Divorce must be subject to the doctrine of marriage; it will be seen that marriage supersedes the idea of divorce and in their struggle, marriage obliterates her foe: divorce.

The King James Version of the Bible is the source of this dissertation. The hermeneutics of the author will be of the literal-historical-cultural school. One important law of interpretation which will not be violated is the law of *"common sense."* I join with Edward W. Goodrich (Professor of Greek and Bible Multnomah School of Bible): "If there ever was a place for common sense, it can be found in the rules for interpreting the Bible." The Bible's autograph languages may be referenced from time to time and will be given their honor.

Sola Gratia, salvation by Grace alone, is the truth that is being contaminated by those who misinterpret the marriage doctrine. (You might consider that statement rather out of place, but please read on for it is central to this dissertation.) If you do not teach salvation by grace alone, you inevitably teach salvation by works. By endorsing remarriage this side of death, the preacher contradicts Jesus and His doctrine of Grace as he attempts to mix Grace with the Law—his use of the Law contaminates Solely by Grace.

The doctrine of works is always condemned by the God of Salvation, "but though we, or an angel from heaven, preach any other gospel unto you than that which we have preached unto you, let him be accursed, *anathema.*" We are assured that God's love for man is long-suffering; He is not willing that any should perish, but that all should come to repentance; therefore, any teacher who promises man salvation without repentance must be accursed. And since God's love calls upon all men everywhere to repent, it must be understood that God's doctrine of repentance, and God's doctrine of marriage apply to all men, all religions, all societies, all political institutions, and all nationalities. The first application of God's matchless grace is to lead a sinner to repentance: "Or despisest thou the riches of his goodness [Grace, my comment] and forebearance and long-suffering, not knowing that the goodness [Grace, my comment] of God leadeth thee to repentance?" (Rom. 2:4). Repentance for one's sin and faith in the shed blood of Christ will cleanse the sin of any man; therefore, there is hope that every marriage can be saved from the complexities of marital sin—providing repentance (departure) of the marital sin has been exercised—often the marital sin is the physical union of a *remarriage*.

In matters of controversy, the student inevitability will face a crossroad. His progress will require a step of faith. That crossroad will clearly be faced by each student of the marriage-divorce controversy. In this study the inevitable intersection is the "exception clause." This entire dissertation surrounds this one clause. My prayer is that the reader will have the courage to study the entire text, and then consider the true meaning of the exception clause. As you will see the fate of marriage and perhaps the fate of mankind may depend on your interpretation of those five words: *"except it be for fornication."*

Jesus defined marriage with this doctrine: "But from the beginning of the creation God made them male and female. For this cause shall a man leave his father and mother, and cleave to his wife; And they twain shall be one flesh: so then they are no more twain, but one flesh. "What therefore God hath joined together, let not man put asunder." *Note: With these exact words Jesus fully endorsed and Blessed the sexual union of heterosexual marriage (one man and one woman for life) and, thus: Jesus condemned all other sexual activity of the human race as sinful, i.e., either as adultery, or as fornication. Jesus said, "For from within, out of the heart of men, proceed evil thoughts, adulteries, fornications (Mk. 7:21). Thus, Jesus condemned polygamy, and all other sexual acts of man outside of His definition of marriage at creation: heterosexual* marriage is the only definition of marriage.

The clincher here is that they twain shall be one flesh, and that flesh is only dissolved by the death of a spouse. Thus, marriage is permanent and indissoluble this side of death. The *axiom* of this book: No-Remarriage-This-Side-Of-Death—the other side of this means that such remarriage is a *continuous act of adultery.* That is the Abomination! Such a practice is in direct conflict with Scripture (I Cor. 6:9, 10) where it speaks of those who will inherit the kingdom of God; and those who will not. This is a matter of Heaven or Hell!

ABOUT THE AUTHOR

John D. Keller is an independent fundamental Baptist; saved in 1960 and married Janet in 1962. A graduate of Philadelphia College of the Bible, and shortly afterward ordained to the Gospel Ministry in 1971. He was the pastor of two churches in Maine, and now resides in North Carolina. Our sixty-one years of marriage have brought us six children and 12 grandchildren and 2 great grandchildren. In his early ministry Rev. Keller was convicted by the Lord to address the doctrine of marriage in his preaching ministry. At that time a debate with a fiery young preacher led him to a full study of the Scriptures regarding the Biblical doc- trine of marriage. His first tract in 1975 was entitled: "Apostasy and Divorce."This present volume is the result of forty years of labor—All for His Glory.

CHAPTER ONE

Whom Hath God Joined Together?

Has God joined together all marriages? Has God joined together the unsaved? Has God joined together the unbeliever with the believer? Has God joined together the divorced and remarried? Has God joined together the innocent partner in a new marriage? Has God joined together the guilty partner in a new marriage? Has God joined together partners of the same gender? Just whom has God joined together?

Regarding same sex unions, be assured that God has nothing to do with such sin and debauchery. He has declared such an act, same sex union, as a capital crime equal to if not the same as bestiality; the word marriage cannot refer to homosexuality, as it cannot refer to bestiality marriage. As a man or a woman cannot marry their horse, dog, dolphin[1] or any other beast, so they cannot marry partners of the same sex. In God's eyes homosexuality is a godless sinful act that is fit for the punishment of a capital crime in the nation of God that adhered to the death penalty:

> If a man also lie with mankind, as he lieth with a woman, both of them have committed an abomination: they shall surely be put to death; their blood *shall* be upon them. *Lev 20:13*

Thus, the Word of God, this commandment of Moses, confirms that the act of homosexuality is a capital crime. The only salvation for such a crime is repentance (the total cessation of the sin) and faith in the forgiveness through the blood of Christ, or the death penalty—the death penalty may await God's final judgment day; then death may mean eternal death in the fires of hell. The Bible equally condemns lesbianism (Rom. 1:26; Lev. 20:13 are gender neutral). If a woman lie

---

[1] YnetNews.com singles—Brit Jew Marries Dolphin, Dec. 79 29, 2005 Joe Kot

with womankind, both of them have committed an abomination: they shall surely be put to death—I once read that one man's definition of lesbianism is atheism—the same death penalty was deemed proper for bestiality:

> If a man lie with a beast, he shall surely be put to death: and ye shall slay the beast. And if a woman approach unto any beast, and lie down thereto, thou shalt kill the woman, and the beast: they shall surely be put to death; their blood *shall be* upon them. *Lev. 20:15, 16*

The Remaining Questions:

The remaining initial questions will be answered throughout this dissertation, and their answers will provide the solution to the entire marriage-divorce-remarriage confusion. *The dilemma is that men refuse to permit God to rule marriage.* Man has the idea that man is the sovereign judge and ruler of marriage. But we shall see that man is not the king of his own castle; he has no sovereign right over his wife or family. It must be mentioned that the woman also has no claim to sovereignty; she is also subject to the Creator of the *Single Pair.* Marriage is literally the creative act of God, and man cannot alter that act: an act where God created one man and one woman and joined them together in a marriage. At this point in creation (Gen. 1-3) marriage was completely defined.

Two thousand years ago, when the Pharisees came baiting Jesus with the inquiry: ("Is it lawful for a man to put away his wife?" Mk. 10:2) the marriage-divorce-remarriage question was in the eyes of that generation as murky and muddled as it is to the children of the twenty-first century. Their question smacked of male sovereignty, although it was intended to test Jesus' understanding of the Law of Moses; but it did more than that, it actually raised the vital subject: marriage. Divorce is a sub-article in the doctrine of marriage, and

Jesus clearly identified that fact. At the heart of Jesus' answer were these profound words, "What, therefore, God hath joined together, let not man put asunder." The only question man can propose from this immortal statement is: Who hath God joined together? To answer this question, we will follow the guiding hand of the Preacher, Jesus. He began his answer to the Pharisees question by sounding the original Genesis marriage text.

The Creation-Marriage Text: Gen. 1:26 -27, 2:7, 20-24

And God said, Let, us make man in our image, after our likeness: and let them have dominion over the fish of the sea, and over the fowl of the air, and over the cattle, and over all the earth, and over every creeping thing that creepeth upon the earth. So, God created man in his *own* image, in the image of God created he him; male and female created he them. (*Gen. 1:26, 27*)

The Lord God formed man of the dust of the ground and breathed into his nostrils the breath of life; and the man became a living soul. (*Gen. 2:7*)

And Adam gave names to all the cattle, and to the fowl of the air, and to every beast of the field, but for Adam there was not found a help meet for him. And the Lord God caused a deep sleep to fall upon Adam, and he slept: and he took one of his ribs and closed up the flesh instead thereof; and the rib, which the Lord God had taken from man, made he a woman, and brought her unto man. And Adam said, this is now bone of my bones, and flesh of my flesh: she shall be called Woman, because she was taken out of man. Therefore, shall a man leave his father and his mother, and shall cleave unto his wife: and they shall be one flesh. (*Gen. 2:20-24*)

When the Pharisees came to Jesus tempting him, they asked: "Is it lawful for a man to put away his wife?" In noting this discourse, we must listen to what Jesus said in His answer *to this question*. At first Jesus offers another parenthetic question of His own: "What did Moses command you?" And the Pharisees said, "Moses suffered to write a bill of divorcement, and to put her away." Please note that the Pharisees offered that there was *NO COMMANDMENT*, but only that Moses suffered (permitted under duress); thus, Moses only permitted but certainly did not command the writing of divorcement. Jesus then acknowledges their reference to the Mosaic permission—given under duress—then Jesus said: "For the hardness of your hearts he wrote you this precept. But from the beginning of creation God made them male and female. For this cause shall a man leave his father and mother and cleave unto his wife; and they twain shall be one flesh: so, then they are no more twain but one flesh. What therefore God hath joined together, let not man put asunder" (Mk. 10:2-9).

By these words Jesus drove His hearers, and now you, the reader, to the actual creation of man. Marriage is to be defined within the context of the first two chapters of Genesis. Jesus does not proceed beyond the Genesis text to define marriage. Therefore, we can conclude that the *definition of marriage is defined within that textual limit.*

Jesus immediately introduces the person of the Creator God as the engineer of marriage. He links marriage with the actual creation of man, stating that the act of creating man, male and female, is the basis of marriage. Some interesting comments surround this text, with one author, Ziegler, stating that the male did not possess *complete sexual distinction* without the creation of the female. Adam was a male in *simple potentiality*, out of which state he passed, the moment the woman stood by his side.[2] Much, has been said regarding creations concluding statement by the Creator, "And God saw everything that he had made

---

[2] C.F. Kiel; F. Delitzsch, quoting Zeigler, (O.T. Commentary; Eerdmans; Grand Rapids, MI; 1978) v.1, p. 88; Abel Isaksson, (Marriage and Ministry in the New Temple trans. N. Tomkinson with J. Gray, Lund: Gleerup, 1965) p. 144, 145; Isaksson argues against androgyny.

and behold, it was very good." It should be pointed out, that before He said it was very good at one point, He stated that something was *not good* in the initial primary creation of man. "And the Lord God said, It is not good that the man should be alone," man was not at this time malformed, he was just not completely formed being alone. Ziegler's thoughts coincide with Laney's comment that the two Hebrew terms male and female literally mean the piercer and the pierced.[3] Would the male plug of an electrical extension cord have a definition without its female receptor. Now if a male electrical connector cannot be defined without its antithesis, can man be defined without a woman? Some have suggested that man was created androgynous (both male and female) but Kiel and Delitzsch are correct and overthrow this theory by stating that God referred to man with the pronoun *them*,[4] "male and female created he them." The revelation which we must see here is not that God created man androgynous, but that he created man *married*. The purpose of removing a rib from Adam in the creation of the woman was not to form a biologically compatible creature, for that could have been accomplished with more dust; the purpose was to create *kinship*.[5]

Isaksson, the author of this idea, concentrated on Genesis chapter two. However, if we examine (Gen. 1:26) with this kinship concept we will discover the meaning of the text. The mystery of the Godhead is suddenly revealed in this marvelous conversation: "Let *us* make man in *our* image." These words have delighted the spiritual mind since their inscription, but most commentators agree that we have never savored their full flavor. However, if we concentrate on the kinship

---

[3] Laney, Carl J., The Divorce Myth (Minn., MN; Bethany House, 1981) p. 16

[4] Kiel, C; Delitzsch, F. Old Testament Commentary (Eerdmans, Grand Rapids, MI) v. 1 p. 65

[5] Isaksson, Abel, Marriage and Ministry in the New Temple (trans. N. Tomkinson with J. Gray; Lund: Gleeup, Copenhagen 1965) p. 20: This idea of kinship is a strong support for the doctrine of indissoluble marriage. Heth, Wenham, Laney, Steele, and Ryrie lean in Isaksson's direction. Gen. 2; Lev. 18; and Deut.24 are pertinent to kinship

concept and meditate on the Triune God for a moment, then a greater light shines through.

Man was created a *single pair*, apparently in contrast to the animals. Kiel and Delitzsch translate Genesis 1:20, "God said; Let the waters swarm with swarms, with living beings, and let birds fly above the earth in the face of the firmament." Their comment, "The animals were created, not only in a rich variety of genera and species, but in large numbers"[6], reflects the opinion that there were many pairs of animals. That is in remarkable contrast to man, the *Single Pair*. Before the Fall the animals only benefit would be in the rapid advance of their numbers, but afterwards their advantage was in marked contrast to the disadvantage of man.

Since man and beast were by creation herbivores (Gen. 1:29, 30), we can confirm that there was no competition between them since neither was the hunted; a remarkable contradiction to Darwin. However, after the *Fall*, man was immediately faced with the dangers of death from: fellow men, beasts, insects, storms, disease, even the possibility of an accident. The odds favored man's extinction. The initial survival of the many paired animals, on the other hand, was a sure thing. Man, the *Single Pair*, was in a peculiar strait. Man lived in fear of extinction until he could produce a sufficient population to ensure his immediate survival. Man's only prospect for his existence was bundled in a single relation with the only other man, woman. This first and only relationship—marriage—was the most delicate alliance in the history of the human race. By faith Adam would build a relationship of hope between his family and his God. It must be remembered that Adam walked away from the tree with God's condemning words, ringing in his head: "In the day that thou eatest thereof thou shalt surely die." We read in Hebrews (2:15) that Adam lived out his days in the fear of death. He would have to hope where he saw little hope. Could he survive to procreate mankind? Would he have faith in the God of Salvation? His fear would have to be conquered. It was

---

[6] Kiel, C; Delitzsch, F. Old Testament Commentary (Eerdmans, Grand Rapids, MI; 1978) v. 1 p. 60

imperative that he find the faith which would permit him to cultivate his marriage with love, peace, and promise. He would have to lead his lady in a life of hope and faith. Conjugal love depends on security and hope; thus, seeking out the promise that the seed of the woman would bruise the head of the serpent; Adam would have to learn to pray. We do know that he and his wife prayed earnestly, for Eve's testimony declares where she believed her first born came from, "I have gotten a man from the Lord", obviously an answer to prayer.

The *creation-marriage*, and the birth of Cain bring a bright new meaning to the truth of man's creation as being in the *image and likeness* of God. The Biblicist believes that God's image and likeness is a united diversity, a tri-unity, a trinity—Father, Son, and Holy Spirit. Many commentators have attempted to define this quality in man; some calling it a trichotomy, (body, soul, and spirit), others attribute it to personality (intellect, emotions, and will). The failure of the traditional interpretation is that it has failed to see the woman in the text. By placing the woman properly in the context, a wonderful truth bursts into bloom. God's image was an image of kinship. The three persons of the Godhead were equally related and were one. Jesus clearly revealed this:

> That they all may be one, as thou, Father, art in me, and I in thee, that they also may be one in us; that the world may believe that thou hast sent me. And the glory which thou gavest me I have given them, that they may be one, even as we are one. (*Jn. 17:21, 22*).

When God removed a rib from Adam, He did more than just create another man. He created a man with the same genes, blood type, DNA and physical characteristics. He created kinfolk. God's existence is an eternal kinship. God's image and likeness would be an earthly kinship; man's existence would be dependent on kinship. With the birth of Cain man reached the ultimate kinship: family. Man was created family. Trinity and Family are divine synonyms. God is a family (Father, Son, and Holy Spirit). Man is a family (father, child, and mother). A Trinity!

Abortion and Man the Family-Trinity

The truth regarding the family as a trinity impacts all mankind. When even one baby is deliberately put to death, by the abortionist, it impacts on the very nature of being human; and it affects all mankind for eternity.

The headlines today, on the fortieth anniversary of Roe v. Wade, read that 55 million Americans have been aborted, deliberately put to death, or murdered; in the past forty years. Isn't this genocide? Who ever heard of 55 million people dying from violence, and it is just a passing comment? How God must be grieving, and grieving! I believe that this act of mass abortion of our babies is the gravest sin of those women (those mothers) of our country. OH! God have mercy on us.

Man and Woman - The Definition Excludes:

I am quite sorry to include this paragraph in this dissertation, however considering the decline of human civilization that we are witnessing in our so-called *modern age*, I have no other choice but to do so. The definition of man and woman excludes any person who chooses to alter their natural born gender in any attempt to become the opposite sex: medically, psychologically, or by any other conceivable method. Remember the word alter means to make different without changing into something else; a man will always be a man and a woman will always be a woman—they say you can tell them by their hands.

Genesis 2:23, 24

And Adam said, This, is now bone of my bones, and flesh of my flesh: she shall be called Woman, because she was taken out of Man. Therefore, shall a

man leave his father and his mother, and shall cleave
unto his wife: and they shall be one flesh. *Gen. 2:23, 24*

The details of the first wedding were planned in heaven, and
Gen.2:23, 24 reveals that all went exactly as planned. God is love (1
Jn. 4:8b), and with this adhesive, love, God bound the first couple, the
single pair. Jesus knew this binding love:

I in them, and thou in me, that they may be made
perfect in one; and that the world may know that thou
hast sent me, and hast loved them, as thou hast loved
me. *Jn. 17:23*

Adam was taught love. First, he was introduced to the agony of,
aloneness, loneliness. He was permitted to explore the satisfaction of
nature. He is obviously befriended by the animal kingdom to whom
he affectionately awarded to each creature a name. His home was a
marvelous garden. But the beauty of flora and fauna, the majesty of
nature, the friendship of every creature, and the companionship of the
triune God did not meet man's most inner need. Even God concluded
that it was not good for man to be alone. The loneliness of man was
broken during the silence of his deep sleep. This is further evidence
that man is not saved by works, but by faith. Man's heartfelt emotions
cried for fulfillment even in his sleep. Carl Laney hears a song from
Adam as he expresses his delight with the gift of the woman; with
sleepy eyes Adam beheld the most beautiful creature of God's creation, and with ecstasy in his voice he declares literally: "This one at
last – Bone of my bones! Flesh – my flesh! This one shall be called
woman, because out of man this one was taken.[7] The dawn of human
love was born in marriage, a marked contrast to the opinion of modern men who have been deceived to believe that marriage is the end of
love. Marriage owns love. Marriage is the instructor of love. Marriage
was God's love gift to the lonely man. Marriage made God's creation

---

[7] Laney, Carl J. The Divorce Myth (Bethany House, MN 1981) p. 18

very good. Man was created married. Man was created in love. It is no wonder that since the garden love scene all creation has been filled with reports of the same; it seems as though the famous English lover was in the Garden:

> What lady is that which enriches the hand yonder knight?
> O, she doth teach the torches to burn right!
> It seems she hangs upon the cheeks of night
> Like a rich jewel in an Ethiop's ear;
> Beauty too rich for use, for earth too dear!
> So shows a snowy dove romping with crows,
> As, yonder lady o'er her fellows shows.
> The measure done, I'll watch her place of stand,
> And, touching hers, make blessed my rude hand.
> Did my heart love till now? forswear it, sight!

I ne'er saw true beauty till this night.[8]

"I ne'er saw true beauty till this night", was the cry of the romantic. The soul of Romeo saw the torches burn bright because of the lady. She stood out as a dove among crows (this would have been literally true in the case of Eve). Adam could have easily said, Amen! to William Shakespeare. The spectacular beauty of creation, especially seen in the symmetry and color of the birds, insects, fish, flowers, and sunsets ensures the knowledge that Adam was a creature of excellent handsomeness. His song raises the woman to his equal. Her silence speaks of a breathtaking experience as she was enraptured with her lover; Adam was irresistible. Her thoughts were expressed by the Shulamite:

> Let him kiss me with the kisses of his mouth.
> *Song of Sol. 1:2*

Eve's passiveness speaks submission and permission. The male announces his intentions with forwardness, the lady submits and sig-

---

[8] Shakespeare W. Romeo and Juliet (Act I, scene V)

nals permission to her lover. Kiss is plural; it requires two players. One alone cannot kiss. The act can only be accomplished with two sets of lips. Each person's lips must desire the others. Kiss is irresistible. Each person is drawn by an energy of love which each cannot resist. Kiss is promise. Each person promises admiration, trust, faith, and sacrifice in the kiss. The drawing power of the kiss has been quaintly explained by our English lover: Love goes toward love as, school-boys from their books, but love from love, toward school with heavy looks.[9]

The Loving God created man in love. Man was created a plurality of being. He was created married. He was created kinfolk. He was created family. He was created with the cement of love. He was bound with the lady with this love cement. The twain "was" one. Man was created a *Single Pair*. Where the animal's depen- dence was upon their numbers, man's survival was dependent on his love. His love was victorious. The *Single Pair* could have joined with Solomon:

> I raised thee up under the apple tree. There thy mother brought thee forth who bore thee. Set me as a seal upon thine heart, as a seal upon thine arm; for love is strong as death. *Song of Sol. 8:5, 6*

Leave His Father and Mother

> Therefore, shall a man leave his father and his mother, and shall cleave unto his wife: and they shall be one flesh. *Gen. 2:24*

Although these words initially appear to be those of Adam, Laney points out that Matthew clearly explains that they are the words of God: "Have ye not read that He who made them at the beginning, made them male and female; and said, For this cause shall a man leave his father and mother, and shall cleave to his wife, and they twain

---

[9] Ibid. (Act II, scene II)

shall be one flesh."[10] The reason they shall leave mother and father is bound in the fact that they are male and female. G. von Rad suggests that the drive behind Edenic love was bound in the physical nature of the rib:

> Whence comes this love 'strong as death' (Song 8:6), and stronger than the tie to one's parents, whence this inner clinging to each other, this drive towards each other which does not rest until it again becomes one flesh in the child?
>
> It comes from the fact that God took woman from man, that they actually were originally one flesh. Therefore, they must come together again and thus by destiny belong to each other. The recognition of this narrative as etiological is theologically important. Its point of departure, the thing to be explained, is for the narrator something in existence; not something 'paradisal' and thus lost![11]

The creation of the woman removed a physical part of man, the loss of which compels man to be rejoined with his missing being. While visiting a nursing home, the author often witnessed to an elderly gentleman who in his youth lost a leg in an industrial accident. The man was usually sad and melancholy since the early death of his dear wife, and only child, his daughter. He was usually unresponsive to the Gospel, however, when it was suggested that his missing leg would be returned to him in the resurrection, he was startled. He sat up at attention as if he was preparing to take up arms and march into battle. He yearned for his limb as he yearned for his wife, and daughter. Adam yearned for his missing rib from the moment the heavenly anesthetic wore off. Adam's missing rib caused his heart

---

[10] Laney, Carl; The Divorce Myth (Bethany House, Minn. MN 1981 p.18
[11] Atkinson, David; quotes von Rad, To Have and To Hold, (Eerdmans; Grand Rapids, MI 1979) p.77

to explode with affection, as his eyes beheld his lovely lady. His song begs her love.

The *Single Pair* were created on the sixth day. God created them male and female. God created them married. Creation married Adam. Marriage is man. Marriage is the natural state of man. The natural must be considered. The English word is derived from the Latin *nasci > natur > natura*, to be born. As natural as it is to be born, so is marriage. Chaucer said, "The day natural, bat is to seyn 24 hour is," (as 24 hours is natural to the day).[12] As the hours of a day cannot change, marriage cannot change. Marriage was born on the sixth day of creation and the truth of marriage is the same today. The New Testament word for *natural* literally means the face of ones, birth, (the idea is that the natural is present from birth). It is no wonder that God cursed the women and the men who changed their natural use:

> For this cause, God gave them up unto vile affections: for even their women did change the natural use unto that which is against nature: And likewise, also the men, leaving the natural use of the women, burned in their lust one to another; men with men working that which is unseemly, and receiving in themselves that recompense of their error which was meet. *Rom. 1:26,27*

The natural is honorable, the unnatural disgraceful. The AIDS epidemic is a fitting recompense for unnatural lust.

The familial relationship satisfies each member's need for security and fellowship, but it is prohibitive for the family to satisfy man's sexual needs. Incest, consanguineous marriage, is forbidden. Should kinfolk, by some unusual circumstance, find themselves in an incestuous relationship, that relationship must be put asunder. Incest is the most unnatural of all sexual acts. Other unnatural acts take place outside of marriage, but incestuous marriage defiles marriage as no other act can. The unnatural sexual lust of women with women, and men with

---

[12] Chaucer in, Compact Oxford Eng. Dict. (Oxford Univ. Press 1984) p.1899

men is cursed with the judgment of hell fire and earthly AIDS, but the judgment of incest is immediate, it must be *put asunder*. Marriage is a sexual union outside the kin of family.

> This union is a totally different nature from that of parents and children; hence marriage between parents and children is entirely opposed to the ordinance of God.[13]

The tragedy of human history is that it seems to follow Murphy's Law: If man can do anything wrong, he will. Shortly after the Lord God rescued Lot from the Sodomites and the destruction of Sodom, Lot gets drunk and commits incest with his two daughters. Today the world continues this record of fornication, porn.

Sons depart to military duty or academic studies, daughters the same, but no living departure should be as acute as the departure to divorce a spouse with children. The *nuclear family* is the natural family. All other unions are unnatural. Families are nuclear or they are not families— the family includes adopted children. The nuclear family can only be severed by death or the departure of the child in marriage; thus, permitting one of its members to join in a new family. A man never ceases to be family. Those born through unnatural union like the leop- ard cannot change their spots; although they can be adopted into a new family—salvation and the new birth will make them completely the children of God. But the naturally born and living are seen to be with their parents till the time of their living departure: marriage. This speaks of marriages that last. Legally broken families do not per- mit their offspring to depart naturally. Natural families help produce sound marriages. Although the departure of the son and daughter produce some trauma, the presence of the parents and their approval of the new union nevertheless speak of something wonderful.

---

[13] Kiel, C; Delitzsch, F. Old Testament Commentary (Eerdmans, Grand Rapids, MI; 1978) v.1 p.60

Cleave Unto His Wife

> There be three things which are wonderful for me
> Yea, four which I know not. The, way of an eagle in
> the air, The way of a serpent upon a rock, The way of
> a ship in the midst of the sea And, the way of a man
> with a maid. *Prov. 30:18-19*

Since Eden there would never be another as lonely as Adam, the *single man*, and the moment his loneliness was removed creation was complete. Creation is marriage. Marriage is a living organization that was ordained by God: *an organic union.* Marriage is an ordinance of God. Marriage is an institution of God, ordained and instituted before the fall. This ordinance requires man to leave and then to cleave. Many have commented on the Greek proskollao, to cleave. The idea is to bind together with glue. As a boy, the author learned the adhesive strength of resin glue when joining wood projects together. At times, after the glue had cured, attempts would be made to undo the glued joints and divide the wood only to realize that the wood would freshly break rather than permit the glued joint to separate. Contemplate this while you consider the words of the Lord Jesus, "What God hath joined (glued) together let not man put asunder."

Jesus the master of language exhausts all possible definitions of the dimensions of marriage with a singular defining thought. He expresses that definition mathematically. He claims that when man was created, he was created male and female and that plurality was singular. And for this reason, the groom and the bride must leave mother and father, because they must again be one.

> Have ye not read that he who made them at the
> beginning, made them male and female; and said, For
> this cause shall a man leave his father and mother and
> shall cleave to his wife and they twain shall be one
> flesh? Wherefore they are no more twain, but one
> flesh. *Matt. 19:4-6*

Jesus explicitly states that the married man and woman are not two, but that they are *one*. One is the smallest indivisible particle. William J. Hopewell makes this fitting comment:

> *One* is the smallest indivisible unit that there is, so it is impossible to divide the unit of one flesh once it has been glued together. Man and woman are two entities before marriage; but following marriage they become an indivisible unit of one in marital status. *Thus, they cannot be divided.*

Hopewell goes on to enforce his comment:

> Tertullian (200 A.D.) said, Again He [Jesus] said, They shall be two in one flesh...not three or four. But if they marry a second time, or oftener, their oneness no longer exists; there will not be two in one flesh, on the contrary, many in one.[14]

The clarion call of marriage throughout eternity is, *No more twain but one.* The consequent command that resounds back throughout eternity is, Quod DEUS conjunxit, homo non-separet, (What, therefore, God hath joined together, let not man put asunder.) To disobey God is violence. Adultery is violence. Divorce is violence. Hatred is violence. Man was created in unity with God, however this blessed unity was broken when he and his woman ate the forbidden fruit; leaving the vicarious sacrifice of the blood of the Lord Jesus Christ as man's only hope for a reunion with God. Salvation.

Why do men commit vicious acts against man and God? Violence speaks of disunity. The O.T. prophets referred to divorce as: Treachery (Mal. 2:16). Man is capable of violence by the nature of his disunity. Jesus is the Prince of Peace because of his perfect unity. The foun-

---

[14] Hopewell, W.J. Jr. Marriage and Divorce, (Niles & Philips; Birmington, NY 1976) p. 3, 4

dation of monotheism was founded in the text: "Hear, O Israel: The Lord our God is one Lord" (Deut. 6:4). This attribute of God, unity, is in contrast to the disunity of man, and man is fully aware of his weakness. Driven by his inability to conquer his disunity, and be like God, man has determined to hate the Unified God and His Son—man's supreme act of violence. Jesus pointed this out, "And the light shineth in the darkness and the darkness comprehended [overcame] it not." Jesus indicated that man's act of trying to overcome the light, actually consisted of an open hatred against Him and God, "If the world hate you, ye know that it hated me before it hated you", and "He that hateth me hateth my Father also." During one particular confrontation, Jesus asked the mob, "Why go ye about to kill me?" The Apostle states that all men were, or are the "enemies of God" (Rom. 5:10). Marriage is a God ordained unity, therefore any doctrine which propagates the unity of marriage will be hated by the creature of disunity, man. It is natural for man to hate, to war, to kill, for man is naturally violent.

> As it is written, There is none righteous, no, not one: There is none that understandeth, there is none that seeketh after God. They are all gone out of the way, they are together become unprofitable; there is none that doeth good, no, not one. *Rom 3:10-12*

Unity

Many factors are uniting to attack the unity of marriage, and the family. Pornography, the literature of prostitutes, is intended to create in the imagination, the violence, and gratification of instant sex. Science in the latter half of the twentieth century has permitted the propagation of porn with life-like electronic internet media. The selfishness of man has feed on the bait of pornography and has strengthened itself in the violence of sex. The exploitation of man's selfishness is profitable; some say prostitution is the world's oldest business. The prostitute, however, cannot be blamed for man's selfish nature.

Science has come to power in the twentieth century. The question is: Has science exploited the selfishness of man? Has science offered man a justification for his selfishness. Science is an instrument of disunity. Its most famous trophy is the Atomic Bomb: the very essence of splitting unity. Its authority is rooted in its disunity. Science is the Paradox, its greatest equation, $E = mc2$, has given us Nagasaki and Hiroshima, and the fear of the destruction of mankind. Its concepts of disunity, and its glory in the same, seem to have endless consequences. Vincent Edward Smith, a philosopher-scientist, who survived World War II, wrote a delightful little book entitled, *Footnotes for the Atom*, in which he chides modern man for abandoning philosophy/religion for the strict science world model.

Modern physics has had no monopoly on the empiriological method. Liberal economics took it over and found men to be only atoms, closed off from one another and mechanically united under the state solely for the protection of property and the preserving of public order, [Marxism, my comment]. Sociology, at least when it began, felt that social and political affairs could be run off with the ease of experiments in the physicist's laboratory. Psychology got a later start than other empiriological studies of human affairs, but it grew very rapidly to the extremism that man is only a bundle of atomic reflexes (behaviorism) or an aggregate of atomic drives (Freudianism).

All of these views, which tend to copy the method of empiriological physics, are powerless of themselves to solve the pressing human problems which the atomism of matter has heightened. They only atomize men. On the social plane, atomism or individualism cuts men off from one another. "Bundle Theories" of man scatter his personality into disorganized and warring atoms, differing from matter only in complexity. The atomic bomb is dangerous because of the atomic man. It is unity that alone can organize.[15]

Smith admits that pure science will increase man's power; but warns that it will kill his love.[16] He continues, "It is already quite clear that physics is atomizing matter and then atomizing the atoms. It aims to explain all physical structures by smaller ones and then resorts to a third particle, like the meson in the nucleus, to show how two others are united. It is analytic even when it wants to synthesize. But where does the division stop? The answer is nowhere: it just keeps going."[17] The killing of man's love is almost prophetic, as we look about our land. There is a twofold nature to mistreated love. Jesus taught that the true lovers of the future would have their love wax cold because of iniquity, and Paul predicts that the self-lovers would wax hot. The latter predicted the perilous days ahead, when men would be selfish (lovers of their own selves), without natural affection, and beside other things trucebreakers. A.T. Robertson identifies covenant breakers in Romans 1:31 with trucebreakers in II Timothy 3:3. Therefore the prediction of II Timothy: "This know, also, that in the last days perilous times shall come. For men shall be lovers of their own selves, covetous, boasters, proud, blasphemers, disobedient to parents, unthankful, unholy, without natural affection, *trucebreakers* (those given to divorce).

The destruction of unity contributes to the progress of physics, but when applied to the walk of man it has produced a modern paganism. "Society has been atomized into individual units, and pagans, seeking nothing but themselves."[18] Smith completes his admonition with the judgment that Science is a false-messiah.[19]

---

[15] Smith, V.E. Footnotes for the Atom Bruce, (Milwaukee, WI 1951) p. 63, 64

[16] Ibid p. 16

[17] Ibid p. 17

[18] Ibid 67

[19] Ibid 40

Existentialism is the religion of physics. It is the religion of the individual atomic man. "Chiefly a Twentieth Century philosophy, Existentialism centers on the analysis of individual existence and the plight of the individual who must assume ultimate responsibility for his acts of free will without any certain knowledge of what is right or wrong or good or bad."[20] Selfishness is certainly a false-messiah.

When Judah, the son of Jacob, discovered that Tamar played the prostitute, and that he was the father of his daughter-in-law's child, he confessed that Tamar was more righteous than he (Gen. 38:12-26). Like Tamar, science may be prostituting mankind with its offer of a philosophy of selfishness.

Selfishness or Sacrifice

A comment from almost a generation ago may be worth noting: A 1980 (AP) news article headline read, "Population Decline Expected in Europe." A Dutch population specialist (Dirk J. van de Haa) reports that a fertility rate of 2.1 per family is necessary to maintain a constant population. He then states, "The statistics recorded in Europe indicate that they will realize a population decline should the present marriage practice continue." Van de Haa claims that the prime factor contributing to the present low fertility rate is *individualism.*

> Marriage and family place heavy demands on individuals, especially women, and tends to limit the freedom of both partners, he observed.

> For a couple, having children imposes limits on opportunities and activities, in addition to the direct costs, van de Haa said. At the same time, he said, children's utility has declined. They are no longer either expected or legally required to support their

---

[20] Merriam Webster's Collegiate Dict. 10th Ed. (Merriam Webster 1994)

parents in old age or help with family finances, he said. The emotional satisfaction of parenthood can be achieved most economically by having one or perhaps two children.

Many sociologists consider the movement toward greater self-fulfillment, available at a time when fertility is relatively easily controlled, a major factor. Cohabitation is increasingly accepted as normal, and as many as half of the men and women in Northern Europe may never marry.[21]

Individualism of marriage partners is a form of marriage hatred. Cohabitation without marriage is violence. The scientific generation is viewing the intricate relationships of life through the prism of the empirical method. William Kirk Kilpatrick makes this observation:

The words *mother* and *father* remind us of what a family ought to be and that without one we are incomplete. But his idea isn't a fashionable idea. Autonomous individuals have a higher priority than families in the social science world.[22]

The social science world is one of unbridled selfishness. Eric Fromm has aptly entitled his volume, *Man for Himself*, and then places this crowning statement on the subject:

Modern science holds the doctrine that the most powerful and legitimate drive in man is selfishness.

It is no wonder that the epigraph to this volume reads;

[21] van de Has, Dirk J. Population Decline in Europe (Bangor Daily News Bangor ME, May 16, 1987)

[22] Kilpatrick, W.A. Psychological Seduction (Thomas Nelson, Nashville 1983) p.126

Be ye lamps unto yourselves
Be your own reliance
Hold to the truth within yourselves
And to the only lamp   (Buddha)

It is fitting that Fromm should quote Buddha, since the psychologist-scientist has chosen to embrace Eastern Mysticism in its quest to define individualism. The Eastern Cults have relied on the *inner solitary light* as the truth which man must seek as the rock of their religion. Science required a prostitute to convey its message, and Eastern Mysticism is that prostitute; included here is the New Age movement; and the so called, Individualistic Society. "It is in the age of the individual that the revolt against marriage has risen to its present irresistible tide." Will Durant made this statement in, *The Mansions of Philosophy*, written in 1941. In the same year America entered World War II, she was in the mist of the new civil war, the divorce war, the family war.

But Christ taught us to march to the tune of a different drummer, the drummer: sacrifice. "This is my commandment that ye love one another, as I have loved you. Greater love hath no man than this, that a man lay down his life for his friends. Ye are my friends, if ye do whatever I command you" (Jn. 15:12-14). Sacrifice is at the heart of the Christian philosophy. Sacrifice is diametrically opposed to the individualism of empiriological physics. The Apostle Peter is a witness to the Christian doctrine of sacrifice:

> For even hereunto were ye called, because Christ also suffered for us, leaving us an example, that ye should follow his steps; who did no sin, neither was guile found in his mouth; who when he was reviled, reviled not again; when he suffered, he threatened not, but committed himself to him that judgeth righteously; who his own self bore our sins in his own body on the tree, that we, being dead to sins, should live unto righteousness; by whose stripes ye were healed. *1 Peter 2:21-24*

Sacrifice is the glue that bonds marriage and the family; selfishness fractures that bond. When that splitting occurs: it is usually the new twigs that have sprouted from our sides that suffer the greatest, those twigs are our children.

The family glue may even reach the supper table. The author had the pleasure of learning the power of a mother's sacrifice as a young lad. In the year 1949 my dad died at thirty-six years of age leaving my mom, Helen Keller—for that is her name, and to me she is as famous as the historical lady—a mountain to climb; that mountain: to raise us five children. For several years following dad's death we struggled, and this struggle often reached the supper table. Mom was seen eating the meanest portions of the meal. When we were fortunate enough to have a whole chicken in the pot, (that means a chicken including the yellow feet) mom would be seen reaching for the neck portion, and the yellow-feet. Several years passed and one day we saw more food on the table. It was this day that I saw my mom reach into the pot and retrieve a whole chicken thigh. She proceeded to eat the thigh with relish. It was at that moment that as a young lad I began to blurt out, "Mom, I didn't know you liked...", and I caught himself and suddenly realized that mom sacrificed those many years and now she was able to relax and enjoy a single meal. The author was overcome with emotion and had to hold back the tears. It has been sixty years since that night, and that moment still brings tears to my eyes. Had mom chose to satisfy herself all those years, her children could have perished. "Love seeketh not her own" (I Cor. 13:5).

It is noteworthy that among some so-called uncivilized tribes as noted by Durant in *The Mansions of Philosophy*, some mothers nurse their children for twelve years, and that among the New Hebrides tribes some mothers kill themselves to take care of their dead child beyond the grave. But the greatest sacrifice the world will ever know took place on an old rugged cross at Calvary. We should love as He loved us. This is where the now disdained clause originated, *till death due us part.* Here again the Apostle declares, "Husbands love your wives as Christ loved the church and gave himself for it" (Eph. 5:25). The glue of marriage is sacrifice.

Choice

W. Fisher-Hunter is wrong regarding the origin of marriage; here he states:

> The idea that marriage is made in heaven is false. The truth is, marriage is a divine institution that pertains only to the earthly existence of mankind (Matt. 22:30). As constituted in the beginning it is a contract which one man and one woman voluntarily enter into; nevertheless, God will hold them responsible in it.[23]

He is partially correct by stating that marriages are made on earth, however marriages are made in heaven and earth. Adam required the Creator of the universe to intercede and find him a wife. Eve was made on the earth, but who would deny that the first marriage was not also made in heaven.

"For this cause shall a man leave his father and mother, and shall be joined unto his wife, and they two shall be one flesh. This is a great mystery; but I speak concerning Christ and his church" (Eph. 5:31-32). The mystery is the awesome merging of the heavenly with the earthly. The romance of this merging event gives birth to our songs and poems. It has been said that the pure sexual act is 99% spiritual (heavenly), and 1.0% physical (earthly). This mixture of heavenly and earthly aroused in Adam the aggressiveness to bond to the woman, exuberantly surrounding her with his masculinity. Her attraction is both spiritual and physical. He senses her promise of companionship as well as being attracted to her physically. Using physical terms, he claims the woman is his bone and flesh. Adam's words speak of the woman as irresistible. Her silence speaks of approval. She was created with the power of speech and could have rejected Adams's advances,

---

[23] Fisher-Hunter, The Divorce Problem (MacNeish; Waynesboro, PA 1952)

  p. 11

but passively and with a sense of delight the woman joins the man and is not ashamed. She immediately consents to his proposal, and in that sense (proposal/consent), I agree that marriages are made on earth.

One major factor that must be established before any successful solution can be found to the marriage/divorce/remarriage question that is addressed in the title of this chapter, and that factor is: "Who hath God joined together?" Mr. Hunter is again incorrect with his assumption: "Moreover, the idea that God is responsible for having united every man and woman who are married is also untrue." Hunter admits by his statement that God is responsible for uniting some marriages. My question to Mr. Hunter is, "Which marriages has God not united."

When discussing this issue, we must not loose sight of the element of choice. This e lement is a divine element which may be the actual heavenly activity joining the partners in marriage. E. Neufeld list two defined lines of marriage: (a) intention and, (b) actual consummation.[24] Heth and Wedham list four lines: (a) consent and intent, (b) ratification of parents, (c) ratification of public witnesses, and (d) physical consummation.[25] Atkinson following Dunstan list five marks of marriage: (a) the initiative of love, (b) vow of consent, (c) obligation of faithfulness, (d) promise of blessing, and (e) the centrality of sacrifice.[26] All these points must be considered but the major points are: (a) choice, (b) consent, (c) a public wedding (d) and consummation. (No one would deny the war veteran, or the lame the right to marry. Where each party is in an agreement—I suppose—the consummation could be defined as the maximum possible physical expression that could be corporately expressed).

Creation dictates the aggressive nature of the male, the passive yet thoughtful nature of the female. The Shulamite speaks, "Let him kiss

---

[24] Heth W.A.; Wenham G. quote Neufeld E. in Jesus and Divorce (Hodder/ Stoughton, London 1984) p. 103

[25] Ibid. p. 103, 104

[26] Atkinson, D. To Have and To Hold (Eerdmans; Grand Rapids, MI 1979) p. 94

me with the kisses of his mouth." She anxiously awaits her aggressor with a permissive spirit. Jacob approached the well, rolled the stone away, and kissed Rachel. Consent must be won. The man must be gentle, strong, romantic, and practical. When the prerequisites have been satisfied the stage is set for the drama of love. The verbs *to have* and *to take* have a special place in marriage. They are terms of common law. The Baptist, when speaking to Herod said, "It is not lawful for thee to have her." And the Apostle reported, "It is commonly reported that there is fornication among you, and such fornication as is not so much as named among the Gentiles, that one should have his father's wife." Abraham told his eldest servant, "Thou shalt not take a wife unto my son of the daughters of the Canaanites, among whom I dwell: but thou shalt go unto my country, and to my kindred, and take a wife unto my son Isaac." Even our children's nursery rhymes carry the thought of to take: *The farmer takes a wife, the farmer takes a wife, heigh ho the der-y-o, the farmer takes a wife.*

There is something final about taking a wife. Choice has been propitiated. Decision has been exercised. Contract has been negotiated. The wedding has been celebrated. What God has instigated in marriage is the act of choice/consent. I will address *arrangement marriage*, but for the moment we must realize that God aggressively guards man's right to choose the bride, and the ladies right of consent. This is the mystery of love. Add this concept to the finality of man's word and vows especially in the Old Testament, and one realizes the power of choice/consent.

Consent

The man's choice is contingent upon the acceptance of the lady. Both are contingent upon social interaction. To leave father and mother, and to obey the command to honor father and mother, implies that parental blessing will be sought by the pair. Note that Heth and Wedham have included parental consent in their definition of marriage, but as mentioned parental consent is bound up in the pair's choice/consent. Nevertheless, should the pair make a choice/

consent which does not receive parental blessings the union is still defended by the Creator who aggressively protects choice/consent. Some may object to (choice/consent) claiming that social *arrangement marriage* annuls it. It must be conceded that in a culture where the parents arrange the marriage that the groom agrees to the custom and thereby knowingly concedes his right of choice. Even where parental arrangement is the norm, should the groom step out of line, his choice is still a binding marriage. Samson ordered his parents to take him a wife of the daughters of the Philistines; and they did so (Jud.14).

Western culture understands parental blessing as a secondary concern, whereas eastern culture looks upon it as a primary concern; but keep in mind that both seek parental blessing. The parent in the east is laboring to ensure the child's happiness, as is the western parent, probably with the same energy and interest. Both customs culminate in the wedding, regardless of eastern or western influence. The wedding is a peculiar cultural custom. There are as many different wedding ceremonies as there are different cultures. Customs precedes laws. Customs are created by people. Groups of people design a common practice which is acceptable by the many and that practice is refined to an acceptable custom. The custom is protected, and cherished, and becomes a tradition. Children in their games act out particular customs which they will mature to experience in actuality. The wedding is a common game among the young girls. Regardless of the culture the custom is honored. Isaac was overwhelmed with the joy of Rebekah, "And Isaac brought her into his mother Sarah's tent, and took Rebekah, and she became his wife; and he loved her." Here the public wedding consisted of the public offering of the parental tent.

Wedding

Public testimony is a vital element to any social contract, and marriage is a social contract. Marriage is a public social act, a wedding. The strongest customs on earth are religious customs, and the public wedding is the most universal custom; and I might say the strongest of all customs at that. This is only fitting since marriages are made in heaven and on earth. The details of the wedding custom are not significant; the historical event is significant. The verbal and written contract is complete in the public testimony. The wedding event is climaxed in the conjugal act of physical consummation, the private physical contract. Thus, the physical consummation is totally part of the wedding.

Marriage is a legal act, not based on the state, but based on the law of creation. Jesus said, "from the beginning, it, i.e. (putting away, or divorce) was not so." He was questioned regarding the meaning of the law of Moses, but Jesus answers to the meaning of a higher law; the Law of Creation-Marriage. More than the Sabbath Day was established in creation; the common laws of God were created. Blackstone concludes that common laws are doctrines "not set down in any written statute, but depending upon immemorial usage for their support."[27] On the seventh day the Sabbath became a Law. Creation-Marriage is now also a universal common law. Antiquity has produced several ancient codes, and most, if not all, contain marriage regulations. But prior to the written codes, marriage was controlled by the common law of Creation. The ancient codes only support the creation-marriage law. Christ invoked the creation-marriage code which was written in the epistle of the Creation with the marriage of Adam and Eve—please note I did not say Adam and Steve. The common law of marriage was written in the creation and the existence of the *Single Pair*. All that Christ decreed regarding His marriage doctrine was imbedded in the *Single Pair*. "From the beginning, it (putting away), was not so"; thus, it was not lawful for a man to divorce his wife for any reason.

The common corporate act of Eden was the basis of God's relationship to Israel. "Thou shalt fear the Lord thy God; him shalt thou serve, and to him shalt thou cleave" (Deut. 10:20). "Turn, O backsliding children, saith the Lord: for I am married unto you" (Jer.

---

[27] Ency. Britannica (1960) v 6:123

3:14). "Thou shalt make no covenant with them, or with their gods" (Ex. 23:32). The Israelites understood the terms of covenant because those terms were marriage terms. This can be seen in the delightful story of Ruth and her mother-in-law, Naomi. It cannot go unnoticed that Ruth clave unto Naomi, not merely remaining her companion but remaining a companion till death due her part; "Where thou diest, will I die, and there will I be buried; the Lord do so to me, and more also, if aught but death part thee and me" (Ruth 1:17). We find Ruth understanding the covenant terms of marriage with keen accuracy: *cleaving till death do us part.* Did this concept generate out of the Genesis marriage? This author believes so. Is not this the idea Adam had in mind when he proclaimed *bone of my bones, and flesh of my flesh.* The simple question is, "When would her bones and flesh cease to be his?" Her flesh would be his flesh till death. Their relationship was bound in blood; life is in the blood. Blood is generated by the bone: therefore, we are assured that Adam and Eve were kinfolk. The *Single Pair* was family. The only way to cease from being family is to cease in death. Till death do us part. Thus: no-remarriage-this-side-of death.

Therefore, marriage is complete when: (a) the man makes a choice, (b) the lady consents, and (c) the wedding is complete. For centuries laws have regulated this act. Even in Eden there was a condition placed on marriage; that it must be sought outside the parental relationship; incest was forbidden. This was not the case of the fornicator of Corinth, who had taken his father's wife, or of Herod who took his brother's wife. The condition was clearly commanded, that the pair would have to leave father and mother. The Mosaic Law (Lev. 18) would clearly define the forbidden degrees of marriage within the limits of family or consanguinity.

God's full doctrine of marriage existed in the Garden. Moses did not define marriage; God did. Jesus said that Moses had to compromise God's will regarding marriage, because man's heart would not permit the creation doctrine of marriage. It actually appears that had Moses codified the Creation-Marriage Law in the Mosaic Law, he would have caused some men to kill their wives. The idea of hardness is all inclusive, indicating that some men were prepared to commit the violent act of wife-murder if they did not get their way in their absolute will to expel (divorce) their wives. Even today, the courts award divorce readily in fear that if they refuse, the woman will be subject to abuse and death. During the decades of the mid-twentieth century the abuse of women was well documented. Strong laws were promulgated to defend the women, and consequently today these laws are still in the books. This in spite of the fact that the table of abuse has in many cases turned, and today some women have become the violent aggressors, recording many criminal cases of abuse against the man; husband abuse. If this continues the state will most likely reverse the laws that now support women.

God's will regarding marriage as witnessed in the Garden preceded the State, Israel, Moses, and the Church. "The idea that God's will is not to be obeyed is an idea quite alien to Jewish thinking.[28] Isaksson comments on the relevance of God's will:

> The distinction between the sphere of the law and a sphere in which God's will is expressed but mankind is not bound to try to obey it, is a distinction foreign to the N.T....In other words, to make a distinction like this is based on conditions derived from a different period and a different environment than those of the N.T.[29]

The Old Testament saint believed that any revelation of God's will has the binding force of law. Jesus called the Psalms, God's law in (Jn. 12:34) when quoting (Ps. 82:6), "Is it not written in your law, I said, Ye are gods." The Jews answered him likewise, "The people answered him, "We have heard out of the law that Christ abideth forever: and how sayest thou, the son of man must be lifted up;" a ref-

---

[28] Isaksson, A. Marriage and Ministry in the New Temple (Lund, Gleeup, Copenhagen 1965) p. 86

[29] Ibid. p. 87

erence to (Psalm 102:26, 27) being understood to be the Law of God. Again in (Jn. 15:25) Jesus said, "But this cometh to pass, that the word might be fulfilled that is written in their law: They hated me without a cause", a reference to (Psa. 35:19, and 69:4). Merril F. Unger in his dictionary defines the law of God as:

> A term employed almost 200 times in the Bible and signifying the revealed will of God with respect to human conduct. It includes all the Divine commands and precepts for regulating man's moral life without and within.

Dr. H. L. Willmington in his *Guide to the Bible* lists a total of 613 commandments in the Old Testament which Israel believed consisted of God's Law. The Biblical term law has a broad range of significance.

Creation-Marriage, therefore, is God's law; a law that was revealed in the very creation of man. It is a law of creation as is the law of gravity. The *Single Pair's* creation-marriage was indissoluble. God's revealed will was that marriage is indissoluble. Indissoluble marriage is the law of God. To change that law would require the same force required to change the law of gravity. It would literally require God to dissolve heaven and earth and create a new universe with different natural laws. Thus creation-marriage is with us today 6,000 years since its inception; listen to these definitions from Black's Law Dictionary:

> Leave: Willful departure with intent to remain away, and not merely a temporary absence with intention of returning.
>
> Join: To unite; to come together, to combine or unite in time, effort, action, to enter into an alliance.
>
> Marriage: As distinguished from the agreement to marry and from the act of becoming married, the civil status, condition or relation of one man and one woman united in law for life, for the discharge to each

other and the community of the duties legally incum-
bent on those whose association is founded on the
distinction of sex.

The wedding is interpreted by culture and custom and these dic-
tate the dreams and fears of the event. Youth of all culture's past,
present and future gather and will gather from society those activities
that are honored as wedding ceremonies. These customs are deeply
ingrained in our social mores. Likewise, the creation-marriage wedding must be embraced by all Bible believing pastors, teachers, evangelists; all of the members of the Body of Christ; the Church. This is
one of the most important soul-winning doctrines neglected by the
evangelist of our day. Heresy will hinder both the soul-winner and the
lost he was sent to win.

Heresy

Creation-marriage, indissoluble marriage, is an absolute literal
commandment. The majority of modern commentators flatly reject
this idea. Lost souls and most saved alike are repulsed by the doctrine
of an indissoluble union; their chorus appears to be: "Let us break
their bands asunder and cast away their cords from us." The scholar's objections include a form of semantic confusion. Men like E. G.
Dobson persuade that since "the Lord God threatened to divorce
Israel, divorce is not an act of sin; because God cannot sin."[30] J.E.
Adams is bold when he persuades for divorce claiming that, "God is
a divorced person;" because He divorced Israel.[31] The commandment
of creation-marriage is foreign to their dissertations. I have chosen
to persuade for the commandment of permanency; they for a false
teaching of divorce.

---

[30] Dobson, E.G. What the Bible Teaches About Marriage, Divorce, and
    Remarriage (Flemming H. Revell, Old Tappan, NJ 1986) p. 42-47
[31] Adams, J.E., Marriage, Divorce, and Remarriage (Presbyterian and
    Reformed Pub. Co. Phillipsburg, NJ 1980) p. 24

The fundamental Bible believer embraces a, grammatical-historical-literal hermeneutics. We boldly claim that the way of truth. We spurn the allegorist and separate ourselves from the modernist-liberal. Vain philosophy is far from our door. But dear reader, are you prepared to measure marriage with the literal-grammatical-historical method? To teach the literal interpretation of Edenic marriage to the Church of Christ is the most difficult task facing the evangelists, and pastors of our day. It is difficult because the saints refuse to hear God's command. "Oh yes", they say, when asked if they believe the literal teaching of Genesis; and "Yes", the Edenic marriage is a literal permanent indissoluble marriage. But when this preacher translates this doctrine into a commandment for modern man, they say, "No!" And then they go on to philosophize the truth away. Rigid rules, or absolute commands have a way of exposing the narrow minds of the Modernist-Liberal. They immediately respond to the absolute with intolerance, and rebellion. Immature children have a like reaction, always interpreting limits as confinement rather than safety. Liberals like children demand thoughts that permit them limitless activity. When confronted with an absolute command, they resort to philosophy; thus, paving the way to liberalism which usually includes sinful conduct. Therefore, when confronted with the doctrine of creation-marriage man is faced with a dilemma. The predicament is obvious. Creation-marriage is sound doctrine. It is simple. It is unobjectionable. It is literally solid as concrete. Therefore, it leaves all men with one of two alternatives; man must believe it, or he must philosophize it away. The philosophy used is as old as sin. It simply teaches that creation-marriage is true, but it is only an IDEAL. This simple philosophical maneuver has succeeded throughout the history of man. It has succeeded as a most fierce cruel weapon of Satan, a weapon designed to destroy the children of men. Let us study the ideal deception of modern philosophy.

Immanuel Kant—his first name should accord him no spiritual honor since his only resemblance to our Immanuel ends there—must be credited with the invention of the ideal scheme. Perhaps he could qualify as one of the false-Christ's who would come in Jesus name? His parent's were members of the Pietist sect, devoted to the strict teaching of New Testament principles, "The new birth must always be preceded by the agonies of repentance and that only a regenerated theologian could teach theology,"[32] is a sample of their belief. Immanuel attended a strict school where as he said, he was exposed to the fearful teachings of an everlasting hell as well as solid Bible courses and was obligated to practice austere piety. Kant later resented this heavy dose of piety and terror; "fear and trembling," he said, overcame him when he recalled those days.[33]

Note that resentment was the reaction of this lad to the rigor of a strict disciplined Christian school. It is regrettable that after a life as a philosopher, Kant at the age of sixty-nine in an attempt to redeem his religious heritage entered into the field of theology. His famous essays, *Religion within the Limits of Reason Alone,* have made him famous to the world and infamous to Biblicists. He preached the innate goodness of man, universal morality, morality does not need divine revelation (Scripture), Christ was the most godlike of men (the ideal man), and that it should not be necessary for a Christian to believe in miracles, or in the divinity of Christ.[34] Reason was his god and savior, and Reason gave him those glorified ideas and ideals. His most notorious convert was the wicked, George Wilhelm Friedrich Hegel.

Hegel was also born into a family steeped in piety. His godly parents mortgaged their property to send George to study theology at Thuringen Seminary. After graduating, Hegel disappointed his parents by refusing to enter the ministry. He later denied the virgin birth, rejected miracles, pictured Christ as a crucified rebel, and he did not mention the resurrection. His definition of God: "Pure Reason, incapable of any limitations is Deity itself,[35] certainly identifies him with Kant. Hegel became a political idealist and invented "Dialectic

---

[32] Ency. Britannica (1960) v17:919

[33] Durant, W. & A. quote T.M. Green in The Story of Civilization (Simon and Schuster, NY, NY 1967) v.10:532

[34] Ibid. p. v. 10:546

[35] Ibid. p. v. 11:645

Logic". It is surprising that Hegel would have been read by anyone, considering the remark of Schopenhauer:

> The height of absurdity inserving uppure non-sense, in stringing together senseless and extravagant masses of words, such as had previously been known only in madhouses, finally reached in Hegel, and became the instrument of the most beautiful mystification that has ever taken place, with a result which will appear fabulous to posterity, and will remain as a monument of German stupidity.[36]

Nevertheless, after his death, two schools of Hegelian thought evolved: the Hegelian Right with its contribution, *Higher Criticism*, and the Hegelian Left with the political philosophy of the atheist, Carl Marx.

Hegel concluded that the true essence of Christianity resides in its great Ideas, not in the historical events that gave birth to them.[37] These great ideas, to the mystical idealist, are mere visions of hope, unattainable but truly honorable goals. Targets higher then anyone can reach; literally impossible dreams. The meaning of a standard capable of existing only as a mental concept by virtue of its unattainable perfection, ideals is the meaning the Liberals need so they can escape the demands of absolute commands. The philosophy of Kant and Hegel would not only produce Higher Criticism and Marxism, but would go on to inspire Ritchl, Schleiermacher, Troeltsch, Darwin, Fosdick and the spirit of Liberalism. Kenneth Cauther makes this observation of Liberalism:

> Liberalism is a certain attitude toward all of life
> and the world as one great process with God at work
> in it to give purpose with man at the center in the

---

[36] Ibid. p. v. 11:645 (Schopenhauer in)
[37] Showers, Robert E. What On Earth Is God Doing? (Loizeaux, Neptune, NJ 1973) p. 79

image of God. This divine deposit is to be developed
to the highest extent through the rule of love. When
it is widespread we will have a world brotherhood living up to the highest ideal [emphasis mine] even as
Jesus did.[38]

Idealism is the father of Liberalism. The Modernist-Liberal
Church has proposed this philosophy since its inception. Then
Evangelicalism embraced this false teaching; but today some professed Fundamentalists have embraced this heresy, preaching and
teaching dissoluble-marriage. Ambrozic has clearly stated this matter:

When Paul gives the Lord's teaching on indissolubility of marriage, he is not offering advice; neither
is he counseling or exhorting his readers to strive for
a beautiful ideal. For him, Jesus' teaching is God's will
which must be obeyed.[39]

The ambiguity of the debate is the fact that Jesus' teaching of
indissoluble marriage is almost a universally accepted conviction. The
liberal, moderate, and conservative commentators all agree that this is
the definite doctrine of Christ. Thus, in order for the liberal and moderate to think of a dissoluble union they must reach out to the drug
of idealism to permit their infraction. But when the Fundamental
Biblicist employs idealism to support his compromise, one can only
look down with sadness, and despair. While refusing to believe and
teach the literal truth of the Garden Wedding, the brethren have
accepted the poison drug of idealism and commit heresy. God has
clearly posted his warning concerning this danger: "Beware lest any
man spoil you through philosophy and vain deceit, after the tradi-

---

[38] Dollar, G.W. quote Kenneth Cauther in A History of Fundamentalism
    (BJU Press, Greenville,SC 1973) p. 91
[39] Ambrozic, Aloysius, Indissolubility of Marriage in the N.T.:Law or Ideal?
    (Studia Canonica 6; 1972) p. 285

tion of man, after the rudiments of the world, and not after Christ." (Col. 2:8).

The leaven of idealism regarding creation-marriage is so subtle that many of the current authors, both liberal and conservative, employ the "ideal" in their writings:

P.E. Steel and C.H. Ryrie, *Meant to Last*, (Victor, Wheaton, Ill. 1983) "He forced them to view the divine ideal in Genesis 2. (p. 88) "This is, without question, the ideal that God declared in His Word. (p. 88)

R.W. DeHaan, *Marriage, Divorce, Remarriage* (Radio Bible Class, Grand Rapids, Mich. 1979) "There are exceptional situations where steps less than ideal are taken." (p. 7)

Edward G. Dobson, *Fundamentalist Journal*, "God's ideal for the permanency of marriage has not changed." (Oct. 1985, p.39) "In Luke 16:18 we find the general teaching of Jesus that presents God's ideal."; "In Luke 16 and Mark 10, Jesus is giving the ideal." (Dec. 1985: p. 35) "Jesus encouraged God's ideal for marriage," (Jan 1986 p. 39)

Guy Duty, *Divorce and Remarriage*, (Bethany House, Minn. MN, 1967) "Jesus is reverting to the original, gave affirmation to the Creator's intent and purpose of marriage. The divine ideal of the New Testament law has its basis in the original." (p. 69)

Lewis Sperry Chafer, *Systematic Theology* (Dallas Sem. Press, Dallas TX, 1948) "It was clearly taught in the New Testament that, because of an advance in the relationship between God and His saints, there should be the most careful recognition of this more exalted ideal of one wife and one husband." (7:234)

A.T. Robertson, *Word Pictures In the New Testament* (Broadman, Nashville, TN, 1930) "The present perfect active of ginomai to emphasize the permanence of the divine ideal. (10:154) Bruce quoted in Ibid. "How small the Pharisaic disputants must have felt in presence of such holy teaching, which soars above the partisan view of controversialists into the serene region of ideal, universal, eternal truth." (Ibid. 10:54)

A command is not an ideal. Men who refuse to obey a command will gladly believe in an ideal. The pulpits of our land are filled with pastors who employ the heresy of philosophical idealism while teaching the saints to compromise God's creation-marriage command. The sermons of these pastors refuse to preach that marriage is indissoluble by employing the following terms: God's intention, God's plan, God's desire, God's institution, God's principle, God's ordinance, and God's ultimate desire. Their language betrays their stubborn refusal to teach God's marriage command. One can understand the rebellion of the Liberal-Modernist and the Evangelicals, but when the true Biblicist's participates in this heresy one exclaims, "His coming draweth nigh," for he said, "Nevertheless when the Son of man cometh, shall he find faith on the earth."

Marriage

We are now ready to define marriage. The definition of which will answer the question,"Who hath God joined together"? Creation-marriage is the axiom of all marriage. Creation-marriage was the emotional/physical joining of one man and one woman (monogamy) to form a new single unit. The two literally became one. This unity is indissoluble and inseparable. It was literally an act of creation. On the sixth day, male and female created He them. Man was created married. Marriage requires the severance of the familial union and the joining of the marriage union. Man was created a plurality, a family.

Marriage has been manifest when one (never been married or widowed) man, and one (never been married or widowed) woman, consent to, and complete a public wedding ceremony.

Therefore, God has joined together every man and woman who meets the above definition—the only exemption would be marriages of Jewish couples during the dispensation of the Law; there both partners were required to be Jewish. Although God advises against the believer marrying unbelievers, He nevertheless will honor such Church Age marriages as holy (1 Cor. 7:13, 14). Thus, God has not joined together anyone who already has a living spouse during the lifetime of a divorced partner, regardless of the conditions; that union is adulterous.

NO-REMARRIAGE-THIS-SIDE-OF-DEATH

CHAPTER TWO

From Whence Cometh
Polygamy and Divorce?

Will Durant, the historian, wrote that man is a secret and ravenous polygamist.[40] This certainly was not true of Adam when created. He was very good: "And God saw everything that he had made, and, behold, it was very good. And the evening and the morning were the sixth day" (Gen. 1:31). Then, when did the change occur? The answer to that question is at the heart of Bible doctrine. Soon after the Fall man realized he was deep into sin. His tendencies were no longer toward innocence but were prone to evil. Adam's delight with Eve was beyond question. Even if God created a Jane, it appears that Adam would have paid her no attention. He loved his bride.

Then Adam's eldest son suddenly betrayed this serenity. It is alarming that the first human death was the result of fratricide. If Cain's jealousy could only be satisfied by murder, what would appease his lust—rape or perhaps a new doctrine of marriage: polygamy? Durant is correct when he portrays man as a ravenous polygamist; for this is a common lust of natural man. Adam's disobedience was transmitted to all his children, even to those who oppress all outward acts of sin. The prophet Jeremiah revealed the common trait of man: "The heart is deceitful above all things, and desperately wicked; who can know it," (Jer. 17:9). God's command is His absolute will. The nature of Eden spelled God's will to be life. The murder of Adam's youngest son seriously defied God's absolute will. God's will was so ingrained in nature that all of nature was excited to vengeance when the shepherd boy, Abel, was murdered. Cain would have been instantly consumed for his sin, for our God is a consuming fire; but God often refrains from immediate judgment. This is an important factor in the equation of human existence. Should God at any time elect to judge the

---

[40] Durant, W. The Mansions of Philosophy (Garden City Pub. NY, NY 1941) p. 226

wickedness of man, He would immediately destroy every sinner; He certainly would have destroyed Cain. But this would have reduced the human population to two men. God generally per-mits the sinner to exist; we call this God's permissive will. He permits sinners to live for a period of time. In the other Garden, Jesus said, "Thinkest thou that I cannot now pray to my Father, and he shall presently give me more than twelve legions of angels"? (Matt. 26:53). Should God choose judgment rather than mercy, we would all die a fiery death. But man's existence is always directly proportional to God's mercy to permit man to exist. Whether there was one man on the earth, or six billion men.

Consequently, God's merciful permission to man is to permit man to exist; to modern man this means he is given three score and ten years. We do not die immediately for our sin, we eventually die. Along with our existence God permits our sin to co-exist; this is directly related to our existence. Therefore, Cain was permitted to exist after committing a violent murder. But this permission was complex. The nature of man also understands justice, and his justice demands vengeance. Cain knew this and fears the hand of man; "It shall come to pass that anyone that findeth me shall slay me." God also knew the vengeance of man, and forbid man to judge Cain. God's permissive will is His voluntary act of grace, and His grace abounds. God mercifully places a mark on Gain and threatens the man that would kill Cain with a sevenfold judgment. Here we find a profound mystery. The mystery is that although God permits the sinner to live He never permits him to sin. He never approves of his sin. But the consequence in permitting the sinner to live means that God must permit the sinners sin to go immediately unpunished. He might even regulate, or mark the sin, so that it does not destroy the man, i. e. Cain. After the Flood, Noah was ordered to form a human government designed with its now God given power of human capital punishment. Gen 9:6 Whoso sheddeth man's blood, by man shall his blood be shed: for in the image of God made He man.

Permit me to explain this with common terms. The history of man is often studied by the articles he leaves behind, as he camps along the hills of life. Unfortunately, these articles are most likely litter, and garbage. His acts of pleasure, and war are even more hazardous, the former produced AIDS, the latter an A-Bomb. Pollution and death is caused by man's existence. Before Noah, God permitted the Cain's to exist by controlling their sin, he *marked* it, and he set rules about it, *seven fold judgments*. But Christ marked a new era. Rather than destroying all sinners, and recreating a new earth, God chose to *bruise his* Son. He permitted the sins of man to destroy His Son, on a bloody cross, so that man might be born again.

He also ushered in a new era, whereby His will would again be absolute, as it was in the Creation. Therefore, during the period of history between the Fall, and the Cross, God regulated sin, or regulated pollution. By permitting man to live, he permitted the pollution of man to exist, however, God did regulate and control the pollution. Two of the artifacts of man's debris are polygamy, and divorce with remarriage.

God initially controlled sin by ordaining that man would be regulated by his conscience, "And the eyes of them both were opened, and they knew that they were naked; and they sewed fig leaves together and made themselves aprons." Conscience was designed to control the sin; sin that God hated. Conscience, the trophy of man, was the weakest of all controls; it almost led to the annihilation of mankind. "Who sometime were disobedient, when once the long-suffering of God waited in the days of Noah, while the ark was preparing, in which few, that is, eight souls, were saved by water." Conscience led man into the deadly Flood-Judgment. God also permitted man to govern man. Human government had a twofold design, (1) it offered man the right to control his own sin, and (2) it would prove to man that he could not govern sin out of his life. Rather than using human government to humble his sin nature, man used human government to inflame himself, "let us make us a name." With a tower to heaven, he believed he could rule the universe. Although human government would be ordained throughout history the judgment which destroyed the Tower of Babel pronounced the sentence of death on the hope that human government would provide man eternal salvation. But human government was in control of sin which existed because of the existence of man. Although this failed, nevertheless, human government did control and regulate the sins of men.

Man has proved that his nature is violent. "The earth also was corrupt before God, and the earth was filled with violence" (Gen. 6:11). As Jeremiah said, "The heart is deceitful above all things, and desperately wicked; who can know it" (Jer. 17:9). The point is that conscience, and human government (human laws), are band-aids on the cancer of man's depravity. Man, labors to conceal his sin. Under human government rather than clubbing his brother, man hid his evil nature under his tongue, but Jesus saw his heart. "Whosoever shall say to his brother, Raca, shall be in danger of the council; but whosoever shall say, Thou fool, shall be in danger of hell fire." Rather than sleeping with Bathsheba, man chose to imagine his way into her bed, "Whosoever looketh on a woman to lust after her hath committed adultery with her already in his heart." The garments of man's sin are filthy rags.

> But we are all as an unclean thing, and all our righteousnesses are as filthy rags; and we all do fade as a leaf, and our iniquities, like the wind, have taken us away. *Isa. 64:6*

As men invented ways to avoid the outward act of sin, he actually covered his sin with sin. His hard heart would not repent, rather he worked on his sin. Man's garment coverings for sin were invisible garments to God, but man believed in them because other men could not see the real sin, the inner man. Rather than clubbing his younger brother the eldest now used those four letter words (Raca, fool, etc.). Rather than hate his wife man now used a new weapon: divorce. Man's nature was particularly violent on the domestic front. The ferocity of man's nature in the home strained God's longsuffering. To Jesus' question, "What did Moses command you?" The Pharisees said, "Moses suffered to write a bill of divorcement, and to put her away." (Dear reader please note here that the Pharisees who were experts on the Law did not have a verse to quote that referenced a divorce *COMMANDMENT.*) Jesus then explains God's reasoning, "Moses, because of the hardness of your heart, suffered (permitted) you to put away your wives, but from the beginning it was not so." *Divorce was not an invention of heaven*, it was one of the manufactured garments of sin, *the invention of man*. It is of the earth, nothing more than a feeble covering for the sin of man. As we shall see its existence predates Moses. *This is very important to the truth we discuss here.*

Another garment of sin was *polygamy*. Rather than commit adultery, a man divorced his wife, and married his paramour. Rather than raping the beautiful young maid, man invented polygamy; he just married another wife. *God permitted man to invent divorce and polygamy*. He permitted man's sin to exist, as he permitted sinful man to exist. These feeble coverings for sin are actually the sinful acts and inventions of man. God did not invent divorce or polygamy. Later we will discuss why God chose to permit these sinful acts to exist in the Mosaic Law; but first let us study the ancient laws of man; laws that *preceded Moses*.

The Antediluvian Society: (Gen. 4-6)

Creation-marriage is the doctrine of God throughout all ages. Time and circumstance have no influence on its content and application. After 4000 years of human history, Jesus clearly stated this fact, "from the beginning, it (to put away) was not so." Idealism, divorce, polygamy, the inventions of man did not alter Jesus' doctrine of creation-marriage. Theologians refer to *progressive revelation* as doctrine that is revealed, gradually, throughout Scripture, but the revelation of marriage was totally revealed in the Garden of Eden (Gen. 1-2). Man's actions that surround marriage require us to study all of history, and the entire Bible; customs play a part in history. Keep in mind that Noah was ordered to form a human government, and that dispensation is with us to this day, and impacts this discussion. Also keep in mind that Moses—notice I said Moses—was ordered to form a unique human government to rule not the world, but the Hebrew Nation; human government is never perfect. The Law could not promulgate righteousness. It was weak in that effect.

The first marriage question that arises out of Scripture is: Who did Cain marry? Since creation-marriage required Cain to leave his mother and father and to be joined to a wife, certainly eliminated

Eve the only woman, of becoming Cain's wife. We read in Gen. 5:4, 5 that Adam lived 930 years and begot sons and daughters. Thus, Cain married one of his sisters, or possibly one of his siblings' daughters. At this period of history his marriage to a daughter of Adam was not forbidden. Incest was limited to a marriage, or sexual act between mother and son, and father and daughter.

Surprisingly the next major objection to creation-marriage is the question: What of Bible polygamy? Creation-marriage was monogamy. In the seventh generation of Adam the Bible records the first act of polygamy. The first recorded sin was the eating of the forbidden fruit, the second was the murder of Abel, and the third was the polygamy of Lamech—Man does appear to be a ravenous polygamist. "And Lamech took unto him two wives", (Gen. 4:19). At first glance this appears to be a simple matter of a man taking two women in marriage; but a closer look will reveal several important elements. Please note that polygamy is not a simple matter; this was an entirely new doctrine regarding marriage, and as we shall see, it was the sinful invention of an evil man—need I say more. It is absolutely void of any blessing or approval from our Holy God.

The statement of Lamech's polygamy is introduced abruptly, as to mark Lamech, as the murderer Cain was marked. The tip off regarding the character of Bible personages is often found in their name: Adam *(adam, adamah, ground)*, Eve *(hawah, life giver)*. Kiel and Delitzsch point out that Lamech turned marriage into the lust of the eye, and the lust of the flesh. "The names of the women (Lamech's women) are indicative of sensual attractions: *Adah: the adorned;* and *Tillah: shady, tinkling* [41] The *adorned* reminds us of Jezebel who while attempting to circumvent the judgment of God by painting her face; actually, making it more appetizing to the man-eating dogs that ate it. Shady was a trait of street prostitutes. It is noteworthy that tinkling is mentioned by Isaiah when referring to the sensual women of his day, "Moreover the Lord saith, Because the daughters of Zion are haughty,

---

[41] Kiel, C; Delitzsch, F. Old Testament Commentary (Eerdmans, Grand Rapids, MI; 1978) v 1:118

and walk with stretched forth necks and wanton eyes, walking and mincing as they go, and making a tinkling with their feet; Therefore, the Lord will smite with a scab the crown of the head of the daughters of Zion" (Isa. 3:16, 17). The uncommon record that a daughter (Naamah) was born to Zilla is mentioned, Naamah: pleasant, lovely, graceful. Kiel-Delitzsch believe her name "reflects the worldly mind of the Cainites."

Henry Morris attributes to Lamech the leadership role of the antediluvian rebellion against God; stating that he initiated his rebellion against God with his polygamy. Further suggesting that the sensuality of this society can be heard in the lyrics of Lamech's song; a song which he sang in the presence of his wives. Morris notes that although there were no paramours present, Lamech's boast to killing two men is actually a warning to all men. He warns them not to seduce his women.[42] This is a fitting commentary on the moral tone of this society; and when one reads the record in Genesis chapter six of the days immediately preceding the Flood it is evident that Lamech's fears were justified; "That the sons of God saw the daughters of men that they were fair; and they took them wives of all whom they chose" (Gen. 6:2); later we will fully discuss this text. Regardless, the first polygamist was a killer. Scripture records his confession, "Hear my voice ye wives of Lamech, and hearken unto my speech: for I have slain a man to my wounding, and a young man to my hurt." Jewish tradition believes that Tubal-Cain while guiding his nearly blind father (Lamech) to shoot a beast of prey, while on a hunt, that Lamech failed to reach, the target, and his shot mortally wounded his grandfather, Cain. Lamech was so jubilant, and excited about his deed that he began to clap his hands heavily, and in his blind condition he failed to regard Tubal-Cain, accidentally striking him in the head also killing him. His song was his celebration and self-blessing.[43]

---

[42] Morris, H.M. Genesis Record (Baker, Grand Rapids, MI 1976) p. 148

[43] Polano, H. The Talmud (Frederick Warne, London, 5636) p. 18

> And Lamech said unto his wives, Adah and Zillah,
> Hear my voice; ye wives of Lamech, hearken unto my
> speech: for I have slain a man to my wounding, and
> a young man to my hurt. If Cain shall be avenged
> sevenfold, truly Lamech seventy and sevenfold. *Gen.*
> *4:23-24*

The survival of the human race was essential to both the generation of Adam and Noah, and this depended on the hope of replenishing the earth with a large human population. Along with numbers man needed power, and the sons of Lamech were powerful. The record tells us that they were tent makers, herdsmen (red meat eaters), inventors of musical instruments, and metallurgists (metal weapons). This raises a question. Since numbers of sons was power, was it possible that Lamech was cheating on the numbers, by committing bigamy? Polygamy is nothing more than the sin of bigamy. Realizing that more than one wife gave him the potential to have many sons, he must have imagined he discovered a doctrine of marriage that would make him the savior of the world: the doctrine polygamy—a Satanic deception. Bible history never fails to document the lives of men who resist the knowledge of God.

Lamech reminds one of the Antichrist of the last day, "Who opposeth and exalteth himself above all that is called God, or that is worshiped so that he, as God, sitteth in the temple of God, showing himself that he is God" (II Thess. 2:4). The Cainites were an ungodly sensual race; thus polygamy satisfied their lust and need for power. It could also satisfy a man's need for at least one son, an heir, as we shall soon see.

The Godly Antediluvians

> And Adam knew his wife again; and she bore a
> son, and called his name Seth: For God, said she, hath
> appointed me another seed instead of Abel, whom
> Gain slew. And to Seth, to him also there was a son;

and he called his name Enos: then began men to call
upon the name of the Lord. *Gen 4:25, 26*

The next major event which affects our thesis is the birth of a
godly seed of Seth and his son Enos; "who called upon the name of
the Lord" (Gen. 4:26). In Paul's letter to the Romans we are assured
that, "Whosoever calleth upon the name of the Lord shall be saved."
Here again, most commentators, see the Sethites as a spiritual race
who found salvation by faith. Salvation is clearly visible in one of
their race, Enoch. The fact that he walked with God is mentioned
twice, perhaps for the reason that he walked with God for 300
years—a just cause for God to honor him by taking him to heaven
via a secret rapture.

But as the world turns, it remains a law of man's depravity that
the good of men is overcome by their evil, and this will continue until
the Lord returns to establish his kingdom—"thy kingdom come."
Man's battle between good and evil often takes the form of war; and
so, we have the first recorded world war, a civil war. The righteous
nation of Seth was at war with his brother, the tribe of the Cainites.
The weapons of Cain were, lust, sensuality, polygamy, and the power
associated with eating red meat, metal weapons, violence, and pride.
Seth was equipped with his faith in God, creation-marriage, peace,
and love. Jesus was successful in his defense against the darkness of
evil, "it overcame him not", but this is not so with Seth. He could have
had victory by putting his total faith in the Seed of the woman, the
promised redeemer. Eve believed this when she announced, "For God
hath appointed me another seed instead of Abel." The protevange-
lium (the promise of redemption Gen. 3:15) was the hope of man, it
was the message which was at the heart of God giving us the Book.
In this marvelous text we are given the hope of man, *the seed of the
woman,* and at the same time we are told of the enmity of the woman,
the serpent.

And I will put enmity between thee and the
woman, and between thy seed and her seed; it shall

bruise thy head, and thou shalt bruise his heal.
Gen. 3:15

The battle of the ages began that day. It would now manifest itself in the battle between Cain and Seth; this battle would be won by the seed of the woman. But before the seed of the woman would enter the scene, man was to wait on him by faith. The vehicle which would deliver this Son of God into the world was marriage, creation-marriage. Early in this battle, the serpent despised marriage, i.e. creation-marriage. Thus the Serpent was bent against creation-marriage, the vehicle of his destruction. His attempt was to corrupt marriage, thus Satan influenced Lamech to choose two wives. If Satan could succeed in corrupting marriage, he would have prevented the godly seed, *Jesus The Messiah*, his destroyer. The corruption was to permit adultery and lust, to be called marriage. Rather than lust after another woman, the married man could just marry the woman of his lust.

Satan was very successful in his early attempt to corrupt the vehicle of the promised Messiah. The proverb was fitting before its time, "Hell and destruction are never full; so the eyes of man are never full" (Prov. 27:20). Immediately before the Flood, Satan nearly succeeded in his effort to corrupt marriage. "And God looked upon the earth, and behold, it was corrupt; for all flesh had corrupted his way upon the earth" (Gen. 6:12). In the judgment of the Flood, God saw it fit to save only four creation-marriage couples.

The Battle of (Gen. 6)

Some have speculated that the *sons of God* in Genesis 6:1-4 were fallen angels, who had sexual relations with the daughters of men, resulting in the breed of beings referred to as giants or nephilim.[44] I believe this view can be refuted with what Jesus said, "For in the resurrection they neither marry, nor are given in marriage, but are as the

---

[44] NSRB (Oxford Univ. Press NY, NY 1967) p. 11

angels of God in heaven:" a clear reference to the asexual nature of the angels. However, Scofield correctly notes that, "The uniform Hebrew and Christian interpretation of (Gen. 6:2) marks the breaking down of the separation between the godly line of Seth, and the godless line of Cain." This breaking down was a marriage breakdown; an attempt to corrupt the generation of the godly seed.

The First World War was a marriage war. The Cainites with their lust-marriage were attacking the Sethites, the possessors of creation-marriage. The true prize was to preserve the *promised seed;* the loss of which would have doomed all man to eternal suffering in the fires of Hell. The Sethites were in possession of the prize. The Canites were bent on its destruction: their weapon lust. The weapon of the righteous was the preaching of the Word of God. Noah, a Sethite, was a preacher of righteousness; Lamech, a Cainite was a killer and a polygamist. The battle seems to be even until men began to multiple on the face of the earth. This comment indicates that there was a rapid population growth. Although it is speculation, but this population explosion begs the question: Was it that the doctrine of lust-marriage, polygamy, and the absence of birth control, contributed to a rapid growth in population. And could it have been that the concept of beauty, sensual beauty, contributed to a new breed of fair women. This combination could have produced an imbalance in favor of the Cainites: (1) Plentiful number of daughters, (2) These daughters were fair in the sense of sexy; (3) sons which possessed lustful physical appeal, *giants of lust and power.*

If the lust-marriage doctrine actually was the practice of the antediluvian society, the final days of that age would read as follows: And it came to pass, when Lamech's lust doctrine succeeded, the Cainites increased in unusual numbers swarming the earth in swarms. Their daughters held unusual physical appeal in a sensual sense they were fair. The Sethites, the sons of God, looked upon the daughters of the Cainites, suggests that they stopped to look at length. These tinkling, shady, lovely, pleasant, graceful, creatures enjoyed this attention. Being trained in the ways of sex-appeal, these daughters of men persuaded the Sethites to say that they were fair. The sons of God were actually saying that these promiscuous sexy females were good—the Hebrew word tohu here translated fair is unanimously translated good in Scripture.

Please permit a short parenthesis here. In the midst of the Garden, the Lord God planted the tree of knowledge of good, tohu, and evil. When the Sethites who were godly priestly men called the sensual women, tohu, they were confusing good and evil. The prophet Ezekiel found the priests of Israel doing the same thing, "Her priests have violated my law, and have profaned my holy things: they have put no difference between the holy and profane, neither have they showed difference between the unclean and the clean" (Ezek. 22:26). And again, Isaiah said, "Woe unto them who call evil good, and good evil" (Isa. 5:20). God is not the author of confusion, and therefore the seduction practiced by these beauty queens may be the basis for the antediluvian confusion.

Immediately after proclaiming that the fair ones were good, the Sethites were trapped. The lasciviousness of the pleasant females further intoxicated the sons of God, and finally the sons of God entered the seduction and "they took them wives of all whom they choose."To add insult to injury, there is something suspicious about the phrase, "all whom they chose." Could it be that the sons of God actually took multiple wives, committing adultery and polygamy? If so, then the story will continue as follows: Therefore, the Sethites, fell into apostasy inciting the anger of God, "My Spirit shall not always strive with man." But God's anger did not deter the apostasy, the Cainites and the Sethites continued in their lust creating tyrants [45] in the land in those days. These tyrants or giants were mighty gibbor men—men who believed they were messiahs. Isaiah tells us that the true coming Messiah would be the El Gibbor, "The Mighty God, the Everlasting Father, the Prince of Peace."These gib-bors were mighty Liberals, false messiahs who had no limits but their reason alone. Their thoughts and

---

[45] Kiel, C; Delitzsch, F. O.T. Commentary (Eerdmans, Grand Rapids, MI; (1978) v.1:137

imaginations were only evil continually, "And it repented the Lord that he made man, and the Lord said, I will destroy man."

There is a sense of urgency about God's decision. It appears that the corruption had reached such a height that it was about to overwhelm every man, woman, and child. But finally, at nearly the last moment, God interceded; there were only eight righteous souls remaining, souls which had not participated in the moral decline of creation-marriage. These eight souls were separated from their society by the preaching of their preacher, by a huge ark (a type of Christ), and now they would be saved from the social corruption as by water. The women who were saved from the swelling tide of social corruption were important women indeed. One of these four women would deliver the seed which would be the Savior of the world. These eight souls were four married couples, creation-marriage couples. They were the only righteous souls on the earth.

Now, this scenario is no more fabulous then, the speculation that the sons of God were fallen angels, who had sexual intercourse with earth's fair women; and that these women bore giants, E.T.'s. (extraterrestrial creatures), or A.L.F's. (alien life forms) nephilim. To the contrary, there are several facts which lend credence to the lust-marriage view. History has duplicated the declension of a nation, or society through moral corruption, and marriage corruption. Egypt grew wicked in domestic violence and became notorious for its practice of incest.[46] The moral decay of the Roman Empire is marked in history as one of the underlying causes of its fall, and Greece can boast of its invention of the word Lesbian, not to mention its contribution to male homosexuality. There is one final statement that may have some relationship to this matter. Jesus may have alluded to an antediluvian polygamy.

> And as it was in the days of Noah, so shall it be in
> the days of the Son of Man. They did eat, they drank,

---

[46] Summer, W.G. Folkways (Boston MA 1906) p. 485; Erman, Adolf Life in Ancient Egypt (Dover Put. NY, NY 1984, reprint of 1971)

they married wives, they were given in marriage, until
the day Noah was entered the ark, and the flood came,
and destroyed them all. *Luke 17:26,27*

Although the primary thought here is to reveal the serene state
of the society during the days that immediately preceded the judgment of the Flood, nevertheless, Jesus mentions that marrying and
giving wives in marriage was as frequent an eating and drinking.
The possibility that that society had an unusual preoccupation with
marriage may be enforced with the verses which immediately follow
this text:

> Likewise, also as it was in the days of Lot; they did
> eat, they drank, they bought, they sold, they planted,
> they builded; But the same day that Lot went out of
> Sodom it rained fire and brimstone from heaven and
> destroyed them all. *Luke 17:28,29*

Here again Jesus describes the tranquility which prevailed in
Sodom prior to its fiery judgment. The social sins prior to the Flood
and the fiery judgment of Sodom were abnormally bent on violence.
The sexual violence of Sodom remains the byword of sexual debauchery. Was the violence which preceded the Flood a sexual debauchery
of adultery-polygamy, and adulterous-remarriage? The reason Jesus
choose to connect the Flood with Sodom may have a relationship to
the nature of sin that prevailed prior to each judgment. Some may
say that this again is speculation, but the sins prior to the Flood were
of an equal nature to the sins prior to the destruction of Sodom; the
former was filled with the violence of adultery-polygamy, the latter
the violence of homosexuality. Both acts infuriated the Lord God who
saw to it that both acts were annihilated. The interesting point is that
both judgments permitted a few righteous souls to escape. The apparent reason to permit Noah, and Lot and family to escape, is because
they did not participate in the corruption. Therefore, the extent of the
violence was just shy of totality—the mystery of iniquity.

The final element that must be considered is that Jesus stated that the same tranquility would prevail in the society which precedes the second coming of the Son of Man. This also enlists the state of the society prior to the Son's return. Do we see massive homosexuality in our land? Do we see a massive declension in creation-marriage? The question is not: How many remain monogamous? But the question is: How many believe in creation-marriage, indissoluble marriage? "No-remarriage-this-side-of-death." How many true believers—believe—in this doctrine of marriage? The irony of the free-love culture is that it breeds violence. Note the words of the Sodomites:

> And they said, Stand back, Stand back, And they said again, This one fellow came in to sojourn, and he will needs be a judge: now will we deal worse with thee, than with them. And they pressed sore upon the man, even Lot, and came near to break the door."
> *Gen. 19:9*

The lust-marriages of Noah's day were comparable: "The earth was also corrupt before God, and the earth was filled with violence." The Apostle Peter, conveys the same message as he also combines the same two societies:

> For if God spared not the angels that sinned, but cast them down to hell, and delivered them into chains of darkness, to be reserved unto judgment; And spared not the old world, but saved Noah, the eight person, a preacher of righteousness, bringing in the flood upon the world of the ungodly; And, turning the cities of Sodom and Gomorrah into ashes, condemned them with an overthrow, making them an ensample unto those that after should live ungodly. *II Pet. 2:4-6*

Billy Graham captured the thought to which I am laboring with exceptionable simplicity: "If God does not judge our generation, He will have to apologize to Sodom and Gomorrah." If the lust-marriage scenario is correct our generation should be witnessing a plague upon creation-marriage. The modern Sethites, true regenerated believers, should be troubled by the modern Cainites and their new assault on creation-marriage. We should be witnessing the sons of God practicing marriage-divorce-remarriage-adultery-polygamy as they are being led by a world of lust and shame. As a matter of fact, we should be witnessing the fall of the pastors as well as the saints in the pew. Our churches will be teaching doctrines which will accommodate the spirit of divorce-lust-remarriage-adultery, or to be teaching that very doctrine. Dear reader, you are living in that day. "As it was in the days of Noah", is a signpost which gives credence to the lust-marriage scenario of Genesis six. Was polygamy the suffocating sin of the antediluvians? Did divorce-remarriage-adultery-polygamy flood the earth with corruption? Will this sin be the downfall of the modern church? Will Durant, a secular writer, made this startling comment of the world in the year 1941:

> Year by year marriage comes later, separation earlier; fidelity finds few so simple as to do it honor. Soon no man will go down the hill of life with a woman who has climbed it with him, and a divorce-less marriage will be as rare as a maiden bride.[47]

The Basis of Human Law

The postdiluvian period was marked by a new economy. Man proved he could not atone for his sins by trusting in his innocence (Adam), or trusting in his conscience (Lamech), therefore God changed His economy and permitted man, Noah, to test his righ-

---

[47] Durant, W. The Mansions of Philosophy (Garden City Pub. Co. NY, NY 1941) p. 221, 222

teousness under a managed political system, *human government*. After God blessed the only remaining men on the earth, the eight, He offered them the power to rule man by man. The antediluvians were forbidden to regulate or bring men to judgment—Cain was marked, the avenger cursed—but now Noah was ordained a magistrate complete with the power of capital punishment.

> And surely your blood of your lives will I require; at the hand of every beast will I require it, and at the hand of man; at the hand of every man's brother will I require the life of man. Whosoever sheddeth man's blood, by man shall his blood be shed; for in the image of God made he man. *Genesis 9:5, 6*

Capital punishment is not some invention of the state; it is a commandment from God. Note that the commandment would specifically put to death any future brother killers; all future Cain's were to be put to death by man. Capital Punishment!

This commandment was planted in the mind of the only holy preacher, Noah, who survived under the dispensation of conscience. The shock of this awesome responsibility forced man to organize his mind to prepare for such an event. It compelled man, the new judge, to judge himself. Capital punishment by man summoned man to not only organize his mind, but his entire life and the life of every other man as well.

It caused him to organize society. In order to control this power, capital punishment, man would promulgate many lesser punishments for lesser crimes before exercising the death penalty. By organizing lesser regulations and punishments, man could prepare men mentally to commit the act of capital punishment. It is one thing to require capital punishment, and it is an entirely different thing to find the man qualified to execute another man. Consequently, capital punishment is the father of *human government*. Note that God prepared man to contemplate shedding the murderer's blood by requiring the capital punishment of any beast which would take the life of man.

Before beast or man was destroyed, it would of course be necessary to prove guilt, thus the court and the seat of judgment were born. Regarding the dynamics of capital punishment and the Noahic law, Luther wrote:

> This is therefore the source [capital punishment], out of which flows all civil rights and international law. Now if God relinquishes to man the power over life and death, actually he also grants power over that which is less important: property, family, wife, children, slaves, and farms. All these God wishes to be subject to the powers of certain men in order that they may punish the guilty.[48]

Keil-Delitzsch agree:

> This command [capital punishment] then laid the foundation for all civil government and formed a necessary compliment to that unalterable continuance of the order of nature which had been promised to the human race for its further development. If God on account of the innate sinfulness of man would no more bring an exterminating judgment upon the earthly creation, it was necessary that by commands and authorities he should erect a barrier against the supremacy of evil, and thus lay the foundation for a well ordered civil development of humanity, in accordance with the words of the blessing which are repeated in (Gen. 9:7), as showing the intention and goal of this new historical beginning.[49]

---

[48] Kiel, C; Delitzsch, F. Old Testament Commentary (Eerdmans, Grand Rapids, MI; 1978) v. 1 p. 153

[49] Ibid. v. 1 p. 153

This is the truth found in America's historical documents:

> When, in the course of human events, it becomes necessary for one people to dissolve the political bands which have connected them to another, and to assume among the powers of the earth the separate and equal station to which the laws of nature and of nature's God entitle them: (Declaration of Independence)

When we refer to the term civilization, we are making reference to capital punishment since it is the source of all national and international law. Walter Berns illustrates this in the introduction to his volume on capital punishment, *For Capital Punishment:*

> In the dark of a wild night a ship strikes a rock and sinks. But one of its sailors clings desperately to a piece of wreckage and is eventually cast up exhausted on an unknown and deserted beach [Was this land inhabited by savages?]. In the morning he struggles to his feet and, rubbing his salt encrusted eyes, looks around to learn where he is. The only human evidence he sees is a gallows, "Thank God," he exclaims, "civilization".[50]

The Ancient Law codes and the Bible:

As with Adam, God now also commanded Noah and his sons, to be fruitful, multiply, and fill the earth. Violence was to be controlled by the law of man. Therefore, the sons of Noah promulgated laws; some of these documents still exist. We refer to these writings as the ancient law codes. Archaeologists have unearthed many fine legal documents inscribed in stone, brick, papyrus, and vellum, of which we will sample and examine, referencing the legal history of

---

[50] Berns, Walter For Capital Punishment (Basic Books, NY, NY, 1979) p. 3

marriage, divorce, polygamy, incest and other related matters. Leon J. Wood has stated in his fine book, *A Survey of Israel's History*, that the oldest actual written code of laws is Sumerian. One would expect that these ancient codes would reflect the man Noah, the preacher of righteousness. But shortly after his deliverance Noah was found drunk and naked, so his grandchildren became intoxicated with idolatry and were found babbling at Babel. Their laws are invariably adjoined to the idol gods—prior to his call we are told that the father of Abraham was an idolater: "Thus saith the LORD God of Israel, Your fathers dwelt on the other side of the flood in old time, even Terah, the father of Abraham, and the father of Nachor: and they served other gods." Let us now look into these ancient laws that preceded Moses.

Code of Ur Nammu (c. 2050 B.C.)

"Ur-Nammu was the founding ruler (king) of the Third Dynasty of Ur, the builder of the best, preserved ziggurat in ancient Mesopotamia, whose reign inaugurated the last great period of Sumerian literary[51] progress antedating Moses by 600 years. "The text states that King Ur-Nammu was selected by the god Nanna to rule over Ur and Sumer as his earthly representative."[52] He banished malediction, violence, and strife from the land. Dealing with such crimes as cattle rustling, (oxen-takers, sheep-takers, donkey-takers), as well as weights and measures. The orphan, widow, and the poor were protected from injustice. But the most interesting inscriptions to our study are those regulations relating to marriage. They especially expose the understanding of marriage as it existed in the mind of the postdiluvian society. Let us discover the state of creation-marriage in the codes:

> CU § 4 If the wife of a man, by employing her
> charms, followed after another man and he slept with

---

[51] Prichard, James B. The Ancient Near East, Supplementary Texts and Pictures (Princeton Univ. Press, Princeton, NY 1969) p. 87

[52] Wood, Leon A Survey of Israel's History (Zondervan, Grand Rapids, MI 1980) p. 40

her, they [the authorities] shall slay that woman, but that male shall be set free.[53]

Here we see that the Noachian code which instituted capital punishment for murder had now been expanded to also include the crime of adultery. Where King Ur Nammu's judgment lashes out at the woman, Moses latter squares off at the male, and then includes the female, the weaker sex:

> And the man who committeth adultery with another man's wife, even he who committeth adultery with his neighbor's wife, the adulterer and the adulteress shall surely be put to death. *Lev. 20:10*

We can understand why God would condemn adultery as a capital crime, but what caused the postdiluvians to aggressively promulgate this law? Is there something inherent in adultery that in itself generates the death judgment? Why did the postdiluvians prejudice the female? We will discuss these questions shortly?

> CU § 5 If a man proceeded by force, and deflowered [lit.: "undeflowered"] a slave-woman of another man, that man must pay five shekels of silver.[54]

The rape of a slave was considered only a minor offense with a mere monetary penalty. This however is not so strange when we consider Moses:

> And whosoever lieth carnally with a woman, that is a bondmaid (slave-woman), betrothed to an husband, and not at all redeemed, nor freedom given her:

------

[53] Finegan, Jack Light from the Ancient Past (Princeton Univ. Press Princeton, NJ 1959) p. 52

[54] Prichard, ANET supplement (Princeton NJ 1969) p. 88

she shall be scourged; they shall not be put to death, because she was not free. *Lev. 19:20*

The male in this case was only required to offer a trespass offering. I will discuss the Mosaic Law at length later.

CU § 6 If a man divorces his primary wife, he must pay (her) one mina of silver.[55]

The year is 2050 B.C. and it marks the world's first record of a state regulated divorce. There is one earlier document, a private legal transaction (not a promulgated law); it is about 50 years younger. These documents obviously reveal that the thought of divorce existed in the mind of man from antiquity. The fact that (CU § 6) addresses divorce is evidence that the act was considered an act of violence by Ur Nammu. Authorities claim that the *"If"* condition, of (CU § 6) is evidence of *casuistically formulated law.*

This means that the code deals with exceptional cases, and not with common daily ones.[56] The State of Ur Nammu saw divorce as a form of unusual violence; thus the law was casuistically formulated. What this author is interested in is the fact that while the law views divorce as violence it does not attempt to prohibit it, it merely regulates the act. Was the desire for divorce so strong that Ur Nammu could only regulate the act. The law could not say, Thou shalt not commit divorce. It could say, Thou shalt not commit adultery. And since adultery was a capital crime man was forced to invent a loophole in the law, and that loophole was divorce and polygamy. Why did Ur Nammu refer to a man's *"primary wife?"*; because *Lamech-Marriage,* polygamy, existed as a common act in Ur Nammu. Now what lies behind this divorce-polygamy passion. Let us look at this from two directions.

---

[55] Ibid. p. 88

[56] Boecker, Hans Jochen, Law and the Administration of Justice in the O.T. and Ancient Near East, (Ausburg Pub. House Minn. MN 1980) p. 58

The first approach sees man viewing himself as a god, or king. Every man has a deep inner self-conceit that he is a king. He may loose this at one time or other, but he has entertained this concept. The word king in English is obviously derived from the word kin (kind, family, tribe, race, nation). The patriarch of a family is a king of his kin. One obsession of the king is ownership. He controls through ownership. This ownership concept spills over into his family, and the king begins to believe he owns his family. And that ownership concept permits the king to certain rights, so he believes. It has been debated whether the basis of Israelite marriage was one of ownership. Millar Borrows in his exhaustive study, *The Basis of Israelite Marriage* argues against the concept of ownership, marriage by purchase.[57] I agree with Burrows, nevertheless, it does appear that ownership-marriage did play a part in the mind of the husband-king. The very law code we are discussing is the law of King Ur Nammu.

It seems when the Lord God gave man the power of capital punishment, man actually began to think he was a god. Man was ordered to exercise the act of capital punishment collectively, "Whoso sheddeth man's blood, by man shall his blood be shed" (Gen. 9:6a). Noah was not a god. But his grandchildren, who turned to idolatry, invented their righteousness by calling on their idols who ordained them king-gods: "Nanna (a god) selected Ur Nammu to rule over Ur and Sumer as his earthly representative." And we were told that King Ur Nammu banished violence from the land. Ur Nammu was a mini-god, a king-god. The Pharaohs and Caesars were believed to be gods.

This invention was easy to create since from the days of Cain, man believed he had the power over life and death. Vengeance is an act of God, not man; vengeance belongeth to the Lord, a prohibition to human vengeance. But ever since the Serpent said, "For God doth know that in the day ye eat there of, then your eyes shall be opened, and ye shall be as (God),[58] knowing good and evil." Man has not ceased to believe in his own righteousness, his own godli-

---

[57] Burrows, Millar The Basis of Israelite Marriage (American Oriental Society, New Haven, CNT 1938)

[58] NSRB, Gen. 3:5

ness apart from God. At times He believes he is God. Sovereign. King. When God permitted Israel a king, He nevertheless knew that a single man now could exempt himself from the power of the law, and that man could indeed be sovereign over man. The concept here is that the state could not execute the king because the king was the state.

God can experience sovereignty with justice because of His holiness. Man's sinfulness does not lend itself to sovereignty; it inevitably results in the abuse of power. Man's sovereignty rests in his possessions. When people are assumed to be possessions of a man's realm, it usually results in some degree of mishandling and exploitation. Men continually develop what is commonly referred to as turf, and the most common turf is in the home. The adage, "A man is the king of his own castle", may not be true. It may mislead some to think as if they were sovereign, or owners of their family, giving them the idea that they can dispose or divorce whom they choose. As we saw in (CU § 6), the violence of divorce was common enough that Ur Nammu penalized it with a mere mina of silver. Nevertheless he did penalize the deed as a criminal act. Notice that the act is assumed that it will be committed by men. The ancient codes see divorce as an act of the man, the woman the victim. The only explanation is sovereignty; man assumed he was the sovereign king of his own castle. Divorce is the act of a king banishing his subject, a subject that he owns.

It is interesting on this point that in around 400 A.D. Augustine a church theologian noted that men in his generation believed that they should not be punished like women for the crime of adultery. They believed that only women were guilty of adultery; they believed men were permitted to sin in this regard without any reprimand of the law:

> When we speak thus to these men, they not only
> are not willing to detract at all from their severity, but
> also become enraged at the truth. They say in answer:
> We are men; will the dignity of our sex sustain this

affront, so that we become like women in paying the penalty for our sins if we have relations with women other than our own wives?

> They [the men] ought not to be less overcome by lustful desire; and, as though, for the same reasons that they are men, they ought not to be less servile to their wanton flesh. Yet they become indignant if they should hear that men, guilty of adultery, pay the same penalty as the adulterous women (their wives), although they should be punished as much (and) more severely.[59]

The mention of a *primary wife* in (CU § 6) speaks of polygamy. It must be assumed that the fine of one mina of silver was reduced if the woman was a secondary or lesser wife. Lamech-marriage, polygamy, revived in the postdiluvian world. Will it flood the world again? The idea of ownership contributes to the act of divorce, ownership also contributes to polygamy. Borrows is correct by defining the basis of Israelite marriage as that of a covenant relationship typical of the Creators relationship with Israel. But sin ruined this idea, and that sin was the idea of husband sovereignty. Although marriage by purchase is not God's will, it nevertheless played and plays a part in the customs of marriage from antiquity. Man assumed that a wife was a mere possession, and he had the right to buy as many as he could afford. If he had enough money, he could afford a harem, and since the king was wealthy it was only fitting that he had the most wives. Harems were the possession of the ancient kings. The Lord God set the rules for Israel's king, "Neither shall he multiply wives to himself, that his heart turn not away", (Deut. 17:17). Nevertheless, we know David had eight wives named, and when he took up residence in Jerusalem, we

---

[59] Augustine, Adulterous Marriages: Book II; The Church Fathers, Wilcox ed. (Catholic Univ. Press Washington, DC 1955) p. 8-9

are told that he took more wives and concubines. Solomon of course had 700 wives and 300 concubines. But God commanded the king not to multiply wives.

The concept of ownership spilled over to other members of the family as well, for even in the Mosaic Law we find legislation which regulated the sale of a daughter, (Ex. 21:7-11). The father, obviously poor, could offer the sale of his daughter to be a maidservant. Keil-Delitszch see concubinage in this text and they are probably correct. Polygamy, like divorce, both violent acts, were not eradicated by God, for to eradicate divorce and polygamy would have required the annihilation of mankind; the heart of man was that hard. The ownership of family was assumed by others as well. The poor widow's words to Elisha tell how the creditors looked upon children. "Thy servant my husband is dead, and thou knowest that thy servant did fear the Lord: and the creditor is come to take unto him my two sons to be bondmen", (I Kings 4:1). The concept of sovereignty, ownership of property, also supported the ownership of slaves, a common act of man.

Vengeance played a significant role in the motive of a man's choice to divorce a wife. In the records we find the wives of Israel were subject to extreme scrutiny. If a wife shamed herself in the eyes of her husband, she often found herself under his judgment. Records indicate that if a wife raised her voice in public to over-rule her husband, and embarrassed him, then her husband had the social approval to avenge his humiliation by divorcing his outspoken wife. It appears that if the law legislated against divorce it would have been responsible for the death of many women, since man's anger may have led him to the violence of wife-murder. Divorce obviously the lesser of two evils. The Canadian Government reported that forty percent of the murders in their country are related to violence in marriage, leading various organizations to open halfway houses for women to find refuge. The present laws in the United States, which favor the woman, were laws which were designed to protect women from domestic violence which was common in America during the first half of the Twentieth Century. A live mother is better than a dead one; therefore the judges of the land awarded divorce. This was the same dynamic experienced by the ancients:

> He, [Jesus], said unto them, Moses, because of the hardness of your hearts [wife murderers] suffered you to put away your wives, but from the beginning it was not so. *Matt. 19:8*

It appears that adultery was a capital crime, and lesser infractions were subject to the punishment of divorce; the next area of concern is the realm of the false accusation or suspicious act. The guilty must be punished, but the innocent must be set free.

> CU § 11 If a man accused the wife of a man of fornication, and the river (ordeal) proved her innocent, then the man who had accused her must pay one-third of a mina of silver.[60]

In (CU § 4) the case is against the woman who slept with another man. Here the woman is accused of fornication by a third party. The ancient women were held to very strict standards of modesty: the act of showing the under arms or other body extremities was thought tantamount to fornication. If a woman was accused of adultery, or suspected of committing such, she was subject to the river ordeal; and if she passed the ordeal she was innocent. In Israel there was a similar regulation; if a woman was suspected of committing adultery and her husband was overcome with the spirit of jealousy, (that is he suspected her of committing adultery); he would bring his wife to the Hebrew priest, who would mix dust from the floor of the tabernacle with water, and have the woman drink it. If guilty the water would be a curse causing her thigh to rot and her belly to swell. If innocent she would go free and conceive (Num. 5:12-31).

In (CU § 12) the code protects the rights of a prospective son-in-law: If a (prospective) son-in-law entered the house of his (pro-

---

[60] Prichard, ANET supplement (Princeton NJ 1969) p. 8-9

spective) father-in-law, but his father-in-law later gave his daughter to another man, he (the father-in-law) shall return to him (the
rejected son-in-law) two-fold the amount of the bridal presents he
had brought.[61] Please note that Ur Nammu, was contemporary with
Abraham. So here we find the justice whereby Jacob was awarded the
increase of Laban's cattle. Remember the Patriarchs preceded Moses
and lived by the rule of these ancient laws as Jehovah God ordained
under Noah.

> CU § 22 If a man's slave-woman, comparing her-
> self to her mistress, speaks insolently to her (or him),
> her mouth shall be scoured with a quart of salt.[62]

This final comment from Ur Nammu gives us a glimpse into
the responsibilities of Hagar. Although it was Ishmael who mocked,
nevertheless Sarah demanded their punishment; but it appears Sarah
went too far.

Code of Eshunna (c. 1925 B.C.)[63]

This code, written in the Akkadian language, has been attributed
to the Elamite King, Bilalama, of the kingdom of Eshnunna. The
Elamites conquered the city of Ur but continued their degree of civ-il-
ization. Again in this code we find an idol-god, Tishpak, bestowed the
kingship to Bilalama. We will examine this code with its marriage
customs and the origin of divorce, and polygamy.

> CE § 25 If a man offers to serve in the house
> of (his) father-in-law and his father-in-law takes him
> in bondage but (nevertheless) gives his daughter [to

---

61 Ibid. p. 88

62 Ibid. p. 89

63 Wood, Leon A History of Israel's History (Zondervan, Grand Rapids, MI
1980) p. 149

another man], then the father of the girl shall refund the bride-money which he received twofold.[64]

This law obviously resembles (CU § 12); notice here the prospective son-in-law bonds himself to his father-in-law in labor, in an effort to purchase his bride; Jacob and Laban.

> CE § 26 If a man gives bride-money for a (nother) man's daughter, but a second man seizes her forcibly without asking the permission of her father and her mother and deflowers her, it is a capital offense and he shall die.[65]

Very similar to (Deut. 22:25), this law does make one interesting comment: "asking the permission of her father and her mother", an obvious custom from antiquity, or perhaps from the beginning of creation.

> CE § 27 If a man takes a(nother) man's daughter without asking the permission of her father and her mother and concludes no formal marriage contract with her father and her mother, though she may live in his house for a year, she is not a "housewife".[66]

This ancient code addresses the modern practice of cohabitation, which here is not recognized as marriage, even though the couple lived-in for one year. A formal contract was required. In the United States cohabitation is being recognized, under certain conditions, as marriage in some states by judges if the couple, cohabit for a relatively short period of time.

---

[64] Goetze, Albrecht The Law of Eshnunna, (Iraq and American Oriental Research/Jane Dows Nies Fund, New Haven, CT, 1956) p. 75

[65] Ibid. p. 76

[66] Ibid. p. 76

CE § 28 On the other hand, if he does conclude a formal marriage contract with her father and
her mother and then takes her, she is a "housewife".
When she is caught with a(nother) man, she shall die,
she shall not get away alive.[67]

This sequence to (CE § 27) indicates that the woman who cohab-
its without a formal marriage contract is considered a prostitute, however a formal contract will qualify her to be a housewife. Again, here
we see adultery considered as a capital crime.

CE § 29 If a man has been [made prisoner]
during a raid or an invasion or (if) he has been carried
off forcibly and stayed in a foreign country for a long
time, (and if) a second man has taken his wife and she
has born (him) a son—should he (i.e. the first man)
return, he shall get his wife back.[68]

This particular law protects the rights of a married soldier-prisoner whose wife, because of his long absence, has remarried. The
regulation makes no mention of a divorce however, the marriage is
considered legitimate providing the soldier-prisoner does not return.
The new marriage was annulled, even though a son was born to the
new husband.

CE § 30 If a man hates his town and his lord and
becomes a fugitive, (and) if a second man takes his
wife—should he (i.e., the first man) return, he shall
have no right to claim his wife.[69]

This law permits remarriage to the abandoned wife. It annuls the
deserter's marriage and denies him any further claims on his wife.

---

[67] Ibid. p. 76-77

[68] Ibid. p. 83

[69] Ibid. p. 84

Some may see the elements of what is referred to as Pauline privilege here (I Cor. 7:15). We will discuss this later.

> CE § 59 If a man divorces a wife after having made her bear sons and takes another wife, he shall be expelled from (his) house and whatever (property) there is and he will go after him who will accept him.[70]

Although it appears this regulation makes no provision for the mother of one son, the mother of daughters, or the childless woman, it nevertheless shields this mother from further violence. As we said, *casuistically formulated law*, the (if - then) concept, admits to the fact that divorce was the idea of the man not the law. The codes attempt to control violence through regulation, and divorce, a form of violence, is regulated by placing penalties on the act. It is assumed that men will divorce their wives. This assumption is based on the nature of man. In other words it is unimaginable for men to think that they do not have the absolute right to expel an unwanted wife—this is the product of what Jeremiah the prophet called the deceitful heart of man (Jer. 17:9). The woman is assumed to be a possession of the king-man. Generally, divorce was an instrument only permitted to the man. The ancient Semitic tribes, including the Jews, believed that men had the right to repudiate their wives at will. They practiced verbal or oral divorce merely by saying, "I divorce you", three times. The king-man can depose of a wife and may procure a new one at will. The king-man becomes the law; he becomes the judge and the jury. He executes the expulsion of the woman.

The Code of Lipit-Ishtar CL (c. 1860 B.C.)

King Lipit-Ishtar was anointed by the idol-gods, He was commissioned to "establish justice in the land", and to "bring well-being to the Sumerians and Akkadians", and to "re-establish equitable family

---

[70] Ibid. p. 142

relations among his subjects."[71] King Lipit-Ishtar refers to himself as the "humble shepherd of Nippur." Regarding domestic regulations he writes, "I made the father support the children and I made the children [support their] father; I made the father stand by his children and I made the children stand by their father; in the father's house."[72] The value of family was of special concern to the government of Sumer. This writer recalls an incident when some of the American public objected to remarks of their vice-president, Daniel Quayle, who stated that a single parent mother, bearing children out of wed-lock, should not receive the honor of a true family. It appears that Lipit-Ishtar would have agreed with the American V.P. Although the extant of this code is fragmentary, we have these interesting remains which enlighten our study.

> CL § 24 If the second wife whom he had married bore him children, the dowry which she brought from her father's house belongs to her children (but) the children of (his) first wife and the children of (his) second wife shall divide equally the property of their father.[73]

Note that, as divorce, polygamy is the assumption of this law. The two actions that we have addressed in the title of this chapter have the same inventor, man.

> CL § 25 If a man married a wife and she bore him children and those children are living, and a slave also bore children for her master (but) the father granted freedom to the slave and her children, the children of the slave shall not divide the estate with the children of their (former) master.[74]

---

[71] Steele, Francis Rue American Journal of Archaeology vol. LII (George Banta Pub. Co., Menahsa, WI, 1948) p. 434

[72] Ibid. p. 441

[73] Ibid. p. 441

[74] Ibid. p. 441

Here we find regulations addressing slaves, as in the social laws of Moses, (compare Lev. 19:20, and Deut. 21:10-17). Regardless, it speaks of the concubinage of slaves. It assumes that the slave-girl, as a possession of the king-man, was obliged to provide her master conjugal, and child bearing responsibilities. Where did the king man acquire this right? From himself! Man is a self-appointed king.

> CL § 26 If his first wife died and after her death, he takes his slave as a wife, [the children] of [his first] wife [are his heirs]; the children which [the slave] bore for her master shall be.[75]

Abram took Hagar while Sarai was alive, for he believed his wife's womb was dead. The elements of both Abram's practice and (CL § are essentially the same. The fragment teaches that Ishmael did not have the rights of the true heir, Isaac.

> CL § 27 If a man's wife has not borne him chil-dren but a public harlot has borne him children, he shall provide grain, oil and clothing for that harlot; the children which the harlot has borne him shall be his heirs, and as long as his wife lives the harlot shall not live in the house with the wife.[76]

This law has overtones of the Tamar incident in the life of Judah, (Gen. 38). Tamar played the harlot, deceiving Judah, and was found with his child. In Israel the penalty for Tamar, had she actually been a harlot, would have been to be burned to death. However, since Judah was her father-in-law, and she was only playing the harlot so as to receive justice, Judah was obliged to confess, "she hath been more righteous than I, because I gave her not to Shelah, my son." Although it is reported that Judah "knew her again no more", it does appear that along with her pardon Tamar was supported by Judah for she was

---

[75] Ibid. p. 441

[76] Ibid. p. 442

given a place the genealogy of Jesus, (Matt. 1:3) where she appears as a wife of Judah.

> CL § 28 If a man has turned his face away from his first wife...but she has not gone out of the [house] his wife which he married as his favorite is a second wife; he shall continue to support his first wife.[77]

This speaks of a live-in divorce—a form of bigamy—which actually might be more just than divorce. Martin Luther said, "In regard to divorce, it is still a subject of debate whether it should be allowed. For my part, I have such a hatred of divorce that I prefer bigamy to divorce."[78] Divorce with remarriage, if divorce is prohibited, as this paper contends, amounts to simple bigamy or adulterous-marriage, which Luther preferred.

> CL § 29 If a son-in-law has entered the house of his (prospective) father-in-law and he made his betrothal and afterwards they made him go out (of the house) and gave his wife to his companion; they shall present to him the betrothal gifts he brought, and that wife may not marry his companion.[79]

The story of Jacob and Laban surfaces again in this section of the code as the son-in-law's rights were protected. God, of course, protected Jacob.

> CL § 30 If a young married man married a harlot (from) the public square and the judges have ordered him not visit her, but afterwards he neglected his wife.[80]

---

[77] Ibid. p. 442

[78] Shaner, Donald W., A Christian View of Divorce (Leiden, E.J. Brill, 1969) p. 49

[79] Steele, AJA vol. LII p. 442, 443

[80] Ibid. p. 443

Steele comments on the word neglect, stating that this word possibly means divorce. If that be so here again we see the man with what he believes to be his natural right in marriage, i.e. his right to execute divorce, with the authority to remarry, and the right to commit bigamy or polygamy; as his sovereign right.

The Code of Hammurabi CH (c. 1700 B.C.)

This is the most celebrated of the ancient laws of the sons of Noah prior to Moses. Although scholars and intellectuals have honored this treatise with their recognition, it is nevertheless the product of the idol-gods. Many of whom are mentioned in its prologue and epilogue. Dagan (Dagon) the Semitic grain-god, the pillars to whose temple Samson pulled down; and Marduk (Merodach) whom Jeremiah called down, "The word that the Lord spoke against Babylon and against the land of the Chaldeans by Jeremiah, the prophet: Declare among the nations, and publish, and set up a standard; publish, and conceal not; say, Babylon is taken, Bel is confounded, Merodach is broken in pieces; her idols are confounded, her images are broken in pieces", (Jer. 50:1, 2). This same Hammurabi who experiences the defeat at the hand of Jehovah, was the king-god who gave obeisance to the false idol-gods said:

> The laws of justice, which Hammurabi, the efficient king set up, and by which he caused the land to take the right way and have good government.

> I, Hammurabi, the perfect king, was not careless (or) neglectful of the black-headed (people), whom Enlil (storm-god) presented to me, (and) whose shepherding Marduk had committed to me;

> I sought out peaceful regions for them; I overcame grievous difficulties; I caused light to rise on them.

The great gods called me, so I become the benefi-
cent shepherd whose scepter is righteous: By the order
of Shamash (sun-god), the great judge of heaven and
earth, (god of justice). May my justice prevail in the
land; by the word of Marduk, my lord, may my stat-
utes have no one to rescind them.[81]

The Lord God did rescind Hammurabi and his idol-god; Babylon
fell in one hour, as will the future Babylon. Nevertheless, we must keep
in mind that the Lord God ordained Noah and his sons to replenish
the earth and to rule it by man, i.e. human government with laws of
the land. Therefore, the Code of Hammurabi is an ordained system
of human government as are the laws of Russia, China, Egypt, and
America. Let us examine Hammurabi's regulation of marriage.

CH § 128 If a seignior acquired a wife, but did
not draw up contracts for her, that woman is no wife.[82]

The International Bible Encyclopedia states that, "though the
Hebrew wife and mother was treated with more consideration than
her sister on other lands, even in other Semitic countries, her position
nevertheless was one of inferiority and subjection. The marriage relation from the standpoint of Hebrew legislation was looked upon very
largely as a business affair, a mere question of property. A wife, nevertheless, was indeed, in most homes in Israel, the husband's 'most val-
ued possession.' Frequently we find this belief regarding the basis for
Israelite and Semitic marriage." But as we have said, Millar Borrows
believes the basis for the Israelite marriage was the covenant nature of
their relationship with Jehovah. The covenant was obviously a powerful force with the sons of Noah, as noted here in (CH § 128); a
marriage contract was required.

---

[81] Prichard, ANET supplement (Princeton NJ 1955) p. 177, 178
[82] Ibid. p. 171

CH § 129 If the wife of a seignior has been caught while lying with another man, they shall bind them and throw them into the water. If the husband of the woman wishes to spare his wife, then the king in turn may spare his subject.[83]

Moses commanded the death of both subjects.

CH § 130 If the seignior bound [raped] the (betrothed) wife of another seignior, who had no intercourse with a male and was still living in her father's house, and he has lain in her bosom and they have caught him, that seignior shall be put to death, while that woman shall go free.[84]

Almost identical to Moses in (Deut. 22:25-27) this law, as the Mosaic, establishes the importance of catching the person, or as Moses states, the act of "being found". This will be an important item to consider when we exposit (John 8 the woman taken in adultery).

CH § 131 If a seignior's wife was accused by her husband, but she was not caught while lying with another man, she shall make affirmation by god and return to her house.[85]

CH § 130 If a finger was pointed at the wife of a seignior because of another man, but she has not been caught while lying with the other man, she shall throw herself into the river for the sake of her husband.[86]

---

[83] Ibid. p. 171

[84] Ibid. p. 171

[85] Ibid. p. 171

[86] Ibid. p. 171

The ancient laws continually place the woman on the defensive. Of course, if she was caught in the act the judgment was swift and final. However, if she was suspected of infidelity, she likewise was subject to a proving process. As noted by Moses, when a man was caught in the "spirit of jealousy" the woman was obliged to submit to the *bitter water* ordeal, (Numb. 5:11-31). She would be forced to drink the bitter water and if she was guilty her abdomen would swell, and her thigh would rot. Here we find a similar test, "thrown into the river."

In (CH § 133 - 135) Hammurabi deals with the wife of a prisoner of war. The wife who had "sufficient to live on" was required to remain in her home and wait for the return of her husband. Had she insufficient provisions she was permitted to leave her home and marry another. In the event her first husband returned home, she was to return to him leaving any of the second husband's children with their father. Should she leave her home where she had sufficient provision, she was to be "thrown into the river." In (CH § 136) we find a law identical to (CE § 30) where the husband deserted the village of his residence, here again he would be denied his wife upon return.

> CH § 137 If a seignior has made up his mind to divorce a lay priestess, who bore him children, or a hierodule [female temple slave (concubine)] who provided him with children, they shall return her dowry to that woman and also give her half of the field, orchard and goods in order that she may rear her children; after she has brought up her children, from whatever was given to her children they shall give her a portion corresponding to (that of) an individual heir in order that the man of her choice may marry her.[87]

The comment, "If a seignior made up his mind", affirms that divorce rests solely in the heart of man. His act is final. This squarely contradicts the mandate of Jesus, "Let not man put asunder." This supports the theory that divorce is thoroughly the invention of man.

---

[87] Ibid. p. 171

> CH § 138 If a seignior wishes to divorce his wife who did not bear him children, he shall give her money to the full amount of her marriage-price and he shall also make good to her the dowry which she brought from her father's house and then he may divorce her.[88]

Childlessness was a failure of the marriage relationship and was considered a breach of contract by the ancients.

We should be thankful that Abram loved Sarai even though she failed to conceive. Had he hated her and put her away, as the codes provided, the *incarnation* of the promised Seed would have failed.

> CH § 141 If a seignior's wife, who was living in the house of the seignior, has made up her mind to leave in order that she may engage in business, thus neglecting her house (and) humiliating her husband, they shall prove it against her; and if her husband has then decided on her divorce, he may divorce her, with nothing to be given her as her divorce-settlement upon her departure. If her husband has not decided on her divorce, her husband may marry another woman, with the former woman living in the house of her husband like a maidservant.[89]

> CH § 142 If a woman so hated her husband that she has declared, "You may not have me," her record shall be investigated at her city council, and if she was careful and was not at fault, even though her husband has been going out and disparaging her greatly, that woman, without incurring any blame at all, may take her dowry and go off to her father's house.[90]

---

[88] Ibid p. 172F

[89] Ibid p. 172

[90] Ibid p. 1725

This is the first mention in the ancient codes of the woman's right to initiate a separation—it would become a common practice among the Gentiles; Jesus addresses the subject, "If a woman shall put away her husband, and be married to another, she committeth adultery", (Mk. 10:12). Jesus condemns the remarried woman as an adulteress. Jesus simply states that any divorce with remarriage this side of death is adultery.

In (CH § 143 - 145) Hammurabi addresses various aspects of marriage, but in (CH § 154 - 158) deserve mention:

> CH § 154 If a seignior has had intercourse with his daughter, they shall make that seignior leave the city.

> CH § 155 If a seignior chose a bride for his son and his son had intercourse with her, but later he himself has lain in her bosom and they caught him, they shall bind that seignior and throw him into the water.

> CH § 156 If a seignior chose a bride for his son and his son did not have intercourse with her, but he himself has lain in her bosom...[he shall pay a fine, and let her go to marry a man of her choice].

> CH § 157 If a seignior has lain in the bosom of his mother after (the death of) his father, they shall burn both of them.

> CH § 158 If a seignior after (the death of) his father, has been caught in the bosom of his foster mother who was the bearer of children, that seignior shall be cut off from the parental home.[91]

---

[91] Ibid. p. 172

Incest, marriage within the forbidden degrees, is the subject of this portion of the code. Notice that intercourse between father/daughter, father/daughter-in-law, son/mother, and son/stepmother are the only forbidden degrees of consanguinity mentioned in Hammurabi. The most prohibitive act was the son/ mother relationship, resulting in a fiery death of both partners. It is no wonder that the Apostle should cry out to the Church at Corinth regarding the man who had married his stepmother, "Such fornication as is not so much as named among the Gentiles." Hammurabi goes on to list twenty other laws that regulate marriage; most of which regulate the betrothal-gift, bride-price, or the dowry. The terms are often used synonymously. Most dictionaries define the dowry as both the gift the wife brings into marriage, and the gift that the man gives to the bride.

The mohar, the payment of a sum to the father of the bride, has created the impression in the mind of most commentators to assume that ancient marriage was an economic transaction, a matter of purchase and ownership.[92] The *International Bible Encyclopedia* is an example of this view: "The marriage relation from the stand point of Hebrew legislation was looked upon very largely as a business affair, a mere question of property." As mentioned, Borrows disagrees and he labors to show that marriage is older than sale, and that the *mohar* was actually a compensation-gift. Regardless the *mohar* was a binding element of the marriage covenant. The words of Jehovah to Israel, "And I will betroth thee unto me forever; yea, I will betroth thee unto me in righteousness, and in judgment, and in loving-kindness, and in mercies. I will even betroth thee unto me in faithfulness: and thou Lord", (Hosea 2:19, 20). The NSRB makes this fitting comment, "The grace of God is beautifully set forth in the verb 'betroth', which signifies to woo a virgin. The pledge that God made to Israel was forever—we will see the ancients applying this concept even to the *engagement* period. Some may question whether the *mohar*, or dowry is practiced today in the west, and most would agree that it is not. Nevertheless, "diamonds are a girl's best friend."

---

[92] Burrows, Millar The Basis of Marriage (American Oriental Society New Haven CNT 1938) p. 1

As mentioned in chapter one, man was created married. Marriage is an act of creation, and that marriage was monogamous. Creation-marriage is an ordinance of creation as is the horizon of the earth. As the horizon of the earth was, is, and forever will be, so creation-marriage was God's will, is God's will, and forever will be God's will. The question then: "From whence cometh divorce and polygamy", there is only one answer. Sinful Man!

As stated, the ancient codes were the result of God's commission to Noah and his sons to ensure human government. They were corrupt by the nature of their idolatry, to which all the codes were dedicated. This idolatry invariably led to immorality. "Babylon was a sink of iniquity and a scandalous example of luxurious laxity to all the ancient world. Even Alexander, who was not above dying of drunkenness, was shocked by the morals of Babylon."[93] Jehovah describes Babylon in the Book of Revelation as, "MYSTERY BABYLON, THE GREAT MOTHER OF HARLOTS AND ABOMINATION OF THE EARTH." (Rev.17:5).

Here is a sample of the immorality of Babylon:

> Every native woman is obliged, once in her life, to sit in the temple of Venus, and have intercourse with some stranger. And many disdaining to mix with the rest, being proud on account of their wealth, come in covered carriages, and take up their station at the temple with a numerous train of servants attending them. But the far greater part do thus: many sit down in the temple of Venus, wearing a crown of cord round their heads; some are continually coming in, and others are going out. Passages marked out in a straight line lead in every direction through the women, along which strangers pass and make their choice. When a woman has once seated herself she must not return home till some stranger has thrown a piece of silver into her lap, and lain with her outside the temple. He

---

[93] Unger, Gordon, C.H. in Archaeology and the O.T. (1954) p. 121

who throws the silver must say thus: "I beseech the goddess Mylitta to favor thee": for the Assyrians call Venus, Mylitta. The silver may be ever so small, for such silver is accounted sacred. The woman follows the first man that throws, and refuses no one. But when she has had intercourse and has absolved herself from her obligation to the goddess, she returns home; and after that time, however great a sum you may give her you will not gain possession of her. Those that are endowed with beauty and symmetry of shape are soon set free; but the deformed are detained a long time, from inability to satisfy the LAW, for some wait for a space of three to four years.[94]

The Future Mystery Babylon

This is a fitting place for the reader to take note. This city state of ancient Babylon will appear again in our world, as revealed in the Book of Revelation 17-18. During the Great Tribulation, Mystery Babylon The Mother of Harlots, will almost rule the world with her immorality and fornication. However, she will be destroyed in the battle of Armageddon by the Lord Jesus Christ the Lamb of God, the King of Kings and Lord of Lords. What will be the condition of creation-marriage during her future reign?

---

[94] Durant, W. & A. quote T.M. Green in The Story of Civilization (Simon and Schuster, NY, NY 1967) v. 1 p. 245

CHAPTER THREE

Do Customs Matter?

Customs are related to costumes. What is accustomed, the habitual practice, may well be thought of in terms of the fashion (dress/costume) of the day, the accepted social behavior. By sheer habitual practice some customs acquire the force of law or right.[95] Therefore the laws reflect the customs and conversely the customs reflect the laws. There is a latent danger in all of this. When an evil practice becomes an accepted custom, it may become a mandated law. The virgins of Babylon were required by law to be spoiled by strangers in the temple of their gods.

After centuries of postdiluvian history, we hear this comment on the sons and grandsons of Noah, "And Joshua said unto all the people, Thus saith the Lord God of Israel, Your fathers dwelt on the other side of the flood in old time, even Terah, the father of Abraham, and the father of Nachor: and they served other gods", (Joshua 24:2). Holy, Holy, Holy, is the Lord of Hosts; the whole earth is full of his glory, (Isa. 6:3, Rev. 4:8). Let God be true and every other god a liar. The other gods were unholy, immoral idols. They were the weak imaginations of men. These gods were the immoral imaginations of men ruling over the hearts of evil men. Their work was to provide a conscience in man for his sin. Their fruit was evil. The attractive virgins were deflowered and released first; the unlovely awaited their ritual fornication, some tarried at the temple for years. Man legislated codes of laws to accommodate his evil immoral nature. Hard-heartedness!

Any attempt by man to exist without reliance upon Jehovah, his God, will inevitably lead him to defeat. Should he attempt to form a government of laws without a reliance upon Jehovah God, the Holy One, he will rely on himself and consequently his customs will eventually become law, and his law will inevitably be a direct reflection of

---

[95] Compact Edition Oxford English Dictionary, (Oxford Univ. Press, Oxford, 1917) v. I: 631

himself; immoral. What God said of man is ever so true: "There is none righteous, no, not one.

For all have sinned and come short of the glory of God," (Rom. 3:10, 23). The question is: How could unrighteous man formulate righteous law? All forms of human government have failed to generate righteous societies; all societies have failed to formulate righteous laws. Noah and his sons were under a mandate to form a human government based on the theocracy of Jehovah; but they formed monarchies, kingdoms built on idolatry. One such early monarchy was the kingdom of Nimrod. He was the *el'gibbor*, the self pro-claimed mighty one. Isaiah identified the true *El'Gibbor* as the Lord Jesus Christ, "His name shall be called *Pele Joez El'Gibbor Abi As Sar Shalom*", (Isa. 9:6). The Authorized Version refers to Nimrod as, "the mighty hunter before the Lord", (Gen. 10:9), but the ancient proverb translates this as, "Nimrod the mighty hunter against the Lord [the Antichrist]."[96] The name of his city kingdom was Babel; that name would eventually reach the city of the Apocalyptic Judgment (Rev. 17:5).

The Origin of the Races and Customs

It was on the Plain of Shinar where the men of the whole earth began to assemble. Here while speaking one language man formed a compact and designed a universal custom. Each man was to make brick and join them together as a symbol of universal unity in the construction of a temple reaching to heaven. In their labor was heard a chant, "Let us make a name, least we be scattered abroad upon the face of the whole earth", (Gen. 11:4). Henry M. Morris suggests that the initial motive for this project was to gain a self accomplished spirituality, but the outcome was a degenerated astrology. He goes on to explain that God placed Virgo in the evening sky to declare the hope of the Promised Seed, (Gen. 3:15), but Nimrod made her the seductive Queen of Heaven.[97] Noah's sons had slipped into mass idolatry. As we all know, this temple tower became an object of consternation

---

[96] K.D. O.T.C., p. 1:166

[97] Morris, The Genesis Record, p. 271

to these worshipers, as suddenly Jehovah the Triune God, judged the builders by confounding their minds causing them to babble in divers tongues. Fear and confusion filled the Nimrodites; in madness and hysteria they scattered themselves upon the face of the whole earth.

The remarkable nature of this judgment is lodged in the human tongue. The speech of man is regulated by his physiology. It is interesting that the only serious theological discussion regarding the origin of the varied races of men is found here at the judgment of tongues, the Tower of Babel. Keil and Delitszch comment on Vitringa and Hofmann who believed that the tongue event of Babel was caused when the omnipotent God changed man's organs of speech, i.e., and anatomical change.[98] Although they refute Vitringa and Hofmann, nevertheless they address the thought of anatomical change.

Creation repudiates the concept of an evolution of anatomy. However, the varied anatomies of the human race indicate that some change occurred to the children of Adam. The eight souls of the ark were obviously of a single racial extract. A study of antediluvian history fails to reveal any time where we might find some event which led mankind into a world of diversity of races with physical anatomical characteristics, like those we see today. But if we examine the Babel Judgment in the light of anatomical judgment the event does lend itself to the thought. It is without question that the Lord God inflicted a psychological curse on man in the Babel Judgment but is it beyond the realm of reason that He also cursed the physiology of man. The voice of the birds is governed by their physiology: the *caw* of the crow is as expected as the *sweet song* of the canary. The *bark* of a dog is as expected as the *me-ow* of the cat. The *snappy* high pitch voice of the Oriental is as expected as the *deep tones* of the African. The anatomy of the creature dictates the voice of the creature. The size of the neck, nose cavities, lips, and tongue appear to contribute to the sound of the man. A Chihuahua cannot make the sound of a St. Bernard. The environment can only affect the cosmetic nature of man, "Look not upon me, because I am black, because the sun hath looked upon me", were the words of the Shulamite. The races are the result of a curse,

---

[98] K.D. O.T.C. p. 1:174

as the races curse the earth with their prejudice and hate, their wars and their death—Are not the races also separated by language barriers and prejudice? This writer believes that the races were created as were the species of birds and the bees. The creation which is the product of a judgment curse is nevertheless pure creation. Thus, the diversity of size, color, and language of the human race that we witness today is the result of a judgment, the Babel Judgment.

(Parenthesis: Creationist Ken Ham and His View)

Since the later days of this study—the later twentieth century scientists, like Ken Ham and his staff at *Answers in Genesis web site* have proposed that the races are in fact a product of the judgment of the Flood of Noah and the Tower Judgment at Babel:

> They believe the sons of Noah probably had several different levels of skin color in their genes. These shades were collected in each of their offspring that spread over the earth as God commanded them: "Be fruitful and multiply and replenish the earth...bring forth abundantly in the earth, and multiply therein." It appears that Noah and his sons did multiply, however they failed to spread out throughout the whole earth. Rather, they accumulated in one area and began to build a city with a tower on the plain of Shinar. God, in judgment, programmed a spirit of many tongues, or languages and sent this spirit into the minds of the builders. Thus, in fear and in practical need for unity these builders were forced to flee the plain and scatter over the face of the whole earth as they were originally commanded. This led to small gatherings of various tribes of like-minded language builders over the whole earth. He also believes that the color genes that Noah and his sons brought with them were now the origin of these new tribes of nations. Thus Mr. Ham then believes that these two judgments com-

bined to scatter the inhabitants of the earth and it was the method God used to eventually create—in judgment—the races we see today.

Hath God Joined the Black and White?

Some believe that the black race was born out of the sin of Ham, seeing the nakedness of his father, Noah. His curse determined that he would be the servant of servants. As stated previously, this author believes that the races were created in judgment at the temple of Babel. Therefore, this author rejects this Hamite doctrine. All races are the result of a curse, consequently all races are cursed, not just the blacks—Thus, Rabbi M.J. Raphall's Civil War tract *"The Bible View of Slavery"* which is a dissertation of the Hamitic doctrine is wrong and is not supported Biblically—"The Phoenicians, along with the Carthaginians and the Egyptians, who all belong to the family of Canaan, were subjugated by the Japhetic Persians, Macedonians, and Romans: the remainder of the Hamitic tribes either shared the same fate, or still sigh, like the Negroes, beneath the yoke of the most crushing slavery.[99] Here Keil and Delitzsch assign several nations to he list of Hamitic peoples; they are not all black. Morris makes the following comment:

> Unfortunately, there have been some interpreters who have applied the Hamitic-Canaanite curse specifically to the Negro peoples, using it to justify keeping the black man in economic servitude or even slavery. It is obvious, however, that the prophecy applies not only to black Africans but also to all other descendants of Ham (most of whom are not blacks), and no more of the Hamitic peoples have experienced such servitude during their history than the non-Hamitic peoples.[100]

---

[99] Ibid. p. 1:158

[100] Morris, Genesis p. 238

If the races were formed at Babel, then the mixed racial marriage takes on an altogether different hue. All skin color is the product of a curse. Color, languages, and race are the product of a universal sin. It is not the sin of one person, Canaan; one tribe, the Canaanites; one color, the blacks. The *Babel-Race* doctrine includes the entire human family. That places all mankind on a spectrum of color tones. Extreme degrees of the spectrum reveal the curse in greater tones than lesser tones, nevertheless all the races are included in the lines of color. Thus, to segregate any of the colors is hypocrisy; all the colors have equally sinned. Race distinction reveals the curse which was aggravated by sin. When a black and white unite in marriage it personifies the curse. This is socially embarrassing to those who have melted into the acceptable background of the spectrum; some people have formed an evil prejudice, that is very strong.

Although mixed racial unions are perfectly legitimate, they nevertheless will be unions that experience social tension, i.e. the tension of societies own embarrassment which is a reminder of the sin of all men at Babel. The loving couple will not personally know the embarrassment; they will however wrestle with the embarrassment of others. Those contemplating this union should be warned of the burden of the mixed-racial marriage, for a pastor to do otherwise would be irresponsible. Therefore: Does God join together the black and white race? Yes.

Abraham and Customs:

As a lad, Abram must have stood in awe of the famous ziggurats and other buildings of Ur, his home city. The well organized society of ancient Ur would have also left a lasting impression on this young man. Abram would have been influenced by Ur-Nammu; Leon Wood states, "For even if the period [of Ur-Nammu] began a few years after Abraham left for the Promised Land, conditions would not have greatly changed in this length of time.[101] The departure of

---

[101] Wood, Leon A History of Israel's History (Zondervan 1980) p. 39

Abram, Terah, Lot, and Sarai from this beautiful city during its zenith of glory, should be recorded among the miracles of the Bible. The code of Ur-Nammu was ordering the peace which contributed to the prosperity of Ur. The element which made the city repulsive to Abram was its idolatry. It was dedicated to the idol-gods. Abram's God was Jehovah Elohim the great Creator.

Abram began a faith relationship with Jehovah through the ancient verbal message of Noah, or perhaps the revelation of Jehovah in His manifold creation. H. Morris suggests, man may have learned the truth of the Godhead from the stars. The Apostle tells us, "For the invisible things of him from the creation of the world are clearly seen, being understood by the things that are made, even his eternal power and Godhead, so they are without excuse,"(Rom. 1:20). Abram knew the Godhead, although his fathers did not, "And Joshua said unto all the people, Thus, saith the Lord God of Israel, Your, fathers dwelt on the other side of the flood in old time, even Terah, the father of Abraham, and the father of Nachor; and they served other gods", (Joshua 24:2). Abraham obeyed Jehovah:

> Get thee out of thy country, and from thy kindred, and from thy father's house, unto the land that I will show thee; and I will make of thee a great nation, and I will bless thee, and make thy name great; and thou shalt be a blessing. And I will bless them that bless thee and curse him that curseth thee: and in thee shall all the families of the earth be blessed. *Gen. 12:1-3*

In leaving his country, Abram was promised with personal blessings, and all the families of the earth were also promised a special blessing. The later would be blessed in a new dimension of *creation-marriage, (Jewish creation marriage)*—throughout the remainder of this dissertation *creation-marriage* will focus on Israel's guardianship of creation-marriage—after all Jesus was born of the house and lineage of David, a Jew. It must be kept in mind that although Abram left his country and forsook his idolatry, he did not sever those customs and laws which comprised the spirit of Noah; this was his reasonable obligation as a world citizen. Those customs and laws which regulated violence as ordained by Jehovah through Noah followed Abram and were practiced by all the Patriarchs. This was not altered until Jehovah appeared to Moses on Mt. Sinai. We shall see that the ancient codes and customs regulated the behavior of Abraham, Isaac, and Jacob. And some of these codes impacted their marriage practices.

Shortly after arriving in the Promised Land, Abram prepared sacrificial offerings to Jehovah. This is the first recorded sacrifice to Jehovah since Noah's at the subsiding of the flood. This is solid evidence that Abram was walking with his God; nevertheless, Abram forsakes his new land for fear of a current drought. He sought refuge in Egypt—some believe this was a lapse of faith—with his half-sister and wife, Sarai. Fearing for his life, because he assumed Sarai's beauty would entice the Egyptians to kill him and take his wife, Abram hid behind Sarai his half-sister-wife. Although Abram was wrong to initiate this scheme, he was correct about the sexual interests of the Egyptians. Their art depicts their women wearing light pervious clothing which was designed to reveal the female body. Their obsession with the sexual delight of their beautiful women reached the height of monomania in this account from Herodotus who records the preoccupation with sex even entered the domain of the mortuary.

> The wives of men of rank when they die are not given at once to be embalmed, nor such women as are very beautiful or greater regard than others, but on the third or fourth day after their death (and not before) they are delivered to the embalmers. They do so about this matter in order that the embalmers may not abuse their women [sexually], for they say that one of them was taken once doing so to the corpse of a woman lately dead, and his fellow-craftsman gave information.[102]

---

[102] Herodotus, The Harvard Classics (Collier, NY, 1937) p. v. 33:

An interesting note was found in the March 14, 1988 issue of *Time* magazine. A team of American biblical scholars deciphered the text of the *Genesis Apocryphon*, a Dead Sea Scroll. Although only a few dozen images have been developed, yet the scholars believe that they shed light on the ancient customs of the Bible. "Most startling are new passages that record in great detail the physical beauty of Abraham's wife Sarah. These include descriptions of the contours of Sarah's breasts."

Pharaoh did take Sarai to wife, however the Lord God intervened and sent plagues upon him revealing that he had taken the wife of another man. Abram was permitted to leave Egypt with his half-sister-wife. It appears that adultery was regulated in Egypt, nevertheless creation-marriage had fallen on bad times in ancient Egypt a place that was unusually corrupt. But before we investigate this act let us follow Abram back to Canaan to the land which was famous for its written alphabet and infamous for its sodomy.

Customs of the Fertility God and Goddess

Expelled from Egypt, Abraham, Sarah, and their nephew Lot returned to the Holy Land with a refreshed determination to trust Jehovah-Elohim. Abraham would go on to grow in grace, while Lot would grow in disgrace, nearly drowning in the corrupt customs of Canaan. The religion of Canaan was at the heart of the matter:

> Canaanitish culture was based on that of Babylonia and begins with the introduction and use of copper and bronze. When Canaan became a Babylonian province, it naturally shared in the civilization of the ruling power. The religious beliefs and deities of Babylonia were superimposed upon those of the primitive Canaanite.[103]

---

[103] ISBE (Grand Rapids MI 1929) v. I pg. 268 I:268

As mentioned, Abraham and Lot were natives of Babylon and therefore would not be terribly startled by the customs of Canaan. This explains why Lot could make Sodom his home; but there was something in Canaan which was actually unnatural even to Babylon—the custom of sexual perversion. One would think that the custom of defiling all virgins through a religious temple rite was the height of corruption, but Canaan would raise corruption to even higher levels, or should I say lower levels.

> It may be stated without exaggeration that the Canaanite religion was the most sexually perverted, morally depraved, and blood thirsty of all ancient history. It was for this reason that God ordered Joshua to exterminate their very culture, citizens, animals and cities. The head god of the Canaanite religion was El. His wife was Asherah. He also married his sisters, one of whom was Asterah.[104]

Asterah was probably the epithet of Istar (Babylon), Asteroth (Canaan), goddess of fertility.[105] As we study the ancients we are impressed with the omnipresence of this female deity. She appears as Astarte (Phoenicia), Isis (Egypt), Demeter (Greek), Aphrodite (Greek), Ishtar (Assyrian), Venus (Roman), Artemis (Assyrian), and Virgo. Henry Morris has this interesting comment:

> Satan is notoriously a corruptor, rather than an innovator. Hence it is probable that the system of paganism, with its astrological emblems and complex mythology and mysteries, represents a primeval distortion of God's true revelation concerning His creation and promised redemption of the universe.

---

[104] Willmington, H.L. Willmington's Guide to the Bible, (Tyndale, Weaton, IL, 1985) p. 931

[105] ISBE, p. 1:268

Thus, the zodiac system of constellations may originally have been devised by the antediluvian Patriarchs as a means of indelibly impressing the divine promises on the consciousness of mankind through marking them on the very heavens themselves. If so, the subsequent system of astrology is a gross corruption of the original evangelical significance of the heavenly bodies, created originally to serve in part for signs and seasons. The Virgin (Virgo), whose sign among the stars once reminded men of the promised Seed of the woman, began to assume the proportions of an actual Queen of Heaven; and Leo, the great sidereal lion at the other end of the Zodiac, became a spiritual King of Heaven.[106]

It is now believed that the origin for the identification of the constellations was universal and not limited to Greek mythology as was once thought.

The principal achievement of the science of astronomy in the centuries during which the books of the OT were written was the arrangement and naming of the constellations, and there can be no reasonable doubt that the same system was known to the Hebrews as that which has been handed down to us through the Greek astronomers.[107]

Morris expands the constellation theory stating that Simiramis, the wife of Nimrod, was the first false virgin, Virgo, the Queen of Heaven. Nimrod was the first false lion, Leo, the King of Heaven. The heavens were intended to declare the Glory of God. The corruption of which caused the Apostle to cry out:

---

[106] Morris, Genesis, p. 265, 271 107

[107] ISBE, p. 1:309

For the wrath of God is revealed from heaven against all ungodliness and unrighteousness of men, who hold the truth in unrighteousness, because that which may be known of God is manifest in them; for God hath shown it unto them. For the invisible things of him from the creation of the world are clearly seen, being understood by the things that are made, even his eternal power and Godhead, so that they are without excuse; because, when they knew God, they glorified him not as God, neither were thankful, but became vain in their imaginations, and their foolish heart was darkened. Professing themselves to be wise, they became fools, and changed the glory of the incorruptible God into an image made like corruptible man, and birds, and four-footed beasts, and creeping things.

Wherefore, God also gave them up to uncleanness through the lusts of their own hearts, to dishonor their own bodies between themselves, who changed the truth of God for a lie, and worshiped and served the creature more than the Creator, who is blessed forever. Amen. For this cause God gave them up unto vile affections; for even their women did change the natural use for that which is against nature; and likewise also the men, leaving the natural use of the woman, burned in their lust one toward another, men with men working that which is unseemly, and receiving in themselves that recompense of their error which was meet. (*Rom. 1:18-27*)

The consequence of false worship is wrong conduct, conversely the result of true worship is moral or right conduct. The Apostle stated: "Wherefore I give you to understand, that no man speaking by the Spirit of God calleth Jesus accursed: and that no man can say that Jesus is Lord, but by the Holy Spirit", (I Cor. 12:3). Jesus said, "God is a Spirit, and they that worship him must worship him in spirit and in truth", (Jn. 4:24). Again, the Apostle adds, "For through him [Jesus] we both have access by one Spirit unto the Father", (Eph. 2:22). The equation simply states that if you do not worship in the true Spirit you will worship in the Evil spirit, and the natural desires of the evil worshipper will be perverted.

Abraham was called out of Babylon by Jehovah God in order to give mankind a new start. Man failed under Adam, and Noah, now he would have a new leader and example. Abraham departed from Babylon and entered the land of Canaan. The natives, however, were thoroughly corrupted by the customs of Babylon, and God would direct Abraham to establish the first literal kingdom of God on earth in this Promised Land, Canaan. The Canaanites included the Phoenicians, Jebusites, Amorites, and the Hittites, with such well known cities as Gaza, Megiddo, Jericho, Sodom, Gomorrah, and Jerusalem. Ham, who was cursed for looking upon the nakedness of his father, was the father of these Canaanite tribes. It is not surprising that his posterity is notably immoral. Asteroth was the supreme goddess of Canaan and the counterpart to Baal. Her cult originated in Babylon. Istar her Babylonian counterpart was known as the morning and evening star. Abraham discovered the city of Asteroth Karnaim, a city dedicated to her worship. Some of the Canaanite tribes have left few physical remains of their culture, but this is not so of the Phoenicians:

> Their religious ideas are important on account of the influence they had on the Hebrews. Derived from the Babylonians, one of the most corrupting tendencies we notice was the ascription of sexual characteristics to the chief deities of their pantheon, such as Baal and Asteroth who was the great Nature-goddess, the Magna Mater, Queen of Heaven (Jer. 7:18). She was commonly identified with Aphrodite or Venus. Her worship was too often accompanied with orgies of the most corrupt kind, as at Apheca.[108]

---

[108] ISBE, p. 4:2398

The Encyclopedia Britannica gives us this description of the immoral Phoenician mind:

> The worship of the female along with the male principle was a strongly marked feature of Phoenician religion. The ghastly practice of sacrificing human victims was resorted to in times of great distress, or to avert national disaster. The god who demanded these victims, and especially the burning of children, seems to have been Milk, the Molech or Moloch of the Old Testament. Another horrible sacrifice was regularly demanded by Phoenician religion: women sacrificed their virginity at the shrines of Astarte in belief that they thus propitiated the goddess and won her favor; licentious rites were the natural accompaniment of the worship of the reproductive powers of nature.[109]

Babylon was apparently preoccupied with the female principle, while the society of Canaan was preoccupied with the male principle. Homosexuality with all it's degrading acts was the accepted custom of Sodom. Some commentators see the act of pederasty, as its identifying sin.[110] (This identifies with the recent scandal of the Roman Catholic Church priesthood.) The men of this infamous city had left the natural use of the woman and burned in their sexual lust one with another: Men with men doing that which is unseemly— Sodom's pederasty and other homosexual acts may have been out done by the Americans. Reports have surfaced of acts of homosexual debauchery that are not fitting to even record in this dissertation— Billy Graham is not far from the truth when he exclaims that God will have to apologize to Sodom, if he further delays the judgment of America.

---

[109] Encyclopedia Britannica v. 17:768, 769

[110] K.D. OTCGen. 19

Just a short note here: The homosexuals of Sodom were violent, although homosexuals claim to be the children of free and unlimited love. Recall the Sodom account: The angels arrive at Lot's door to visit him. They refuse Lot's offer to lodge with him, telling Lot that they prefer to sleep in the street. Lot, knowing the sexual perversion of the men of Sodom persuades the angels to abide with him. After enjoying a feast with unleavened bread—a sign of religious devotion—the angels prepare to retire for the night. A mob, the men and boys of the city, gather outside Lot's door and demand to know the angels, i.e. to know them sexually. Lot closes the door behind him and begins to admonish the crowd, "I pray you, brethren, do not so wickedly." He judges their homosexual wickedness. The backsliding Lot then offers the Sodomites his two virgin daughters. He declares, "Behold now, I have two daughters who have not known man; let me, I pray you, bring them out unto you, and do ye to them as is good in your eyes: only unto these men do nothing." The homosexual mob then cry out in unison, "Stand back." Who are you, Lot, to judge our homosexual custom as wickedness. Then they threaten to kill him. Their custom was universally accepted as good. Lot was threatened with death because he condemned their sinful custom. The men were prepared to murder Lot. These homosexuals were violent, unloving people who were killers—some believe this is true of all homosexuals if they are legally denied to practice their cursed custom; their wickedness. The angels then pull Lot into the house and reveal to him that they were sent by Jehovah God to save him and his family from the violence of Sodom, and the coming judgment. The angels then instantly afflict the men of the city with blindness, both small and great. Then after the safe escape of Lot, his wife, and his two virgin daughters, Jehovah God burns the city to the ground destroying all the perverted boys, girls, men, women, and all living things. Did the evil custom reach to every soul of Sodom? The account states that all the people of Sodom were united in their judgment of Lot: "the men of the city, even the men of Sodom, compassed the house round both old and young, all the people from every quarter." God judged the entire city—He incinerated it; literally cremated it. The question that bids an answer: Did all the living creatures of Sodom have AIDS? Think about that!—I observed a sympathizing American AIDS activist wearing a T-shirt that read, "We All Have AIDS" (a reference to all Americans). Are we the next to be judged? Perhaps our enemies could use this for an apology to nuke us.

The custom of Sodom had become a terrible weapon, a Satanic attack upon the Seed of the woman. The success of the Sodomites would have resulted in the destruction of man's power to propagate, preventing the birth of the Savior, and causing the death of man. Homosexuality is atheism and death. The United States of America is failing to control the sin of homosexuality because the government is protecting this evil custom by promulgating laws in its defense. Had the U.S. Congress been the government of Sodom they could have issued-in the possible extinction of the human race. God interceded to govern Sodom—he destroyed the city and its inhabitants. The Sodomite generation melted in the fire of sulfur. Will this American generation melt from the slim disease, the ugly death of AIDS? The fiery annihilation of Sodom and the plague of AID's is God's opinion and view of homosexuality. Our God is a consuming fire.

> The sun was risen upon the earth when Lot entered into Zoar. Then the Lord rained upon Sodom and upon Gomorrah brimstone and fire from the Lord out of heaven. And he overthrew those cities, and all the plain, and all the inhabitants of the cities, and that which grew upon the ground. But his wife looked behind him, and she became a pillar of salt. And Abraham got up early in the morning to the place where he stood before the Lord. And he looked toward Sodom and Gomorrah, and toward all the land of the plain, and beheld, and, lo, the smoke of the country went up as the smoke of a furnace. And it came to pass, when God destroyed the cities of the plain, that God remembered Abraham, and sent Lot out of the midst of the overthrow, when he overthrew the cities in which Lot dwelt. *Gen. 19:23-29*

Smoking in defeat, the weapon-custom, homosexuality, failed to overcome the world. Satan was again defeated, as God gave men a new start in Abraham. Lot is the example of the salvation that was offered through the following of Abraham. The question might be expanded, "Were all the Canaanites homosexuals?" If so, then the annihilation of Sodom was only the beginning of God's judgment. Later God would require the Israelites to exterminate the remainder of the inhabitants of Canaan, and this He did. It is not beyond comprehension that all the inhabitants of Canaan had contracted AIDS, and that they were a threat to all mankind; therefore, its judgment was the righteous act of God in saving mankind. Regardless, Sodom was gone, removed from the earth. Nothing remained but the fallout of their ashes from the smoke of their furnace.

But this is not the end of the story. Babylon, The Mother of Harlots, as we said, had propagated the doctrine of harlotry and adultery throughout Canaan through the idol deity, Asteroth. This female devil had one preoccupation, harlotry and adultery. The dilemma of Asteroth is that her desire can only be satiated on the earth, and since she knows that the earth is temporal, she tries to satisfy her appetite for sex before she will be judged in the Day of the Lord. God's Word gives us some insight into her ways:

> My son, keep thy father's commandment, and forsake not the law of thy mother: bind them continually upon thine heart, and tie them about thy neck. When thou goest, it shall lead thee; when thou sleepest, it shall keep thee; and when thou awakest, it shall talk with thee. For the commandment is a lamp; and the law is light; and reproofs of instruction are the way of life: to keep thee from the evil woman, from the flattery of the tongue of a strange woman. Lust not after her beauty in thine heart; neither let her take thee with her eyelids. For by means of a whorish woman a man is brought to a piece of bread: and the adulteress will hunt for the precious life. *Prov. 6:22-26*

Proverbs chapter seven describes the "means of the whorish woman" with a vivid description of the "the adulteress who hunts for the precious life." (Prov.7:1-27)

> My son keep my words, and lay up my commandments with thee. Keep my commandments, and live; and my law as the apple of thine eye. Bind them upon thy fingers, write them upon the table of thine heart. Say unto wisdom, Thou art my sister; and call understanding thy kinswoman: That they may keep thee from the strange woman, from the stranger which flattereth with her words. For at the window of my house I looked through my casement, and beheld among the simple ones, I discerned among the youths, a young man void of understanding. Passing through the street near her corner; and he went the way to her house. In the twilight, in the evening, in the black and dark night: and behold, there met him a woman with the attire of an harlot, and subtle of heart. She is loud and stubborn; her feet abide not in her house, now is she without, now in the streets, and lieth in wait at every corner. So she caught him, and kissed him, and with an impudent face said unto him, I have peace offerings with me; this day have I payed my vows. Therefore, came I forth to meet thee, diligently to seek thy face, and I have found thee. I have decked my bed with coverings of tapestry, with carved works, with fine linen of Egypt. I have perfumed my bed with myrrh, aloes, cinnamon. Come, let us take our fill of love until the morning: let us solace ourselves with love. For the goodman is not at home, he is gone on a long journey: he hath taken a bag of money with him and will come home at the day appointed. With her much fair speech she caused him to yield, with the flattering of her lips she forced

him. He goeth after her straightway, as an ox goeth to the slaughter, or as a fool to the correction of the stocks; till a dart strike through his liver; as a bird hasteneth to the snare, and knoweth not that it is for his life. Hearken unto me now therefore, O ye children, and attend unto the words of my mouth. Let not thine heart decline to her paths. For she hath cast down many wounded: yea, many strong men have been slain by her. Her house is the way to hell, down to the chambers of death.

The metaphor has a literal value which cannot be denied, as we watch the cunning craftiness of this Asteroth, the strange woman of the corner. I have always been intrigued by the religiosity of this whore. She boasts of having peace offerings and of paying her vows on the very day of her adultery—Was it the Sabbath? What was she trying to say? It appears she thinks adultery is a religious act, an act which in her eyes is holy. She seems to have the idea that she could commit adultery and at the same time preserve her conviction that she was a perpetual virgin. Asteroth's worshipers praised her as "The Virgin", "The Virgin Mother", and the "Holy Virgin." Regarding her title Will Durant comments, "this merely meant that her amours were free from all taint of wedlock." He continues: "In Babylon she was the goddess of war as well as love, of prostitutes as well as mothers; she called herself a compassionate courtesan."[111]

The concept which permits a man to commit adultery without the taint of adultery is the fuel of hell, the philosophy of harlots. The spirit of adultery amazingly promotes a claim of innocence and a strange idea of rightness. The harlot of Proverbs calls her sin, love. Knowing her time is limited she became aggressive, "So she caught him, and kissed him, and with an impudent face said unto him: let us take our fill of love until the morning." Although she is dead wrong, she is oblivious to the truth. She is a whore, who thinks she is a holy virgin.

---

[111] Durant, History, p. 1:235

Abraham, Hagar, Ishmael, Rebecca, Jacob, and Custom

The lives of the Patriarchs often leave us with many unanswered questions. Why were Abraham and Jacob permitted to practice polygamy? Why did Jacob serve Laban so faithfully? The answers to these questions are often found in the customs and laws that existed during the lives of these men. It must be remembered that the laws that Noah and his sons promulgated were ordained of God. The customs which preceded those laws were often just as binding to the ancient societies—this did not mean that these customs and laws were perfect; they were as all law: weak. Paul confirms this idea with his text: For what the law could not do, in that it was weak through the flesh, God sending his own Son in the likeness of sinful flesh, and for sin, condemned sin in the flesh (Rom. 8:3). Laws were promulgated to control the sinful acts of men; divorce was a sinful act of man. But until Moses, the ancient codes would prevail as the law of the land.

As we stated from (CU § 6) divorce and polygamy were accepted customs in Ur Nammu: "If a man divorces his primary wife, he must pay her one mina of silver." However, the polygamy of Abraham and Jacob were produced by yet other customs. These men were holy men therefore it is no surprise that there are no recorded divorces in their lives.

Recall (CU § 22), where the slave-woman who spoke insolently to her mistress was penalized by having her mouth scoured with a quart of salt, and (CL § 26) where the children of the true or first wife become the rightful heirs of their father's estate even though their father has had children by a slave-wife. The children of the slave-wife are disinherited. These ancient laws shed some light on Abraham's conduct with Hagar, and Ishmael. In 1925 archaeologists discovered thousands of tablets in the ancient city of Nuzi, or Nuzu. Cyrus Gordon states that these tablets draw the most intimate picture we have of the ancient customs which reflect the culture of Abraham.[112] Abraham complained to the Lord God that he had

---

[112] Godron, Cyrus The Living Past (John Day, NY, 1941) p. 156

no heir, save Eliezer, of Damascus. In the light of the Nuzi texts we have support for Abraham's adoption of his house-born slave son, Eliezer. Gordon states that at Nuzi adoption played a significant role as the childless couple adopted an heir as an insurance policy to support them in their golden years. The adopted heir would look after them, repair their home, supply food, as well as mourn their death, and prepare their grave.[113] The custom of adoption secured Abraham an heir. He left his homeland and idolatry, but he could not forsake what he believed to be acceptable customs and the legal ideas of his world. Nuzi was located in northeastern Mesopotamia, the homeland of Abraham. Marital customs from Nuzu as well as the code of Hammurabi provided that, if a man's wife had no children, the son of a handmaid could be recognized as the legal heir. Hagar's relationship to Abraham and Sarah is typical of the customs that prevailed in Mesopotamia.[114]

Abraham may be justified in acquiring an heir through the provisions of the ancient codes and customs, but his failure to trust the Lord God for a son from the bowels of his marriage to Sarah should be marked as one of the greatest sins of mankind. The son of custom, Ishmael, became the father of Islam. Later giving rise to the likes of Mohammed, Kohmeni, Kadaffy, Hussein, Arafat, and Osama Bin Laden. What would the world have been like without Ishmael, Islam, the Taliban, and Isis—One of the most profound verses in the Bible for the twenty-first century must be the prophesy regarding Ishmael: "And he will be a wild man; his hand will be against every man—revealed in the assault on the Twin Towers; New York City 9-1-1—and every man's hand against him; and he shall dwell in the presence of all his brethren" (Gen. 16:12). God had promised Abraham greatness if he would walk by faith. What would have been the greatness of the nation of Abraham, Israel, without their natural Arabic adversaries.

---

[113] Ibid. p. 159

[114] Schultz, Samuel The Old Testament Speaks (Harper, San Francisco 1990)

Abraham was apprehensive when Sarah drove out Hagar and her son, and rightly so for the ancient custom-law did not support this act. Finegan raises the custom to law when he states, "there was a legal basis for this apprehension."[115] Abraham employed another custom when he chose a wife for Isaac. This would be unacceptable in the west today however it must be noted that Isaac loved Rebecca. Not only did he love the lady of his father's choosing, but he also expected his father to acquire him a wife. And Abraham did just that. The price of Rebecca was paid in jewels of gold, jewels of silver, and garments. Burrows debates the meaning of these gifts: on the one hand they could have been a purchase price, and on the other hand they could have been compensatory to a family who was losing a daughter.[116]

It should be pointed out that oriental women feel sorry for the brides of America, and the west because they are given away for nothing. They take the bride in their price, believing that the higher the price the greater their self worth. It was also unlikely that the man who invested good money in his bride would divorce her over a whim.[117] Jacob's life suggests further interest in the ancient customs.

> In Nuzu men sold themselves into slavery in order to obtain, for instance, a wife. In other words, men who knew that they would never have enough money to pay the bride price for a wife on their own, held that it was better to be a married slave than a free bachelor. This nearly parallels the story of Jacob, who worked so long (though not technically as a slave) to win his bride from her father.[118]

---

[115] Finegan, Jack Light from Ancient Past (Princeton U. NJ 1959) p. 67

[116] Burrows, Millar The Basis of Israelite Marriage (American Oriental Society, New Haven, CNT 1938)

[117] Gordon, Cyrus The Living Past (John Day, NY, 1941) p. 170

[118] Ibid. p. 162

When Jacob awoke and found that he married Leah—the fellowship of publicly tenting together constituted marriage—he had reason to be angry with Laban. Though the tenting ceremony was binding, Jacob was permitted, by custom, more than one wife—polygamy, an invention of the hard heart of men as well as divorce and remarriage were approved customs of Jacob's society. Consequently, he could serve another seven years for Rachel. This was compounded by another marriage custom that permitted Jacob to father children by the handmaids of both Leah and Rachael—This was another invention of man. Thus, Jacob became the husband of four women. Perfectly acceptable with the human invented customs of the day— this took place before Moses—remember Moses was at times also regulating customs, because to do otherwise would have cost him an insurrection: (but for the hardness of your heart Moses suffered you to put away your wives, but from the beginning it was not so Mt. 19:8).

Like Abraham, his first wife, Sarah was eventually blessed with the promised seed, so Jacob's first wife, Leah, gave birth to both Levi and Judah. Leah was the mother of Israel's priests and the mother of the promised seed, for "the scepter shall not depart from Judah, nor a lawgiver from between his feet, until Shiloh come; and unto him shall the gathering of the people be", (Gen. 49)—Shiloh, a reference to Christ. That seed, Jesus the Messiah, was destined through Leah. But some may object: Was not this marriage a matter of fraud? That is a fact, for it was just that. Nevertheless, Leah would give birth to the serpent crusher—Most civil judges would award an annulment to the victim of a fraudulent marriage; God here blesses the union of the first married wife, Leah.

Rachael's act of stealing her father's images appears as a theft motivated by idolatry, but the Nuzu library reveals that her intention was aimed at acquiring her father's estate. "The possession of the household god was tantamount to the title to Laban's estate; thus she in the place of one of her brothers became Laban's chief heir."[119] At

---

[119] Ibid. p. 178

first glance her act smacked of an angry daughter who recoiled from the agony of having to share her husband with her older sister, but perhaps we see a form of ancient justice in Rachel's larceny.

Before we leave the land of Canaan we should take note of the customs recorded in Genesis 38. The Roman Catholic Church attempts to support their doctrine of birth control with the recorded act of Onan; "And Onan knew that the seed should not be his; and it came to pass, when he went in unto his brother's wife, that he spilled it on the ground, least he should give seed to his brother. And the thing which he did displeased the Lord: wherefore he slew him also," (Gen. 38).

This was not exactly polygamy; although it is seen here as a custom that God directed and demanded. It was a "duty of marriage" that the brother-in-law was obligated to perform; to raise up the name for his brother. The custom of levirate marriage was obviously common to this society. It would be formally codified by Moses in Deut. 25:5-10 where the sister-in-law is actually called a wife ("the wife of the dead...her husband's brother shall go in unto her and take her to him to wife").

The last custom we will discuss in this section is found in the judgment that Judah sentenced upon Tamar. When Judah learned that his daughter-in-law was pregnant by harlotry, he unleashes the ultimate condemnation on this lady, "bring her forth, and let her be burned." The ancient's penalty for harlotry, as in the case of Tamar, was a bitter form of capital punishment: to be burned to death.

Immunity

"L'etat c'est moi", a thought believed to be spoken by King Louis XIV, seems to be the thought of Judah as he recoils from his sin. The Divine Right of Kings, was in existence from antiquity past. Judah a Patriarch was bound in the tribal setting. The father tribesman was the civil authority by divine right. Noah was the supreme court as would be the claim of the Pharaoh's. Some believe that the law cannot be illegal. Government immunity is a requirement of human government. The King is the law. Immunity is the birthstone of infallibility.

The Judge of the court cannot judge himself. Noah would judge Ham and sound the degree as a righteous one, even though he was drunk. Human law has always been weakened by spiritual wickedness in high places, and especially by kings. The Pope's claim to infallibility rests in his kingship. Yes, Louis XIV was the state "The State Is Me"; L'etat c'est moi is what he said.

A Theocracy was in place at the advent of the lawgiver, Moses, and the following course of the judges, however with the arrival of a king it now took on a threat to the peace of the Theocracy. The Lord God warned the nation regarding the nature of a king and of the effect the king would have upon the people. In Deuteronomy, God established a standard for the king of Israel because He saw that when His people secured the Promised Land they would willfully demand a king, like their neighbors. The cry the Lord God heard was a dreadful sound. Departure was in the whine of His own children. A nation He protected and blessed was now forsaking Him as their King. When they turned from Him they turned to another, their king. They now put their trust in the leader of their nation, a man. Since a man would rule over the people, his very existence in that state was a cause of concern. The initial regulation of the standard was to the people of the king. They were to permit God to choose the king. The king was not to multiply horses in an attempt to return to Egypt. Neither could he multiple to himself gold or wives, for the multiplication of wives would cause the king's heart to turn away from his God. The king was to write a copy of the law, and to read and keep the law all the days of his life; that his heart be not lifted up above his brethren.

The king was caught in a dilemma. A man with his human sinful nature was chosen to be the sovereign over the nation. The people were subject to him. Their children were subject to him. Their service was subject to him. Their material wealth was subject to him. Their governors were subject to him. Their law-givers were subject to him. Consequently, the king believed that the law of the land was subject to him. Although this was not immediately the case, yet unfortunately it was eventually the case. King Louis the XIV believed he was the law. Even in the United States we support the king with what we call: presidential immunity, on matters less than criminal.

Egypt - the Danger Greater Than Bondage

The sexual deviants of Babylon, Canaan, and Sodom had a sister deviant in Egypt. Previously we mentioned that the lust of Egypt even reached to the coffin of a beautiful female corpse, but that was not the only depravity of the Egyptians. The theme of this study is investigating the methods that Satan employed in an attempt to corrupt creation-marriage, and here in Egypt we find a new contaminant. The purpose of which was to hinder and prevent the seed of the woman from being born. For his birth marked the death of the Serpent with a crushing head wound. The clue that leads us to consider the evil nature of the Egyptian attack is found in the book of Leviticus. Here Moses specifically names the abominations of the Egyptians.

Joseph was welcomed to Egypt with open arms and a gripping hand:

> And it came to pass after these things, that his (Joseph's) master's wife cast her eyes upon Joseph; and she said, Lie with me. But he refused, and said unto his master's wife, Behold, my master knoweth not what is with me in the house, and he hath committed all that he hath to my hand; there is none greater in this house than I; neither hath he kept back anything from me but thee, because thou art his wife, how then can I do this great wickedness, and sin against God? And it came to pass, as she spoke to Joseph day by day, that he hearkened not unto her, to lie by her, or to be with her, and it came to pass about his time, that Joseph went into the house to do his business; and there was none of the men of the house there within. And she caught him by his garment saying, Lie with me: and he left his garment in her hand, and fled, and got him out. *Gen. 39:7-15*

In Egypt, the land of artifacts, it is surprising that no ancient code of laws has been uncovered, nevertheless we have evidence that reveals the nature of its supreme court; since Pharaoh believed he was the supreme court who protected the rights of his people. The rights of the people are their customs. Therefore, knowledge of their customs will reveal their laws, or the rights of the people, and the book of Leviticus indirectly reveals the accepted customs of Egypt. The following is a list of certain customs that were practiced in the land of the pharaohs:

- They uncovered the nakedness of their fathers.
- They uncovered the nakedness of their mothers.
- They uncovered the nakedness of their step-mothers.
- They uncovered the nakedness of their sisters.
- They uncovered the nakedness of their step-sisters.
- They uncovered the nakedness of their grand-children.
- They uncovered the nakedness of their daughters-in-law.
- They uncovered the nakedness of their aunts.
- They uncovered the nakedness of their sisters-in-law.
- They uncovered the nakedness of their step-children.
- They uncovered the nakedness of their step-grandchild.
- They approached a woman during her uncleanness.
- They lay carnally with their neighbor's wives.
- They burned their children to death in sacrificial worship.
- Their men would sexually lay with other men.
- They sexually laid with animals.

(Paraphrase - Lev. 18)

Uncovering the nakedness is a Hebrew idiom for sexual intercourse; thus, the customs of Egypt included incest of every kind, homosexuality, and bestiality. The Lord God introduced this section of Leviticus with these words:

> And the Lord spoke unto Moses, saying, Speak unto the children of Israel, and say unto them, I am the Lord your God. After the doings of Egypt [customs], wherein ye dwelt, shall ye not do; and after the

doings of the land of Canaan, to which I bring you, shall ye not do; neither shall ye walk in their ordinances [laws]. *Lev. 18:1-3*

God then goes on to state the case exactly: "None of you shall approach to any that is near of kin to him, to uncover their nakedness: I am the Lord." The peculiar custom of Egypt was incest, and sexual perversion. From the language of Leviticus it appears that incest and wife swapping was ordained as a right of an Egyptian. William J. Hopewell and others commenting on (Deut. 24) make this observation: "When Deuteronomy 24 was written, the Jewish people had followed the terrible sin of the Egyptians in wife-swapping:"[120] perhaps the thirteenth item listed above refers to this custom. Leviticus 18 closes with this admonition:

> Ye shall therefore keep my statutes and mine judgments and shall not commit any of these abominations [those of Egypt]; neither any of your own nation, nor any stranger that sojourneth among you. For all these abominations have the men of the land done, who were before you, and the land is defiled.
>
> *Lev. 18:26-27*

"After the doings of the land of Egypt, wherein ye dwelt, shall ye not do," the doings of the land were their customs, and as we said, it appears that the listed items may have been the legal rights of the citizens of Egypt. This is not surprising since America protects the rights of the homosexual, the adulterer, and the abortionist. But, unlike the U.S., it appears that Egypt ordained incest, and protected the rights of their citizens to marry within the forbidden degrees of consanguinity. In his volume, Folkways, William Graham Sumner writes concerning the incest of the Egyptians:

---

[120] Hopewell, W.J. Marriage and Divorce (NJ 1976) p. 5

In the Egyptians mythology Isis and Osiris were sister and brother as well as wife and husband. The kings of ancient Egypt married their sisters and daughters. The doctrine of royal essence was very exaggerated and was applied with quantitative exactitude. A princess could not be allowed to transmit any of it [family wealth] away from the possessor of the throne. There is said to be evidence that Ramses II married two of his own daughters and that Psammetik I married his daughter. Artaxerxes married two of his daughters. The Ptolemies adopted this practice. The family married in and in for generations, especially brothers and sisters, although sometimes of the half-blood. "Indicating the Ptolemies by numbers according to the order of their succession, the II married his niece and afterwards his sister; IV his sister; VI and VII were brothers and they consecutively married the same sister; VIII married two of his own sisters consecutively; XII and XIII were brothers and consecutively married their sister, the famous Cleopatra.[121]

Adolf Erman in his work, Life in Ancient Egypt, continues this thought:

There existed also another custom foreign to our ideas, the marriage with a sister; This became common in Egypt during the Ptolemaic and Roman periods. Most of the Ptolemics married their sisters, and under the Emperor Commodus two-thirds of all the citizens of Arsi had done the same. Marriage with a sister shocks our moral sense, but seemed most natural to the Egyptians, just as in modern Egypt marriage with a cousin is considered to be most sensi-

---

[121] Sumbner, W.G. Folkways (Ginn, Boston 1906) p. 485-486

ble and right. The gods set an example in point; the brothers of Osiris and Set having married their sisters, Isis and Nehthys.[122]

Water seeks its own level, as the people their leaders. It is not surprising to find the Egyptians committing incest since it was the practice of their gods and pharaohs. Will Durant commenting on the morals of Egypt stated, "The government of the Pharaohs resembled that of Napoleon, even to the incest." He goes on to say:

> Very often the king married his own sister—occasionally his own daughters—to preserve the purity of the royal blood. It is difficult to say whether this weakened the stock. Certainly, Egypt did not think so, after several thousand years of experiment; the institution of sister-marriage spread among the people, and as late as the second century after Christ two-thirds of the citizens of Arsinoe were found to be practicing the custom. The words brother and sister, in Egyptian poetry, have the same significance as lover and beloved among ourselves.
>
> In addition to his sisters the Pharaoh had an abundant harem, recruited not only from captive women but from the daughters of the nobles and the gifts of foreign potentates [Solomon's 1000 wives, my comment]; so Amenhotep III received from a prince of Naharina his eldest daughter and three hundred select maidens. Some of the nobility imitated this tiresome extravagance on a small scale, adjusting their morals to their resources.[123]

Satan would fail to corrupt the generation of the promised seed through incest. The Lord God destroys the first-born males and

---

[122] Erman, Adolf Life in Ancient Egypt (Macmillan, NY 1894) p. 153, 154

[123] Durant, Story, p. 1:164, 954

drowns their fathers in the Red Sea, he then prohibits his children to re-enter the land of Egypt. The death custom of Sodom was destroyed by sulfur-fire, and the death custom of Egypt by the death-angel. God went one step further, he attached the death penalty to anyone who would practice the customs of Egypt and Canaan: "For whosoever shall commit any of these abominations, even the souls that commit them shall be cut off from among their people;" to cut off means to put to death (capital crime = capital punishment). It is not surprising that Western Civilization is built on the morals and customs of Moses. In the State of Maine we find this list of forbidden degrees:

> No man shall marry his mother, grandmother, daughter, granddaughter, stepmother, grandfather's wife, son's wife, grandson's wife, wife's granddaughter, sister, brother's daughter, sister's daughter, father's sister or mother's sister.

> (Marriage Law, State of Maine, Sec. 31)

An interesting (AP) Moscow news release read, "Soviet paper blames incest for infant deaths in village." In order to prevent paying dowries the people of the Central Asian Republic of Turkmenia resort to incest. The Russian medics attribute the high mortality rate here on intermarriage within the bonds of consanguinity. "We are powerless in the case of the death of a child of related parent."

The Apostle declared that the truth of God's will is known by the heathen because it is revealed to them, "For the invisible things of him from the creation of the world are clearly seen, being understood by the things that are made." Therefore, it is not strange to learn of the sexual inhibitions of some native tribes. "The Savages Dread Of Incest", is the chapter title of Freud's book, Totem and Taboo. The basis of the prohibition of the members of the totem was their dread of incest. Sigmund Freud, a non-Biblicist, aptly confesses his ignorance of the origin of their dread of incest:

> This sternly maintained prohibition [incest] is very remarkable. There is nothing to account for it in

anything that we have hitherto learned from the conception of the totem or from any of its attributes; that is, we do not understand how it happened to enter the system of totemism.

[Freud's comments go on to reveal the fear of these tribesmen.] Among the Battas of Sumatra these laws of avoidance affect all near relationships. For instance, it would be most offensive for a Battan to accompany his own sister to an evening party. A brother will feel most uncomfortable in the company of his sister to an evening party. If either comes into the house the other prefers to leave. Nor will a father remain alone in the house with his daughter any more than the mother with her son. The Dutch missionary who reported these customs added that unfortunately he had to consider them well founded. It is assumed without question by these races that a man and a woman left alone together will indulge in the most extreme intimacy, and as they expect all kinds of punishments and evil consequences from consanguineous intercourse, they do quite right to avoid all temptations by means of such prohibitions.

Among the Akamba (or Wakamba) in British East Africa, a law of avoidance is in force which one would have expected to encounter more frequently. A girl must carefully avoid her own father between the time of her puberty and her marriage. She hides herself if she meets him on the street and never attempts to sit down next to him, behaving in this way right up to her engagement. But after her marriage no further obstacle is put in the way of her social intercourse with her father.

The most widespread and strictest avoidance, which is perhaps the most interesting one for civilized races is that which restricts the social relations between a man and his mother-in-law. It is quite general in Australia, but it is also in force among the Melanesian, Polynesian, and Negro races of Africa as far as the traces of totemism and group relationships reach, and probably further still.

On the Banks Islands these prohibitions are very severe and painfully exact. A man will avoid the proximity of his mother-in-law as she avoids his. If they meet by chance on a path, the woman steps aside and turns her back until he is passed, or he does the same. In Vanna Lava (Port Patterson) a man will not even walk behind his mother-in-law along the beach until the rising tide has washed away the trace of her footsteps. But they may talk to each other at a certain distance. It is quite out of the question that he should ever pronounce the name of his mother-in-law, or she his.

On the Solomon Islands, beginning with his marriage, a man must neither see nor speak with his mother-in-law. If he meets her he acts as if he did not know her and runs away as fast as he can in order to hide himself.[124]

In the west today, it appears that men have some peculiar propensity which repels them from their mothers-in-law, but perhaps that repulsion is actually a secret attraction. Nevertheless, the Egyptians were not inhibited with any fear of sex within the forbidden degrees.

In the end, one must consider the cause of the fall of the Egyptian Empire. A civilization which introduced the world to medical procedures, the chemistry of dyes, cosmetics, and embalming, they excelled in letters (hieroglyphics and demotic) as well as inventing the paper to write on, constructed the pyramids and sphinx, raised up the Pharaoh's, King Tut, and Cleopatra, and left behind that mathematical solution of the measurement of a circle: Pi (in Egypt 3.16), (today, after 4000 years: 3.14159265-ad infinitum). It is difficult to precisely identify

---

[124] Freud, S. Totem and Taboo (Vintage, NY, 1960) p. 7, 6, 18

what disease caused this nation to fall from brilliance, but we should not eliminate the corruption of incest.

Did incest weaken the stock of Egypt? Were the Jewish woman birthing as the women of Egypt proclaim, "The Hebrew women are not as the Egyptian women; for they are lively, and are delivered before the midwives come in unto them," (Ex. 1:19). The small family of Jacob had in a mere four hundred years threatened the nation of Egypt with their numbers, "Behold, the people of the children of Israel are more and mightier than we. Come on, Let us deal wisely with them, lest they multiply, and it come to pass, that, when there falleth out any war, they join also unto our enemies, and fight against us, and so get them up out of the land,"(Ex. 1:9, 10). As we mentioned the Lord God added to the affliction of Pharaoh, he destroyed their first-born and their fathers. His judgment of Egypt began on that first Passover, and it has never ceased, for the prophet Ezekiel predicts, "It shall be the basest of the kingdoms, neither shall it exalt itself any more above the nations; for I will diminish them, that they shall no more rule over the nations," (Ezek. 29:15). This judgment has never ceased and will never cease. Could the sin of incest be the everlasting reason? Is the judgment of this nation bound up in its genes? Could this custom (an accepted social practice), or law (the protected right by a state sovereign) be the cause of such judgment? Yes! A thousand times, Yes! Listen to the anger of the Apostle when he discovered incest in the Church of Corinth:

> In the name of our Lord Jesus Christ, when ye are gathered together, and my spirit, with the power of our Lord Jesus Christ, To deliver such a one unto Satan for the destruction of the flesh. *I Cor. 5:4, 5*

This custom, incest, was practiced prior to the fall of the greatest of ancient empires. Dear reader we are living during the fall of the greatest civilization since Egypt, and that is not the most fearful thing. The most fearful fall we are experiencing is the fall of the true church, the true body of Christ. The church today has reached the apostasy predicted by the Apostle:

Now we beseech you, brethren, by the coming of our Lord Jesus Christ, and by our gathering together unto him, that ye be not soon shaken in mind, or be troubled, neither by spirit, nor by word, nor by letter as from us, as that the day of Christ is at hand. Let no man deceive you by any means: for that day shall not come, except there come a falling away first... *II Thess. 2:1-3a*

Now the Spirit speaketh expressly, that in the latter times some shall depart from the faith, giving heed to seducing spirits, and doctrines of devils. *(ITim. 4:1)*

This know also, that in the last days perilous times shall come. For men shall be lovers of their own selves, covetous, boasters, proud, blasphemers, disobedient to parents, unthankful, unholy, without natural affection,

trucebreakers [covenant breakers: divorcers], false accusers, incontinent, fierce, despisers of those that are good, traitors, heady, high-minded, lovers of pleasures more than lovers of God: having a form of godliness but denying the power thereof: from such turn away. For of this sort are they which creep into houses, and lead captive silly women laden with sins, led away with divers lusts. *II Tim. 3:1-6*

Dear reader, we are at the cross-road. The battle has been drawn. Can we stem this rising tide of evil custom, and permit another generation the peace of living in a creation-marriage world? The Egyptian customs were more dangerous than the bondage. Joseph escaped. Will we?

CHAPTER FOUR

Why Does Moses Permit Polygmy and Divorce?

Noah and his sons were commissioned to promulgate laws, but The Law came by Moses. Although the codes of the ancient societies marked the advancement of civilization, the Law of Moses was a masterpiece of ancient and modern jurisprudence. It has rightly been said that if the tables of stone were preserved, they would have become objects of worship today. But the fact of the matter is that the Law of God actually became an object of worship in the form of a religion. Not that it became Judaism, but that it became to some a belief in a way of salvation, a salvation of good works. The loftiness of the Law appeared to promise righteousness to the true follower. But this the law could not do. The Apostle was clear on this point, "Moreover, the law entered, that the offense might abound," (Rom. 5:20). Here Paul directly states that the law's purpose was to condemn man, not to justify man. This is at the heart of understanding the Gospel and understanding the Bible as a whole.

> Now we know that whatever things the law saith, it saith to them who are under the law, that every mouth may be stopped, and all the world may become guilty before God. Therefore, by the deeds of the law there shall no flesh be justified in his sight; for by the law is the knowledge of sin. *Rom. 3:19, 20*

Some would say that Martin Luther was at the heart of the Reformation, but the heart and soul of the Reformation was the cry, Sola Gratia, by grace alone, i.e. faith alone in the finished work of the Lord Jesus Christ. This is the central dynamic of the Gospel; without this truth there would have been no Luther. The Law teaches that all have sinned and come short of the glory of God, and therefore by the deeds of the law shall no flesh be justified. In spite of these driving words, men secretly reach to the law for their righteousness. The law proves a man unjust, but it has no power to regenerate him; to justify him. There are just some things the Law cannot do; in that light the Law is weak. When man expects the law to provide him a system to obtain righteousness, he is barking up the wrong tree. Every purpose of the Law is destined to prove to man that he is guilty of sin—capital sin. This fact must be kept in mind when we approach any element in the study of the Law; polygamy and divorce are elements of the law.

> For whosoever shall keep the whole law, and yet offend in one point, he is guilty of all. *James 2:10*
>
> For as many as are of the works of the law are under the curse; for it is written, cursed is everyone that continueth not in all things which are written in the book of the law, to do them. *Gal. 3:10*

To the non-Jew the Decalogue is the Law (the Ten Commandments), but to the Jew the entire revelation of God is the Law. When considering the specific number of commandments, we find there are actually 613 commandments.[125] Most scholars agree that the Law of Moses is divided into three elements: a civil code, a religious code, and a moral code. The latter is the distinctive feature of the Law. It reveals a righteous God, as compared to the immoral idol-gods of the ancient codes. The Gentile world today establishes their idyllic on the Ten Commandments, the Decalogue. Throughout this dissertation all nations other than Israel are Gentile. The problem is compounded because the church as a whole regarding marriage has embraced the Gentile governments dictates of marriage-law. The state promulgates laws regulating marriage, and the church foolishly over-embraces those laws. This creates a problem. The problem is that the church because of their belief in and embracement of governmental marriage-laws is failing to regulate marriage according to

---

[125] Willmington, H.L. Willmington's Guide to the Bible, (Tyndale, Weaton, IL, 1985) p. 940

the dictates of the God of Creation. Regarding marriage, believers often see the state and the church as the same law-giver. Believers trust that they have certain God given rights which apparently seem imbedded in some state regulations, but these are just the rights of the sovereign man-king. And when the old legal philosophy is excited, that obedience to the law is righteousness, some believers and some churches practice legalism by employing the states marriage laws into the church's marriage discussion, practice, and doctrine. They use the law to stop some mouths and to open others, but God said, that His Law was intended to stop every mouth.

Marriage Is Not a Sacrament:

Please permit this parenthesis: (Marriage is not a Sacrament). Before we continue any further keep this very important fact in mind: Marriage is not a Sacrament. Marriage in and of itself does not impart Grace. Marriage is the right thing to do, but it does not impart grace; the righteousness of Salvation. The word sacrament means an act that acquires the Grace of God. The only way to acquire the Grace of God is to put faith in the substitutionary blood sacrifice of the Lord and Savior Jesus Christ.

As we continue, keep this point in mind, regarding the law. There is another sub objective of the law, i.e., to temporarily control sin. The concept of controlling sin ensures the existence of sin. The law cannot eradicate sin. To do so would require the extermination of mankind. The law cannot make even one man righteous, nor could it eradicate one sin. The law is weak in that light. But before we discuss this let us just consider these points.

The Mosaic Law Was a Marriage Covenant?

Yes, Israel married Jehovah in the giving and acceptance of the law at Mount Sinai. The Scriptures speak of Israel as the wife of Jehovah and Jehovah as the husband of Israel—this does not apply to any Gentile.

Thus saith the Lord, The people who were left of the sword found grace in the wilderness, even Israel, when I went to cause him to rest. The Lord hath appeared of old unto me, saying, Yea, I have loved thee with an everlasting love; therefore, with loving-kindness have I drawn thee. *Jer. 31:3*

Now when I passed by thee, and looked upon thee, behold, thy time was the time of love; and I spread my skirt over thee, and covered thy nakedness. Yea, I swore unto thee, and entered into a covenant with thee, saith the Lord God, and thou becamest mine. *Ezek. 16:8*

The marriage ceremony took place in the wilderness of Sinai:

And Moses took half of the blood and put it in basins; and half of the blood he sprinkled on the altar. And he took the book of the covenant and read in the audience of the people; and they said, All that the Lord hath said will we do, and be obedient, and Moses took the blood, and sprinkled it on the people, and said, Behold the blood of the covenant, which the Lord hath made with you concerning all these words. *Ex. 24:6-8*

It must be kept in mind that the law was unique to Israel and Jehovah. It was literally their personal marriage contract. It was their intimate exchange of vows. What the Law was to these two it could not be to any other. This covenant was not made with any Gentile or any Church. We must remember that stubborn fact. Although the many Gentiles want to share in the blessing of the Law, they never-theless do not want to share in the curses, and in the plagues of the Law. Israel is the Chosen Nation; she is His, God's beloved nation. When Israel camped before Sinai, she looked up to heaven and said, "I am Ruth, thine handmaid, spread therefore thy skirt over thine handmaid; for thou [Jehovah] art a near kinsman." And Jehovah returned, "I spread my skirt over thee, and covered thy nakedness. Yea, I swore unto thee, and entered into a covenant with thee, saith the Lord God, and thou becamest mine." God was the courtesan, providing security for his beloved:

> Then a cloud covered the tent of the congrega-tion, and the glory of the Lord filled the tabernacle. And Moses was not able to enter into the tent of the congregation, because the cloud abode thereon, and the glory of the Lord filled the tabernacle. And when the cloud was taken up from over the taber-nacle, the children of Israel went onward in all their journeys; But if the cloud were not taken up, then they journeyed not till the day that it was taken up. For the cloud of the Lord was upon the tabernacle by day, and fire was on it by night, in the sight of all the house of Israel, throughout all their journeys. *Ex. 40:34-38*

The quality of the Sinai marriage was as magnificent as you would expect from the Creator, the Father of creation-marriage. It was bound permanently. Inseparably!

> Thou shalt fear the Lord thy God; him shalt thou serve, and to him shalt thou cleave, and swear by his name. For if ye shall diligently keep all these com-mandments which I command you, to do them, to love the Lord your God, to walk in all his ways, and to cleave unto him. *Deut. 11:22*

Leaving Egypt and cleaving to Jehovah, Israel was married as she confesses that she would keep the commandments. Moses was the preacher who performed the ceremony:

And Moses came and told the people all the words
of the Lord, and all the ordinances; and all the people answered with one voice, and said, All the words
which the Lord hath said will we do.*Ex. 24:3*

The courtship led the bride into the tabernacle of her lover
where the Shekinah Glory entered and the marriage was consummated. The vehicle of the seed of the woman, creation-marriage was
now in the hands of the children of Abraham, the Jewish Hebrew
Nation, Israel.

The Mosaic Law Established a Religious Sect

Judaism is bound in the Law. It was to be legally administered by
the Levitical priesthood, a requirement attainable by a single nation,
the Chosen Nation. Their marriage to Jehovah was marked with the
union of faith. The wedding ring of Israel was a golden memorial, the
Sabbath. Although marriage is not a sacrament, the law raises Israelite
marriage to the lofty heights only surpassed by the Savior's wife, the
church. In Israel the marriages of priests were regulated to a greater
extent than other marriages. Abel Isaksson in his volume, Marriage
and Ministry in the New Temple, suggests that the N.T. church
should have a higher standard for marriage than others because the
church is a kingdom of priests.[126]

The Law regulated every aspect of Jewish life, including their
time, civic, and religious duty. The Sabbath, the primary holy day,
was followed with numerous holy days, holy weeks, and holy years.
Their clothing, diet, and sacrifices were regulated. Their slaves were
to be governed with the Law's fair civil regulations. Their worship
was to be exercised in a tabernacle to be constructed in the most
precise detail. However, the law could not transfer grace or righ-
teous-ness; it could only transfer guilt. Nevertheless, the law was a

---

[126] Isaksson, Abel, Marriage and Ministry in the New Temple (trans. N.
Tomkinson with J. Gray; Lund: Gleeup, Copenhagen 1965) p. 36

religious code; it was the religious creed of Israel, designed to lead them to the atonement for sin that is provided in the Lamb of God, their own Passover Lamb.

The Law Was a Moral Code

From a moral standpoint the law surpassed the ancient codes which fell away like the hoarfrost to the burning rising sun. David's comments on the law of the Lord are fitting:

> The law of the Lord is perfect, converting the soul; the testimony of the Lord is sure, making wise the simple. The statutes of the Lord are right, rejoicing the heart; the commandment of the Lord is pure, enlightening the eye. The fear of the Lord is clean, enduring forever; the ordinances of the Lord are true and righteous altogether. More to be desired are they than gold, yea, than much fine gold; sweeter also than honey and the honeycomb. *Psa. 19:7-10*

The reader may object: You dear writer have just said that the Law could not make one righteous, yet David proclaims that the law of the Lord is perfect, converting the soul. Let me explain: Taken as a whole the law includes the three sections of the O.T., i.e. the books of Moses (the Pentateuch: the first five book of the Bible referred to as the books of the Law), the poetic books, and the historical/prophetic books. To understand the whole O.T. as the law of God is to understand Psa. 19. Thus, a true understanding of the entire O.T. will lead the believer to the real Lamb of God who taketh away the sin of the world. To understand one's sin in light of a coming sacrificed Messiah Savior is to have the experience of having one's soul converted; one who's sins are forgiven and atoned for. What we are talking about in this chapter is the Law of God, the Decalogue, the Ten Commandments, as a legal instrument to convict the sinner. As Paul so aptly wrote:

Now we know that what things soever the law
saith, it saith to them who are under the law: that
every mouth may be stopped, and all the world may
become guilty before God. *Rom. 3:19*

The moral beauty of the law led some to idolize it with their
worship, thus missing its purpose: to reveal the true sacrificial Lamb,
their Messiah. Jehovah God created the Law to teach man his need
for a Messiah, a Savior who men could worship, and man could
believe in with all his heart, to the converting and saving of his soul.
But men missed the point of the law: the Messianic Lamb, Jesus
Christ. Realizing its moral loftiness, and being unable to worship two
masters, they chose to worship the law and kill the Messiah-Savior,
The Lamb. They could not accept the force of the law. A Jewish man,
the Apostle Paul, came to understand the truth of the law, and he
fully learned its moral lesson: "I had not known sin but by the law—
that sin by the commandment might become exceedingly sinful. For
we know that the law is spiritual; but I am carnal, sold under sin,"
(Rom. 7). A study of the ancient codes will lead the reader to see the
superior moral quality of God's law; David's conclusion was that the
"Law of thy mouth (of God) is better unto me than thousands of
gold and silver," (Psa. 119:72). Unlike the casuistic (if - then) nature
of the ancient codes the Decalogue sets a strong moral tone, "Thou
shalt have no other gods before me; Thou shalt not make unto thee
any graven image; Thou shalt not take the name of the Lord thy God
in vain; Remember the Sabbath day, to keep it holy; Honor thy father
and thy mother; Thou shalt not kill; Thou shalt not commit adultery;
Thou shalt not steal; Thou shalt not bear false witness; Thou shalt
not covet thy neighbor's house, wife, manservant, maidservant, ox,
ass, nor anything that is thy neighbors." Where the ancient codes
regulated the exceptional cases,[127] God's law regulated the entirety
of sin.

---

[127] Boecker, Hans Jochen, Law and Administration of Justice in the O.T. and
Ancient East, (Augsburg, MN) p. 58

This present discussion is vital to the dynamic of this dissertation; so, I encourage the reader to read on.

The Mosaic Law Was a Civil Code, the Constitution of Israel

> And Moses came and told the people all the words of the Lord, and all the judgments; and all the people answered with one voice, and said, all the words which the Lord hath said will we do. And Moses wrote all the words of the Lord, and rose up early in the morning, and built an altar under the hill, and twelve pillars, according to the twelve tribes of Israel. And he sent young men to the children of Israel, who offered burnt offerings, and sacrificed peace offerings of oxen unto the Lord. And Moses took half of the blood, and put it in basins; and half of the blood he sprinkled on the altar. And he took the book of the covenant, and read in the hearing of the people; and they said, All that the Lord hath said will we do, and be obedient. And Moses took the blood, and sprinkled it on the people, and said, Behold the blood of the covenant, which the Lord hath made with you concerning these words. *Ex. 24:3-8*

The civil nature of the law has too often been overlooked. Immediately after Jehovah stated the Ten Commandments He regulates the slave-master relationship. One of the later laws regulating slaves reads: "If he (the slave-owner) smite out the manservant's tooth...he shall let him go free for the tooth's sake" (Ex. 21:27). The civil regulations make up a large section of the law. One scholar who has not missed the importance of the civil nature of the law is Leon Wood. Noting the ceremony recorded in Exodus 24:3-8 where Moses sprinkles the altar and the people with the sacrificial blood after preaching all the words of the Lord, and hearing the people vow to

to enter when the first marriage is restored after the consummation of the second."[131]

The O.T. divorce debate is centralized in this Deut. 24 text. When all is said and done, the victor of this debate will emerge from this ring of Scripture. While analyzing this text theologians speak of it's protasis and the apodosis. The protasis is the subordinate clause, and the apodosis is the main clause of a conditional thought. The former refers to the "if" of the proposal, while the latter refers to the "then" of the condition, i.e., (condition/conclusion, or the if/then). Verse 1 thru 3 of (Deut. 24:1-4) deal with certain if conditions, while verse 4 deals with the then of the conditional statement. The majority of commentators see divorce as the subject of this text; this is incorrect. It is a special-remarriage text. The driving concern of the text is found in (v. 4) which states: the abominable act is a certain prohibited remarriage. When God said that the abomination would defile the land, cause the land to sin, He uses the same language as he used in Leviticus 18, the incest chapter.

> Defile not ye yourselves in any of these things; for in all these the nations are defiled, which I cast out before you. And the land is defiled; therefore, I do visit the iniquity thereof upon it, and the land itself vomiteth out her inhabitants. Ye shall therefore keep my statutes and mine judgments and shall not commit any of these abominations; neither any of your own nation, nor any stranger that sojourneth among you: For all these abominations have the men of the land done, who were before you, and the land is defiled; That the land spew not you out also, when ye defile it, as it spewed out the nations that were before you. *Lev. 18:24-28*

---

[131] Heth and Wenham, Jesus and Divorce, (Hodder and Stoughton, London, 1984) p. 107

The abomination in the Deut. 24:1-4 text is akin to the acts of incest listed here in the Leviticus text. Was this prohibited remarriage of Deut. 24 an act of incest? As we shall see the combined scholarship of Isaksson, Yaron, Wenham, and Heth have collectively reached the summit of understanding regarding the abomination in Deut. 24. Therefore, since the abomination is the primary object of this text, we will reveal this truth before we discuss the meaning of the unclean thing or divorce.

As we noted there are three if conditions in this text: (1) If a man found some uncleanness in his wife, and (2) If a man divorced that wife, and (3) If that woman married another man, then that man (the first husband) could not remarry that woman (his first wife) because she was defiled. As mentioned the three if clauses are subordinate, while the then clause is the main clause. And here the main clause (the then clause) states that when the woman in question meets the criteria of all the three subordinate conditions she is defiled and it is then that it becomes an abomination for her first husband to have her again in a remarriage. Now divorce and remarriage are permitted in the law, save for this one exception, i.e the man could not marry a former divorced wife who had been another man's after he put her away. However, she was permitted to marry another eligible man.

As we simplify this text to the if-then interpretation we see a similarity of this text with the Matthew 19 exception clause. In Matthew divorce was forbidden except for one cause, and here we find that remarriage is permitted except for one cause. (Just a note on exceptions: they are rare and complicated if they exist at all in Scripture.) The real question of Deuteronomy 24 is not the meaning of some uncleanness, but the meaning of defiled in (v. 4). Along with Murry, P.C. Craigie forces his New Testament teaching into this text:

> The language (defiled) suggests adultery (see Lev. 18:20) the sense is that the woman's remarriage after the first divorce is similar to adultery in that the woman cohabits with another man. However, if the woman were than to remarry her first husband,

after divorcing the second, the analogy with adultery would become even more complete; the woman lives first with one man, then another, and finally returns to the first.[132]

Heth and Wenham continue to comment:

> Yet in this statute the second marriage is regarded as perfectly legal. It is the restoration of the first that is prohibited (v. 4). Commentators advancing this position seem to be reading New Testament ideas back into the Old (cf. Matt. 5:32). The language (defiled v.4) is suggestive, but that it anticipates the teaching of Jesus in the New Testament that remarriage after divorce is adultery is by no means certain.[133]

The majority of the Deuteronomy 24 commentators labor the unclean thing, "some uncleanness" (v. 1) in what seems as an endless speculation; with very little discussion of (v. 4). This is done in their attempt to prove that divorce was permitted in the law for infidelity, or adultery as per their interpretation of the N.T., (Matt. 5 and 19). But their interpretation is so wrong; it should go without saying, since the law plainly required the death penalty for adultery, not divorce. But in the discussion of Deut. 24 the defiled of (v. 4) and the abomination has been given little mention. Dobson like Hopewell suggest that the prohibition to remarry the defiled wife was aimed at preventing the abominable custom of Egypt, that of wife swapping.[134] Their explanation is that Moses, by requiring a bill of divorce, was placing a written legal requirement in the way of hasty divorces.

---

[132] Ibid. p. 108 Heth and Wenham quote Craigie

[133] Ibid. p. 108

[134] Dobson, E. G. What the Bible Really Teaches About Marriage, Divorce, and Remarriage (Revell, Old Tappan, NJ 1986) p. 39

Some may contend that the custom of wife swapping was made easy with the ancient custom of verbal divorce.[135] As it remains a custom in Arabic lands today, the man had only to pronounce this verbal statement over his wife three times: I "Tom D." divorce "Nancy D." my wife.[136]

> The proponents of the prevention doctrine teach that the writing of the bill of divorce was intended to cause the man to stop and think more about what he was doing; thus, a way of preventing hasty divorce. But Yaron argues; "the Deuteronomic provision would hardly serve to deter an angry husband intent on divorcing his wife. The one thing he would want at that moment is to be free of his wife for good. Beside in biblical times the chief deterrent to divorce was financial. Usually, the husband forfeited the dowry and sometimes had to make a divorce payment as well."[137]

Murry sees the defilement as: a matter of "gross sexual immorality," gross abnormality," or "gross irregularity."[138] He struggles with the meaning of the word defile because he labors to ensure that remarriage as a whole is permissible:

> It should be noted that it is only with reference to the prohibited return to the first husband that the defilement concerned is mentioned. The remarriage on the part of the divorced woman is not expressly stated to be defilement irrespective of return to

---

[135] Adams, Jay Marriage, Divorce, Remarriage p. 29

[136] Ibid. p. 29

[137] Thompson, J.A., JJS 17, p. 5 quote Deut. (London 1974) p. 244, The sort of payments may be gauged from extra-biblical sources, e.g. Laws of Eshunna 59, Hammurabi 137ff, Middle Assyrian Laws A 37f.

[138] Murry, John, Divorce, p. 13

the first husband. For these considerations we are required to exercise great caution before stigmatizing the remarriage as adulterous.[139]

Murry wrestles with his New Testament problem—that remarriage after divorce is adultery—when he attempts to define the word defiled. Here he is drifting aimlessly, as do the other "adultery group" scholars, but there is hope on the horizon. The total truth of the (Deut. 24:1-4) comes to light when with R. Yaron who sows the seed of thought which when combined with Isaksson's contribution of the new view of consanguinity, the kinfolk nature of Adam and Eve in marriage, and with the final touch of Wenham, and Heth are all combined; then the secret of the (v. 4) text is unlocked. Isaksson's initial contribution:

> To be someone's bone and flesh as a common expression to denote kinship (see, for example, Gen. 29:14; Jdg. 9:2; II Sam. 5:1, I Chr. 11:1). Very likely it is used here also in allusion not only to the fact that woman was created from Adam's rib but also to the consequence of this, viz. that man and woman are closely related to each other. If we accept the translation of "rib", the text says, strictly speaking, only that woman was of man's bone but not of his flesh. When the man nevertheless says shortly afterwards, on seeing the woman, that she is bone of his bone and flesh of his flesh, the combination of these two words, "bone" and "flesh", must have been chosen as a common expression for kinship. What is to be explained in this context is, of course, just how it could have come about that man feels the attraction of forming a unity with his wife more strongly than his affinity to his closest relations—his father and his mother...

---

[139] Ibid. p. 13

With this background of the use of the word to denote kinship, it is reasonable to translate it [bone - flesh] in Gen. 2:24 also by the word "relation", since in this context it is a question of how the original relationship between man and woman forms the explanation of man's strong desire to cleave to his wife. Since man and woman were originally of the same bone and flesh, a man leaves his father and his mother and cleaves to his wife, in order that they may become one flesh, i.e., together form a family.[140]

Yaron, building on Isaksson saw in the defilement: the abomination of incest:

It is submitted that Deuteronomy 24:1ff is to be explained not in terms of adultery but by reference to another sphere, namely to that of incest. This has one immediate advantage; there is no need for stigmatizing the (lawful) marriage of the divorcee as an "implicit" crime. The second marriage puts the wife finally beyond the reach of her first husband; this—and nothing more—is expressed by her being "defiled" (verse 4). More than that, the reference to incest allows us, finally, also to arrive at the true purpose of the law. Rules of incest, it is widely held, are designed to protect the family and to isolate, or insulate, existing socially approved personal relationships from the disruptive influences of sexual tension. Ordinarily, it is true, rules of incest apply within the family group, and in this point Deuteronomy 24:1ff is different; nevertheless, the basic aim is the same. We wish therefore to submit that the prohibition expressed in verse 4 aims at the protection of the second marriage. When the divorcee has married another man, we have

---

[140] Isaksson, Marriage,

before us the possibility of tension within the "trian-
gle" which has come into being. The first husband
may wish to get back his wife, having repented of dis-
missing her, the wife may draw comparisons between
her two husbands unfavorable to the second one and
may indulge in overtures disruptive of the second
marriage. Or, nothing of the kind may have actually
happened, but the second husband may go through
agonies of jealousy and apprehension, making life
a hell for the wife also. All these possibilities are
avoided once the reunion is prevented. And it can be
prevented effectively only by outlawing it, by declaring it to 'evah, an "abomination before the Lord."
This, then, is the very opposite of the approach taken
by Matthew and followed by the "adultery-group" of
scholars. Not only does Deuteronomy not object to
the second marriage, it takes effective steps to ensure
its stability and continuation.[141]

Yaron viewed Deuteronomy as regulating the psychological
aspects of incest, but incest has a darker side. It was Gordon Wenham
who seized upon the opportunity offered by Yaron's insight and captured the analogy of Scripture. His initial thoughts were expressed in
his commentary on Leviticus published as part of The International
Commentary on the Old Testament. Wedham would team up with
William Heth and publish the marvelous scholarly volume, Jesus
and Divorce, and it would be in this book that the bushel was finally
removed to reveal the light of (Deuteronomy 24:1-4). As we watch
Wenham open up the concepts of incest in Leviticus, we get a full
view of the truth:

> The Lord spoke to Moses as follows: Speak to the
> Israelites and say to them, I am the Lord your God.
> You must not behave as they do in the land of Egypt

---

[141] Yaron, R. Journal of Jewish Studies 17 (1966) p.8-9

where you have been living: and you must not behave
as they do in the land of Canaan, which I am bringing
you to; you must not follow their rules. You must do
my laws and keep my rules to follow them; I am the
Lord your God. You must keep my rules and my laws;
if a man does them, he will enjoy life through them: I
am the Lord. (*Wenham: Lev. 18:1-5*)

Wenham notes that the phrase, "I am the Lord your God", is
almost identical to the phrase which introduces the ten commandments in (Ex. 20:2).[142] He points out Israel's familiarity with the
heathen customs, and notes that she is warned to avoid, and at the
same time, she is taught what she was expected to imitate; quoting
that standard of Leviticus, "For I am the Lord your God: ye shall
therefore sanctify yourselves, and ye shall be holy; for I am holy (Lev.
11:44).[143] Wenham goes on to title verses 6-18 of Leviticus 18 the
Forbidden Unions:

No man among you may approach any of his
close relatives to have sexual intercourse: I am the
Lord. Do not have intercourse with your parents: she
is your mother: do not have intercourse with her. Do
not have intercourse with your father's wife; she is
one with your father. Do not have intercourse with
your sister, your father's daughter or your mother's
daughter, whether she belongs to local kindred or
distant kindred. Do not have intercourse with your
granddaughter, because she is one with you. Do not
have intercourse with your step-sister, if she belongs
to your father's kindred; she is your sister. Do not have
intercourse with your father's sister; she is your father's
relative. Do not have intercourse with your mother's

---

[142] Wenham, Gordon J. The Book of Leviticus, NIBC (Eerdmans, Grand
Rapids, MI 1979) p. 250

[143] Ibid. p. 251

sister, because she is your mother's relative. Do not uncover the nakedness of your uncle; you shall not approach his wife; she is your aunt. Do not have intercourse with your daughter-in-law; she is your son's wife; do not have intercourse with her. Do not have intercourse with your brother's wife; she is one with your brother. Do not have intercourse with a woman and her daughter; do not take her son's daughter or her daughter's daughter to have intercourse with her; they are relatives, it is wickedness. Do not marry a woman as well as her sister to distress her by having intercourse with her while she is alive. (Wenhan translation/ *Lev.18:6-18*)

Here Wenham is quick to point out that "close relative" is literally "flesh of his flesh."[144] Adam and Eve were a family. The family is the building unit of mankind, and this unit was protected by the prohibitions of certain sexual unions within the family. Wenham makes this interesting comment on the forbidden degrees mentioned in Leviticus 18:

> There is one striking omission from this table. Marriage with one's daughter is not proscribed. This is probably because it was already accepted that such a union was illicit (Gen. 19:30ff) [Lot and his daughters]. It was forbidden both in the laws of Hammurabi (LH 154) and in the Hittite laws (HL 195). In other words these regulations extend the prohibition on incest already accepted in other parts of the ancient Near East.[145]

Wenham and Heth then go on to reach the summit of this mountainous text:

---

[144] Ibid. p. 253

[145] Ibid. p. 254

Through her first marriage the woman entered into the closest form of relationship with her husband; divorce did not terminate this relationship; she still counted as a very close relative. If a divorced couple want to come together again, [the wife having another marriage in the interim, my note] it would be as bad as a man marrying his sister. That is why it is described as 'an abomination before the Lord' that 'causes the land to sin.'[146]

In the final analysis this text might be translated: When a man divorces his primary wife, he is permitted to marry again, except he cannot remarry his former wife if she had remarried during the interim of their separation. Thus, we see a universal statement with an exception clause—the divorcee may remarry with one exception: he could not commit the abomination of incest. Fornication. The marriage would have been a fornication-marriage. The marriage to the first wife would be equal to a man marrying his own daughter.

Deut. 24:1 Some Uncleanness; Some Indecency (erwat dabar)

When a man hath taken a wife, and married her, and it come to pass that she find no favor in his eyes, because he hath found some uncleanness [some indecency] in her; then let him write her a bill of divorcement, and give it in her hand, and send her out of his house...*Deut. 24:1*

Now let us get back to the sub-article of Deut. 24:1-4 (divorce). Here it just appears as an act that will occur. That is because it was an accepted custom of all the ancient world, and the present world at Mount Sinai, with Moses and the children of Israel. We are not

---

[146] Heth and Wenham, Jesus and Divorce, (Hodder and Stoughton, London, 1984) p. 110

directly told why God permitted this custom other than the words of Jesus: "For the hardness of your hearts he (Moses) wrote you this precept." Here the only condition that permitted a man to put away his wife was: "if he (her husband) found some uncleanness in her." The Hebrew words for some uncleanness (erwat dabar) have been debated for centuries. In order to keep one's focus on these two words remember that these are just part of the sub-article of Deut. 24:1-4 which is a text regarding the Abomination related to the Command that prohibited of a special remarriage. Two other background considerations are important: (1) the Law required the death penalty for both the adulterer and the adulteress; (2) the Law required the "river ordeal" for the woman suspected of adultery.

Heth and Wenham are correct when they say, "The interpretation of 'some indecency' (erwat dabar) in verse one is not really that important in this argument."[147] They follow Abel Isaksson, R. Yaron, and P.C. Craigie; the last of whom they quote:

> ...strictly speaking, the legislation relates only to particular cases of remarriage; the protasis [v.1-3] contains incidental information about marriage and divorce but does not specifically legislate on those matters. The verses do not legislate divorce but treat it as a practice already known.[148]

It is interesting to note that Abel Isaksson was the earliest pioneer to begin beating this drum that (erwat dabar) is incidental information. Other modern writers such as John MacArthur, J. Carl Laney, Paul E. Steele, Charles C. Ryrie, David Atkinson, John Murry, and as mentioned Heth, and Wenham all see the protasis in v. 1-3 and the apodosis in v.4. Murry points out that the Septuagint "adopts this construction" and older commentators like Keil, Delitzsch, Calvin,

---

[147] Ibid. 107

[148] Ibid. 107

Driver, and Reider all favor the position that (Deut. 24:1-4) be interpreted as a prohibition of the specified remarriage.[149]

The unclean or indecent thing (erwat dabar) is of little consequence to this text, or to the subject of divorce. Divorce was an accepted custom for all the reasons previously presented. As we said, both divorce and polygamy were the ancient inventions of man—his private customs that he alone owned, and God disowned:

> For the LORD, the God of Israel saith that He, "hateth putting away [God hateth divorce!]; for one covereth violence with his garment, saith the LORD of Hosts: therefore, take heed to your spirit, that ye deal not treacherously [to divorce is an act of treachery]. *Mal. 2:16*

Thus, God did not legislate creation-marriage in the Law; to do so would have caused a revolt in the heart of men. Moses suffered to permit the ancient sinful custom: divorce and remarriage. The law came by Moses, but grace and truth came by Jesus Christ, (Jn. 1:17). The "When" in Deut 24:1 has led some to believe that this was a nuptial event, and some revelation of the marriage bed on the wedding night. Although not relating their comments to the wedding night, Chase and Edersheim make the following comment:

> In itself, therefore, the expression (erwat dabar) need not denote more than something which is disgusting or unwholesome; or even it would appear, some bodily flaw which might cause disgust and aversion.[150]Alfred Edersheim alludes to the problem of physical unpleasantness (erwat dabar) as being a cause of divorce: "On the other hand, the wife could

---

[149] Murry, John; Divorce (Presbyterian and Reformed, Phillipsburg, NJ 1961) p. 15

[150] Chase, Frederic Henry; What Did Christ Teach About Divorce (Society of Promoting Christian Knowledge, NY, 1921) p. 9

insist on being divorced if her husband were a leper or affected with polypus.[151]

Donald W. Shaner quotes Chase:

> Chase agrees, however, that "some unseemly thing" (Deut. 24:1 erwat dabar) does not mean unchastitly (adultery punishable by death) but rather "some improper or indecent behavior" or possibly some bodily flaw.[152]

Regarding the timing of the "when" of the jealousy text we are sure it was nuptial:

> If any man take a wife, and go in unto her and hate her, and give occasions of speech against her, and bring up an evil name upon her, and say, I took this woman, and when I came to her, I found her not a maid; then shall the father of the damsel, and her mother, take and bring forth the tokens of the damsel's virginity unto the elders of the city in the gate. *Deut. 22:13-15*

On the nuptial eve, during the act of copulation, the man found reason to deplore his bride. During his attempt to consummate the marriage the man found a barrier. He sensed that his wife, who obviously claimed to be a virgin, was not. In his mind he believed he married a harlot. Therefore, at that instant, before the conclusion of the wedding day, the marriage was in a serious crisis. Is it possible that the "when" of (Deut. 24:1) is a reference to the marriage night? Could it be that the man saw some bodily flaw, physical disease, or other phys-

---

[151] Edersheim; Sketches, p. 158

[152] haner, Donald w.; A Christian View of Divorce (Leiden E.J. Brill, 1969) p. 16

ical unpleasantness which caused him to loath the woman he married: "she found no favor in his eyes."

The text in Ephesians is appropriate here:

> Husband's love your wives, even as Christ also loved the church, and gave himself for it, that he might sanctify and cleanse it with the washing of water by the word; that he might present it to himself a glorious church, not having spot, or wrinkle, or any such thing; but that it should be holy and without blemish. *Eph. 5:25-27*

One final comment regarding the timing of the "when" of Deut. 24:1:

> When a man hath taken a new wife, he shall not go out to war, neither shall he be charged with any business, but he shall be free at home one year, and shall cheer up his wife whom he hath taken. *Deut. 24:5*

Regarding the "When" of (v. 1) it is interesting that the "When" of (v. 5) should be injected right in this place in the Bible. Immediately after the so called "divorce text of the O.T. Deut. 24. 1-4" here in Deut. 24:5 we read another statement with the word when that obviously means the wedding night. Also, the idea of marriage in this text is: pregnant i.e., great with love and joy.

Now let us go on to the meaning of the words some uncleanness, some indecency, (erwat dabar). Most commentators believe the term is used to identify a myriad of minor offences (certainly not adultery); offences that triggered divorce; the definition of which was amplified by N.T. times where we find the school of Rabbi Hillel permitting divorce for "any cause." Here Edersheim comments:

> We know that it included every kind of impropriety, such as going about with loose hair, spinning in the street, familiarly talking with men, ill-treating her

husband's parents in his presence, brawling, that is,
'speaking to her husband so loudly that the neighbors
could hear her in the adjoining house' (Chethub, vii.
6), a general bad reputation, or the discovery of fraud
before marriage."[153]

Others include: poor cooking, no sons, or anything else that displeased her husband.[154] "They divorced them for the most frivolous
reasons: if she burnt his biscuits, or didn't season his food right, or if
he did not like her manners, or if she was a poor housekeeper, even
if he finds a woman more handsome than she."[155] Another mentions
the "violation of the Law of Moses, or of Jewish customs, such as
the woman causing her husband to eat food on which a tithe had
not been paid; not setting apart the first dough; appearing in public with disheveled hair; spinning and exposing her arms in public;
conversing indiscriminately with men; speaking disrespectfully of her
husband's parents in his presence; brawling in the house; or spoiling
a dish for him."[156] William J. Hopewell agrees: "When Deuteronomy
24 was written, the Jewish people had followed the terrible sin of the
Egyptians in wife-swapping, putting away their wives for the least
cause, and had degenerated marriage to a very primitive status."

There also existed another school of thought during N.T. times,
those of Rabbi Shammai: he believed that the indecency, (erwat
dabar), was unchastity: adultery. Many N.T. commentators place Jesus
on the side of Shammai, earning them Edersheim's censure: "It is a
serious mistake on the part of commentators to set the teaching of
Christ on this subject by the side of that of Shammai."[157] There is no
question of what the Law taught regarding adultery. It was not a matter of divorce. It was a capital crime: the death penalty.

---

[153] Ibid. p. 16

[154] Hopewell, Marriage and Divorce, p. 2

[155] Duty, Guy; Divorce and Remarriage, (Bethany, Minn. 1967) p. 23

[156] Dobson, E.G.; What the Bible Really p. 35

[157] Edersheim, Life and Times…p. 2:332

If a man be found lying with a woman married to an husband, then they shall both of them die, both the man that lay with the woman, and the woman. So shalt thou put away evil from Israel. *Deut. 22:22*

And the man who committeth adultery with another man's wife, even he who committeth adultery with his neighbor's wife, the adulterer and the adulteress shall surely be put to death. *Lev. 20:10*

Edersheim exhorts NT commentators to remember the absolute position of the Law concerning unchastity. By putting Jesus on the side of Shammai they were misrepresenting the position of Jesus regarding adultery and the law. Sexual intercourse on the part of the woman with any man other than her husband was a capital crime: (1) In the "law of jealousies", (Deut. 22:13) the woman was put to death if she was found not to be a virgin on her wedding night; (2) If a betrothed virgin was forced by another man to lay with him, and she did not cry rape, both the man and the damsel were to be stoned to death; (3) and the married adulteress and adulterer were to be put to death. In the law adultery was always a capital crime. The erwat dabar could never mean adultery.

Edersheim goes on to say that erwat dabar was translated: "a matter of shame, [literally nakedness]." Regarding this idea Abel Isaksson presents this interesting comment regarding erwat dabar (exposure or the nakedness of a thing):

> This expression is usually interpreted to mean something shameful or repulsive, without going into any detail as to what it is that arouses the husband's loathing for his wife. The expression occurs in another passage in the O.T., viz. in Dt. 23.14. Verse 12 of chap. 23 mentions that there is to be a place outside the camp at which all feces from the camp are to be buried. This is to be done lest Yahweh, when he walks through the camp, should find (something exposed). It is clear that here dabar stands for human

excrement. It is accordingly an euphemism. Yahweh must not see excrement lying about exposed. The expression is similarly used as an euphemism in Dt. 24:1 but here it does not stand for human excrement but for the female pudendum [with reference the mention of the female token in Dt. 22] here means a cloth or garment of some kind, as a covering for the female pudendum, which the husband gave his wife at their marriage as a sign that she was his (cf. for example, Ezek. 16:8: "And I spread my skirt over you and covered your nakedness", cf. Ru. 3.9). While Leviticus speaks of uncovering the nakedness of a father (Lev. 18:7 f., 20:11), Deuteronomy speaks of uncovering the skirt of a father (23:1, 27:20). Thus here also Deuteronomy avoids directly mentioning the pudendum. In Dt. 24.1 it cannot be a matter of some other man having lifted the covering and exposed the wife's pudendum. This would have been tantamount to adultery and in that case, there could be no question of a new marriage for the wife, since both parties would be stoned to death.

Probably it is a question here of the wife having exposed herself voluntarily or involuntarily. All other exposure of his wife's pudendum than that which the husband himself is responsible for arouses his loathing. That the husband's improper exposure of himself in the presence of any other person of the opposite sex than the woman he was married to aroused, the wife's contempt is clear from the story of how Michal despised David when in his dance before the ark of the Lord he accidentally exposed himself to the crowd (2 Sam. 6:12-20). Michal interpreted David's involuntary exposure of himself as a deliberate exposure to the servant maids. But it is only licentious people (2 Sam. 6:20) who expose themselves in this way.

No modest Israelite woman will do so. The wife will no longer find grace in her husband's eyes when he discovers her exposing her nakedness. This is also clear from Ezek. 23:18, in which it is said that the man's soul turns away from the wife who exposes her nakedness.[158]

Isaksson goes on to support this view with the translation of LXX and the conservative rabbis. With reference to his comment that (erwat dabar) was used as a euphemism for human excrement it should be pointed out that the Englishman's Hebrew and Chaldee Concordance of the Old Testament lists 51 references to the word dabar, and in 49 of those references it means nakedness. Therefore, the two remaining uses belong to Deut. 24 and here:

> Thou shalt have a place outside the camp, whither thou shalt go abroad; and thou shalt have a paddle upon thy weapon; and it shall be, when thou wilt ease thyself abroad, thou shalt dig therewith, and shalt turn back and cover that which cometh from thee: for the Lord thy God walketh in the midst of thy camp, to deliver thee and to give up thine enemies before thee; therefore shall thy camp be holy; that he see no unclean (dabar) thing in thee, and turn away from thee. *Deut. 23:12-14*

Kiel and Delitzsch comment:

> For the camp was to be kept holy, because Jehovah walked in the midst of it, in order that he might not see the nakedness of a thing, i.e., anything to be ashamed of in the people, and turn away from thee. There was nothing shameful in the excrement itself;

---

[158] Isaksson, Marriage and Ministry, p. 25-27

but want of reverence, which the people would display through not removing it, would offend the Lord and drive him out of the camp of Israel.[159]

Exposed excrement, the erwat dabar the camp of Israel, would have been the act which would have caused Jehovah to be offended, thus driving him out of the camp. Likewise, in Deut. 24:1 the erwat dabar, unclean thing, would have caused the wife to find no favor in the eyes of her husband.

As we said, the meaning of erwat dabar in the context of Deut. 24:1-4 is of little consequence. Edersheim concludes:

> And the Jewish law unquestionably allowed divorce on almost any grounds; the difference being, not as to what was lawful, but on what grounds a man should put the Law in motion and make use of the absolute liberty which it accorded him.[160]

One of the barriers against divorce in the OT was its financial cost. Since a bride price, dowry, was essential to the contract, the paramour had to literally count the cost of investing in and additional wife. Perhaps the anticipation of wealth provoked the admonition to Israel's future king, "Neither shall he multiply wives to himself,"(Deut. 17:17). This remains a problem to the divorced-remarried polygamist in the West: they must pay alimony to their previous wives, even though the law only permits one wife at a time. Multiple wives are still expensive. Traditionally many believe that Moses was erecting a barrier to the easy divorce of the day by requiring the man to write a Bill of Divorce, but Heth and Wenham disagree:

> Deut. 24:1-4 cannot be taken as evidence that Moses sought to limit the husband's absolute right to divorce his wife whenever he wished and for what-

---

[159] KDOTC, p. 3:415

[160] Edersheim, Life and Times, p. 2:333

ever reason. Furthermore, this Deuteronomic concession would hardly deter an angry husband intent on divorcing his wife. When a man divorced his wife, he would not want her to return to him. Since the law accurately mirrors his feelings when he is giving the divorce it can hardly have discouraged him. Besides, probably the strongest deterrent to divorce in Israel and all over the ancient Near East was financial, since the husband had to forfeit the dowry and may have been involved also in other payments to his former wife.[161]

These traditionalists also claim that the bill of divorce would have listed the wives faults and along with the time required to write the document would have in itself regulated hasty divorce—Here is an example of a typical divorce document.

On the_____day of the week in the month _____
of the year_____from the beginning of the world,
according to the common computation in the province of_____, I____ son of _____
by whatever name I may be known, of the town of
_____ with the entire consent of mind and without
any constraint, have divorced, dismissed, and expelled
thee,_ daughter of by whatever name thou art
called, of the town of_____so as to be free this
day forever. Thou art therefore free for anyone (who
would marry thee). Let this be thy bill of divorce from
me, a writing of separation and expulsion according to
the law Moses and Israel.

Witness_____
Witness _____

---

[161] Heth and Wenham, Jesus and Divorce, p. 108

Obviously, the woman's faults were not documented in all divorce bills as evidenced here. To the contrary the bill leads one to believe that divorce was rather simple, and if anything, the bill made it a greater reality and seems to ensure the idea of permanency. Men like Jay Adams become ecstatic with the revelation that divorce was legal. They then violently drive the O.T. concepts into the NT. Dwelling on the word, divorce, as found in the bill he attempts to convey the message that the marriage was forever put asunder: "kerithuth > karath> (1) to cut off; hew down; is used for hewing down timber (I Kings 5:18); (2) amputation (Lev. 22:24); (3) decapitation (I Sam. 17:51). It indicates severing of what was once a living union."[162] The following statement is typical of Jay Adams: "Contrary to some opinions, the concept of divorce is biblical." He goes on to say, "Divorce, for some persons, under some circumstances is altogether proper, and not the object of God's hatred.[163] But as we have seen, regardless of those who like Adams labor to declare that divorce is a tool to put marriage asunder, we have proven that divorce is impotent in its determination to defeat creation-marriage. Adams is incorrect, for he failed to regard the main clause of the text, the abomination. A man could not return to his divorced wife if she in fact had been married to another during the interim of their separation. To do so would be an abomination; and so it was since that man and that woman were still organically married. She was kinfolk. To marry kin was an abomination. Period! She was through marriage equal to his sister, or his daughter. The words to divorce, to cut off, to hew down, to amputate, or to decapitate, contrary to Jay Adams do not, and cannot put asunder the marriage bond, which was created in the garden, creation-marriage, that is man's first marriage. The law could not separate what God hath joined together, therefore the only thing the law could do was permit man to legally separate from the woman he was bound to, permanently, and technically marry a second wife. Polygamy!

---

[162] Atkinson, D. To Have and To Hold (Eerdmans, Grand Rapids, 1979) p. 103

[163] Adams, Jay E. Marriage, Divorce, and Remarriage (Presbyterian and Reformed Pub. Co., Philipsburg, PA) p. 23

Thus, the law permitted polygamy, and divorce because the heart of man was so totally evil that man could not conceive of a marriage that was permanent. We read the words of the disciples—who after walking with and becoming followers of Jesus, for some time as proof that even believers cannot easily accept the doctrine of permanency:

> His disciples say unto him, If the case of a man be
> so with his wife, it is not good to marry. *Matt. 19:10*

Dear reader, please keep in mind, that Jesus abolished, thus totally invalidating, the concession of Moses that is referenced in (Deut. 24:1-4) with His definition of creation-marriage; as an indissoluble-marriage (Mk. 10:2-12) "they are no more twain, but one flesh. He supported this doctrine of marriage with His life; sacrificing Himself at the Cross to provide a man and woman with the gift of the new-birth by which man could live a virtuous life. Since Jesus' doctrine of marriage is permanent then the abomination of Deut 24:1-4 in this Church Age is non-existent. It cannot occur. Period!

Comment on Deut. 24:2-4 Defiled

> 24:2 And when she is departed out of his house, she may go and be another man's wife. (The Law of Moses clearly permitted remarriage however with one exception as noted in the next two verses.)
> 24:3 And if the latter husband hate her, and write her a bill of divorcement, and giveth it in her hand, and sendeth her out of his house; or if the latter husband die, which took her to be his wife; [These are the two final IF clauses of this sentence.]
> 24:4 Her former husband, which sent her away may not take her again to be his wife, after that she is defiled; (This is the THEN clause of this sentence.) for that is abomination before the LORD: and thou shalt not cause the land to sin, which the LORD thy God giveth thee for an inheritance.

The woman's first husband is prohibited to remarry his first wife because she is defiled ONLY TO him; please note that without her first husband she is not defiled. Here the Scripture specifically states that the woman is only defiled to the first husband; she may remarry other qualified candidates. The definition of defiled in this verse CANNOT mean adultery in any sense of the word. Adultery was a capital crime, by that fact, it cannot mean defile in this verse. In the O.T. adultery always carried the death penalty.

The word, defiled, here means that any further sexual union of these two partners would be a sinful act, akin to INCEST if not incest itself. The act of incest in this case has the narrow limit that since this couple—because of their first marriage—remain consanguineous partners. Their remarriage, after the wife had remarried was not permissible; it was equal to incest. Thus, God pronounces His judgment: that specific remarriage is an abomination before the Lord. Thou shalt not cause the land to sin, which the Lord God giveth thee for an inheritance.

I repeat that those four verses in the KJV Bible are actually one verse; as noted in the JPS version of the O.T. The primary subject of the verse is the Abomination. The Law here states this law: Her former husband may not take her again to be his wife.

Then we have the COMMANDMENT" of Deut. 24:1-4: Thou shalt not cause the land to sin. This sin was a special abominable remarriage-sin as stated. It had very little to do with divorce. The sin was a special remarriage prohibition. This text has little to do with divorce. Yet, the whole world screams that it is all about divorce: Is this honest? Is it!

What is the NT Application of This Abomination?

This abomination was only possible in the O.T. where the ancient custom of divorce was suffered to exist as explained. This paper declares that all remarriage-this-side-of-death is forbidden; and therefore, an act of Adultery. The incest Abomination of Deut. 24:1-4 cannot be committed in the Christian World today. Yes, the abomination of

Deut. 24:1-4 is a sin that is now out of reach for the Church; since all divorce with remarriage is adultery—as per the marriage doctrine of the Lord Jesus Christ (Mk. 10:11-12).

As noted, it is believed by some exegetes, as well as this author, that the Egyptians, during this period of Israel's history, practiced wife swapping which includes the specific abomination referenced here. Since the law permitted divorce and remarriage this exception to prohibit a special remarriage is only reasonable, and it certainly was a possibility, and if so then wife-swapping could have been committed legally under the cover of God's Law. So, then the exception of Deut. 24:1-4 with it's Abomination is rather complex and rare, nevertheless necessary in the face of an Almighty and Holy God.

Thus, Jesus abolished the divorce concession of Moses and did what the Law could not do: Jesus mandated the Edenic creation marriage doctrine. Under Christ, marriage is now permanent and indissoluble as it was under the Creation Law of the Creator. Since marriage is permanent all other sexual unions outside of creation marriage are an abomination of adultery. The abomination of Deut.24:1-4 cannot be committed under the rule of the Lord Jesus Christ. Therefore, Jesus sets a new law in order:

> But from the beginning of the creation God made them male and female. For this cause shall a man leave his father and mother, and cleave to his wife; And they twain shall be one flesh: so then they are no more twain, but one flesh. What therefore God hath joined together, let not man put asunder.
>
> And in the house his disciples asked him again of the same matter. And he saith unto them, Whosoever, shall put away his wife, and marry another, committeth adultery against her. And if a woman shall put away her husband, and be married to another, she committeth adultery. *Mk. 10:6-12*

The Law Permits Polygamy

What was true about the law and divorce is true about the law and polygamy. It appears the heart of man was so hard and stubborn that he could not be legislated away from his sin. As we have shown from the ancient law codes man assumed, he has certain rights; rights that he believed were his birthright. If the sovereign king-man wanted several wives, or if his primary wife could not provide offspring, or whatever he expected, he believed he had an unalienable right to acquire more than one wife.

If a man have two wives, one beloved, and another hated, and they have borne him children, both the beloved and the hated, and if the first-born son be hers that was hated; then it shall be, when he maketh his sons to inherit that which he hath, that he may not make the son of the beloved first-born before the son of the hated, which is indeed the first-born. *Deut. 21:15,16*

Without any apology, the law acknowledges that polygamy was the acceptable custom of all men, even at Sinai. This regulation governing inheritance rights is relatively minor, but a major problem when one considers the doctrine of creation-marriage—God only created one wife for man. Notice that the man was permitted to continue his hatred towards the wife of his first-born, although it protected her honor in her child.

> If brethren dwell together, and one of them die, and have no child, the wife of the dead shall not marry without the family unto a stranger; her husband's brother shall go in unto her, and take her to him as his wife, and perform the duty of a husband's brother unto her. And it shall be, that the first-born whom she beareth shall succeed in the name of his brother who is dead, that his name be not put out of Israel. *Deut. 25:5, 6*

As mentioned regarding Onan in Genesis 38: levirate marriage was not exactly polygamy. If the child of this marriage belonged to the deceased brother, then the mother also belonged to the brother. Most commentators agree that the levirate custom or law did not interfere with the living brother's existent marriage. In other words, within these limits the brother-in-law's marriage might co-exist with the prohibition of marriage with a brother's wife; whereas, if the deceased brother had a son or children, such a marriage was forbidden as prejudicial to the fraternal relation.[164] The levirate however speaks well for procreation, on which God obviously places a very high value. Progressive spiritual development, or what is referred to in the discipline of hermeneutics as progressive revelation, seems to play a role in the man's understanding of marriage. Edersheim makes this observation:

> Of course, against all this may be set the permission of polygamy, which undoubtedly was in force at the time of our Lord, and the ease with which divorce, might be obtained. In reference to both these, however, it must be remembered that they were temporary concessions to "the hardness" of the people's heart. For, not only must the circumstances of the times and the moral state of the Jewish and of neighboring nations be taken into account, but there were progressive stages of spiritual development. If these had not been taken into account, the religion of the Old Testament would have been unnatural and an impossibility.[165]

As progression implies a growing knowledge base from premature to mature, it appears that man's understanding of creation-marriage had reached such a low ebb that God had to gradually recover man from his demise. Man's premature understanding of marriage includes the following idea introduced by Isaksson:

---

[164] KDOTC p. 3:424

[165] Edersheim, Sketches, p. 142

The Israelite matrimonial code is also formulated entirely with regard to the husband's interests. Thus the wife may not have liaisons outside marriage, but the husband may do so, provided that he does not thereby infringe another man's rights. As the primary purpose of marriage is to maintain the man's lineage through numerous offspring, polygamy is a natural form of marriage.[166]

If a man find a damsel who is a virgin, who is not betrothed, and lay hold on her, and they be found; then the man who lay with her shall give unto the damsel's father fifty shekels of silver, and she shall be his wife; because he hath humbled her, he may not put her away all his days. *Deut. 22:28, 29*

The law here assumes the right of the damsel's father to deny the perpetrator the right of marriage which is mentioned in Exodus 22:16-17, however it makes no mention of the possibility that the perpetrator was previously married. Actually, it assumes that possibility and the reflection is that the man would simply be obligated to practice polygamy. It was not a capital crime for a married man to deflower a virgin. The penalty for the seduction simply required the seducer to marry the victim and prohibited the right to divorce the woman. So in this text we see the man's right to divorce is denied, and it is actually a form of punishment.

And whosoever lieth carnally with a woman who is a bondmaid (slave girl) betrothed to an husband, and not at all redeemed, nor freedom given her; she shall be scourged; she shall not be put to death, because she was not free. *Lev. 19:20*

---

[166] Isaksson, Marriage…; p. 35

Apparently, the woman did not resist with a scream; her punishment, scourging, while the perpetrator was obviously unpunished.

> When thou goest to war against thine enemies, and the Lord thy God hath delivered them into thine hands, and thou hast taken them captive, and seest among the captives a beautiful woman, and hast a desire for her, that thou wouldest have her as thy wife, then thou shalt bring her home to thine house; and she shall shave her head, and pare her nails, and she shall put the raiment of her captivity from off her, and shall remain in thine house and bewail her father and her mother a full month; and after that thou shalt go in unto her, and be her husband, and she shall be thy wife. And it shall be, if thou have no delight in her, then thou shalt let her go where she will. But thou shalt not sell her at all for money; thou shalt not make merchandise of her, because thou hast humbled her.
> *Deut. 21:10-14*

Polygamy may or may not be involved here but it appears that this law sheds a favorable light on the possibility of such.

As previously mentioned, Jehovah knew the heart of the people would demand a king when they secured the Promised Land. He also knew the propensities of man's hard heart as a ravenous polygamist, was to multiply wives. As previously explained, man's insatiable sin nature could not be redeemed by the law, the law simply attempted to control man in his sin. As we pointed out polygamy was tolerated within the realm of the law. Polygamy was a sin which was not directly acknowledged by the law. It seemed the only conditions it required was that the polygamist chose an unbetrothed wife, and that he faithfully support all his wives.

> Among the unacknowledged sins which God tolerated because of the hardness of Israel's heart was

polygamy, which encouraged licentiousness and the tendency to sensual excesses, and to which but a weak barrier had been presented by the warning that had been given for the Israelitish kings against taking many wives (Deut 17:17), opposed as such a warning was to the notion so prevalent in the East both in ancient and modern times, that a well-filled harem is essential to a princely court.[167]

An Israelite king would now advance an additional threat to creation-marriage, in that he was in a new position to acquire wealth, and the consequence of his wealth would increase his power to support a multitude of wives. The Lord foresaw the king drunk with wives, to the turning away of his heart:

> But King Solomon loved many foreign women; in addition to the daughter of Pharaoh, women of the Moabites, Ammonites, Edomites, Sidonians, and Hittites, of course the nations concerning which the Lord said unto the children of Israel, Ye shall not go in to them, neither shall they come in unto you; for surely they will turn away your heart after their gods. Solomon clave unto these in love. And he had seven hundred wives, princesses, and three hundred concubines; and his wives turned away his heart. For it came to pass, when Solomon was old, that his wives turned away his heart after other gods, and his heart was not perfect with the Lord his God, as was the heart of David, his father. *I Kings 11:1-4*

Jesus said that Moses permitted it so because the heart of man was so callous, that it appears for God to permit man to exist, He had to permit divorce and polygamy to exist. Jesus would however abolish

---

[167] KDOTC p. II Sam. 11

that permission for not only would he prohibit polygamy and divorce, but He would also provide the power and grace for man, to live lovingly while under that prohibition; the man could now by faith in the Gospel experience the new-birth in Christ, and through the Spirit of God he could walk in the newness of life. This gift of the Gospel in Christ is the unspeakable gift of God to man.

Slavery and the Law of Moses; Divorce and Polygamy

One might ask: What does slavery have to do with divorce and polygamy. The question is further exasperated by the current political correctness and righteousness of those who view America's initial use of slavery as uncommonly sinful; but the Law of Moses permitted slavery. As declared: man was the inventor and master of divorce and polygamy; as driven by his hard-heart—the same is true, of among other things, the invention of slavery. The average American today believes that the Civil War was fought to emancipate the enslaved black race from the evil tyranny of the bondage of slavery. The righteous say: the South had no right to employ the ancient custom of slavery as a means to literally, i.e. physically build the nation of America.

I am not saying that slavery is righteous; but I am saying that the custom of slavery—like divorce and polygamy—was ubiquitous from antiquity; it was permitted in the Bible. It was so entirely ubiquitous that the Law of Moses was impotent to remove this custom from an accepted practice of Israel, and the United States. It is another article of evidence that the Law could not institute righteousness because of the absolute indurate hardness of the heart of all men.

In this case as we examine the Law of Moses we discover that in the giving of the Law, God did not condemn slavery; but, as with divorce and polygamy, He chose to permit slavery and then to regulate it. In Exodus chapter twenty we read the record of the Ten Commandments of the Law—As we have mentioned earlier, the Law was composed of 613 commandments. As we proceed from the Ten Commandments, one discovers that the Eleventh Commandment— if that can be said—in Ex. 21:2 regulates the master who purchases a Hebrew born slave. There were two basic levels of slaves in Israel: native Hebrew slaves and Heathen slaves. The Hebrew slaves fared better then the Heathen. Nevertheless, the life of both was in the hand of their master:

> Exo 21:1 Now these are the judgments which thou shalt set before them. [the next sentence is the Eleventh Commandment]
> Exo 21:2 If thou buy an Hebrew servant, six years he shall serve: and in the seventh he shall go out free for nothing.

Of the many regulations that dealt directly with slavery Kiel and Delitzsch see that Ex. 21:3-4, 26, 27 as common to both the Hebrew and the Heathen slave:

> Exo 21:3 If he came in by himself, he shall go out by himself: if he were married, then his wife shall go out with him
> Exo 21:4 If his master have given him a wife, and she have born him sons or daughters; the wife and her children shall be her master's, and he shall go out by himself.
> Exo 21:26 And if a man smite the eye of his servant, or the eye of his maid, that it perish; he shall let him go free for his eye's sake.
> Exo 21:27 And if he smite out his manservant's tooth, or his maidservant's tooth; he shall let him go free for his tooth's sake.

So where does this place the uncommon sin of American slavery, and the righteous prohibitionist of the Civil War? Jehovah God clearly permitted slavery in the O.T. In 21:4 should the slave be given a wife and she bore him children, if he should gain his freedom, then he must leave his wife and children or remain a slave to his master for life. Should the master, in his permitted act of slave discipline, strike out the eye or even one tooth of a slave; that slave was to go free. The real problem here is the stubborn fact that God permitted slavery. Therefore, when the American settlers employed the custom of slavery, they believed that it was an institution of God as per the Mosaic Law—this is the same as the Church, in error, believes that divorce and remarriage are the institution of God as ordained by the Law of Moses. This is caused by the fallacy that the Church, especially the Southern States churchmen, believed that they were God's chosen people—the Church was the new Israel and the true Israel was the Church. They saw no distinction between Israel and the Church. Therefore, they interpreted slavery as a God given right. The truth of the matter is that the Church is not Israel and Israel is not the Church. But if you do not understand this very important distinction you may have believed that the custom of slavery was a God given right absolutely based on the Law of Moses. This was true, yet very unfortunate, since Jesus abolished slavery with His doctrine of the equality of man. The Apostle Paul defined this with these marvelous words:

> For ye are all the children of God by faith in Christ Jesus. For as many of you as have been baptized into Christ have put on Christ. There is neither Jew nor Greek, there is neither bond [slave] nor free, there is neither male nor female: for ye are all one in Christ Jesus. (*Gal: 3:26-28*)

Thus, there is a grave danger in the misinterpretation of the Scripture regarding these important themes: divorce, remarriage, polygamy, and slavery. This is revealed by America's southern Bible believers who by misapplying the Law of Moses, believed they had Jehovah God on their side of the conflict; thus, assuming that their war was a righteous war. So, it is with many in the Divorce-Remarriage War of this treatise. The wrong interpretation of the Law of Moses has led man into the dangerous practice of dissoluble marriage; yes, as it led many into the Civil War.

An interesting footnote here is seen when we look into the life of the truly godly Mr. George Whitefield. Mr. Whitefield had an enormous passion for the orphans that were scattered about the land when he visited the southeastern colonial states in the early to mid-Eighteenth Century. Their desperate need pressed upon his heart and in the middle of his evangelistic campaigns he stopped everything to establish an orphanage, called Bethesda, in Georgia. Bethesda would be a working farm, a southern plantation, a place to provide food, shelter,and an income for its new residents—an orphanage.

Mr. Whitefield had two major problems: (1) the climate of Georgia, especially during the growing seasons, was brutal for the white European settlers who were not physically able to work under the sun in the heat of the day. He concluded that only the Negro had the physical ability and endurance to work in the sun and heat of a Georgia summer. (2) His second problem was that in the early to mid-18th Century slavery was illegal in Georgia.

The interesting thing here is that Mr. Whitefield became a dedicated pro-slavery advocate and in 1749 he began to politically campaign for the legalization of Slavery in Georgia. His letters and public pleas appealed to the Georgia Trustees. In 1751 partly through his campaign Georgia legalized slavery. His writing during that period appealed to the Biblical righteousness of slavery. His success permitted Whitefield to purchase slaves to work the Bethesda Orphanage Plantation. It is reported that his slaves loved him, and many poor orphans had a wonderful home.

There is a nice and true story that took place in the historical city of Philadelphia. Mr. Whitefield was preaching in the city. He was known for his magnificent voice. Without a sounding board he was gifted with almost an angelic voice with angelic volume. As he was preaching this day, one in the crowd was amazed at the phenomenon, his name was Benjamin Franklin. Being the scientist that he was, as well as a knowledgeable citizen of the city, Mr. Franklin began to mathematically calculate the number of people that were drawn to this evangelistic meeting in the streets of downtown Philadelphia. He first estimated the total square feet of the streets that were filled with this outdoor crowd. He then measured the total number of people that could actually be inside that space. This gave him the total number of the congregation: thirty thousand could clearly hear Mr. Whitefield's beautiful voice filled with heavenly appeals.

But the really amazing thing that happened to Mr. Franklin that day is when Mr. Whitefield began to make appeals for an offering for his Bethesda Orphanage. Mr. Franklin said to himself, "I will only give a few pence to this preacher." When the offering container was passed by him, he found himself in tears for the orphans in Georgia and he emptied his pockets of all his money; even to the last coin.

CHAPTER FIVE

Was God a Divorce´?

As we descend Mount Sinai, we must wade through the serpent filled swamps of the wilderness of Sin before we reach the Promised Land. Come along as we join with the band of Israel who carry the cherished cargo, the creation-marriage doctrine. This would be the vehicle of the one who would preach that creation-marriage sermon in (Mk.10:2-12). As we trek along, we will keep our eyes on the progress of this cargo of love. Will the serpent's venom poison her?

Israel the Wayward Wife of Jehovah God

As we stated earlier, Jehovah was married to Israel. The Law was a marriage contract with His beloved lady. He loved her. In His Song of Songs, He composes her sonnet of sonnets, and pledges His love, "Set me as a seal upon thine arm; for love is strong as death," (Song 8:6). His love to Israel is everlasting. We will see throughout this treatise that as Israel deserted Him, He wooed her return, always keeping the door of reconciliation open. His perfect love required Him to discipline her, but He never forsook her. We shall see that although Israel was the blessed chosen nation, and the wife of Jehovah, she nevertheless was given to marital apostasy. As God and Moses were planning salvation worship in the heights of Sinai, Satan and Israel were committing fornication with a golden calf at its base; in nakedness and sensual dance, the nation worshiped in the customs of Egyptian idolatry.[168] The fertility cult would represent idolatry throughout their desert journey, and each time the nation strays into idolatry she will experience fornication, i.e., physical and spiritual fornication. Some may object to that thought; they may change their minds as we proceed.

The news of Israel's Red Sea victory, terrified Balak: (name meaning destroyer), a Moabite king, as he watches the nation of Israel

---

[168] Wycliff Bible Commentary, Ex. 32

march across the Plains of Moab. Realizing his foe was the Mighty God of the Jews with His prophet Moses, Balak chooses to hire his own prophet, Balaam, whom he ordered to curse the children of Israel. Initially Balaam failed, but then conceived a demonic scheme to defile the children of God in hopes of requiring Jehovah to curse His people. Balaam apparently knew that it was prohibitive for Israel to have, i.e., to have as a wife, the daughters of Moab, or of any other nation. Israel was under a special regulation of Jewish-creation-marriage, they were required to marry solely within the tribe of Israel.

> For thou shalt worship no other god; for the Lord, whose name is jealous, is a jealous God; lest thou make a covenant with the inhabitants of the land, and they go a whoring after their gods, and do sacrifice unto their gods; and one call thee, and thou eat of his sacrifice; and thou take of their daughters unto thy sons, and their daughters go a whoring after their gods, and make thy sons go a whoring after their gods. *Ex. 34:14-16*

With this idea as a concept of deception, Balaam convinced Balak, to arrange for the daughters of Moab to play the harlot with the children of Israel on its Plains of Moab. These women were experts in the sin of licentiousness, and the prostitution of idolatry.

> And Israel abode in Shittim, and the people began to commit whoredom with the daughters of Moab. And they called the people unto the sacrifices of their gods; and the people did eat and bowed down to their gods. And Israel joined himself unto Baalpeor; and the anger of the Lord was kindled against Israel. And the Lord said unto Moses, take all the heads of the people, and hang them up before the Lord against the sun, that the fierce anger of the Lord may be turned away from Israel. *Num. 25:1-4*

The worship of Baalpeor was known to be attended by women and virgins who prostituted themselves to this Moabitish Priapus,[169] the god of fertility. Archaeological discoveries have revealed that the devotees of Baal practiced prostitution as a part of their worship. This sordid practice was adopted by the Israelites.[170] In the Book of Revelation (2:14, 15) it is revealed that this fornication was associated with the doctrine of the Nicolaitans. Although some see Nicolaitanism as clerical hierarchy, others see it as a licentious sect advocating complete and free love. So, the daughters of Moab prepared their licentious worship which required the participation of the standing men of Israel. The Moabite harlot decked her bed with tapestry and perfumed it with aloes. She whispered her offer of lust/love to the interested Jewish males who swarmed the desert floor. The army of Israel soon fell into the idolatry of sexual and spiritual fornication. This was the plan of Balaam to curse Israel. Revelation states that it is Balaam who cast this stumbling block before the children of Israel.

But to the surprise of Balaam, the children of Israel were not consumed. Jehovah's anger was kindled, and He began cursing the people with a plague, and ordering Moses to "hang up" the heads of those guilty of fornication. This hanging consisted in a form of crucifixion which was practiced by the ancients. Keil and Delitzsch suggest that a thousand men were crucified and the remainder perished in the plague. But suddenly a miracle occurred which averted this judgment of death. A mediator was raised in Israel who interceded in behalf of God and the people. Phinehas, the son of the high priest, upon seeing a young Israeli soldier return from Baalpeor with a temple prostitute whom he took into his tent, in the sight of Moses, and in the sight of all the congregation, became overcome with a holy rage, took a javelin in his hand, then running into the tent he executed both the man and the woman, thrusting them through with his spear of death. This act was immediately honored by Jehovah who turned away the plague of

---

[169] KDOTC: p. Numb. 25:P1-5

[170] Wycliff Bible Commentary

death; He praised Phinehas for his act of atonement. Another assault on creation failed.

A beam of hope springs out of Jericho. Here in this heathen fortress abides the harlot of this city, Rahab. The miracle of Jericho was more than the fall of its walls. It was the conversion of its harlot—the LXX translates the Hebrew word, harlot, as porne. The fear of Jehovah and his captain, Joshua, drove the harlot, Rahab, to her knees in repentance for her sinful life. She thrust her life into the hands of this gallant soldier-savior and finds atonement for her soul. She is born-again, converted from harlotry to become the great grandmother of the promised Seed. What a miracle. The power of God's men is always salvation, and when that salvation is the salvation of his enemies, Oh, so Great Salvation!

So, with the opening of the Book of Joshua—Rahab's conversion—creation-marriage appears healthy and promising, unfortunately this was for a moment. By the time Israel reaches the end of the Book of Judges we will find Israel at the lowest moral state in their recorded history. Shortly after the death of Joshua we read:

> And the children of Israel dwelt among the Canaanites, Hittites, and Amorites, and Perizzites, and Hivites, and Jebusites: and they took their daughters to be their wives, and gave their daughters to their sons, and served their gods. And the children of Israel did evil in the sight of the Lord, and forgot the Lord their God, and served Baalim and the groves. *Jud. 3:5-7*

Although polygamy was practiced in Israel, as pointed out it was limited by its cost, however it appears that this barrier and whatever others that previously existed were now somewhat removed. It was during this period where we find perhaps its holiest man practicing a brand of polygamy which was previously without record. Gideon, who otherwise had an impeccable and courageous life, had "many wives." Of the exact number of wives, we do not know. We do know he had seventy sons, with no mention of the number of daughters. Perhaps the fate of these men was spawned by the sin of the father. Beside his many wives, Gideon had a concubine, and by this maid he begot a son, Abimelech. Keil and Delitzsch refer to him as Gideon's bastard son.[171] It was this son, Abimelech, who murdered all but one of his brothers. Plurality of wives proves to be a plurality of trouble.

Samson, the thirteenth judge, violated Israel's special marriage code by choosing a bride over his father's wish, and choosing that woman from the ungodly Philistines. Fortunately, Jehovah oversaw the entire affair and redeemed Samson by inflicting judgment upon Philistia via Samson's anger. It would be good if we could end the declension of Israel as recorded in Judges right here. We cannot. Chapter nineteen opens a cesspool with a reeking stench.

Here in (Jud.19) a traveling Levite, attempting to embrace ritual purity, refuses to lodge in the Jebusite city of Jebus, choosing rather to board in Gibeah, a city belonging to Benjamin. The Levite was returning to his home in Mount Ephraim, with his wayward concubine—concubinage was the invention of man's polygamist nature. One might wonder as to what, was his actual fear—what would the Jebusites inflict upon him and his concubine. Perhaps he feared that history might repeat itself, i.e., the impurity of the Sodomite attack on Lot, and the angels. Well, his worst fear of heathen violence was realized in the home of his brethren. Finding lodging with an old man, also of Mount Ephraim, he settled in for the night. The old man washed his visitor's feet and prepared a meal and drink for this friend from his home state. But suddenly the peace is disturbed:

> Now as they were making their hearts merry, behold, the men of the city, certain sons of Belial, [Sodomites], beset the house round about, and beat at the door, and spoke to the master of the house, the old man, saying, Bring forth the man who come into thine house, that we may know him. *Jud. 19:22*

To say the least, history repeated itself, as these worthless fellows, sodomites, employed the very words of the men who attacked Lot.

---

[171] KDOTC; Jud. 9:1

A similar compromise is offered to these homosexuals, i.e., the old man's daughter and the concubine were offered to appease their desire. The record then reveals that in their anger the homosexuals accepted the offer of the strange concubine, abusing her throughout the night. By "knowing her", a reference to sexual knowledge, they abused her until she died. In anger the Levite took a knife and divided her dead body into twelve pieces, as they divided butchered animals. He then sent a portion of this divided body to each of the twelve tribes of Israel. The outcome was a civil war; the eleven tribes of Israel battle Benjamin. The war was vicious against Benjamin as Israel turned its rage on their brethren as they did upon the Canaanites, destroying man, woman, child, and livestock. The tribe was nearly annihilated. At the last moment Israel turned away its wrath permitting a remnant to live. Creation-marriage in the tribe of Benjamin was saved.

The Book of Samuel opens with another sad story. Here the priest Eli fails as a father, his son's, Hophni and Phinehas, taught and practiced heathen doctrine of the worst type. Although unsaved, "they knew not the Lord", they performed the sacrificial rites of the temple. Not only desecrating their offerings by intruding into the priests office, they offered unacceptable sacrifices to Jehovah. But their most notorious act was their propagation of the doctrine of temple prostitution. Hophni and Phinehas committed sexual acts with the women who assembled at the door of the tabernacle of the congregation. Did they actually commit fornication in the compound of the tabernacle?

Jehovah God the Faithful Husband of Israel

During this period of gloom—suddenly—a ray of hope shines into this dark valley, that of Ruth the Moabite. This beautiful story is actually heightened by the background of all this sin. This love story is a picture poem of the day that the Son of God would offer his Holy Life as a ransom for his friends; you and me. It is a poem of marriage; the levirate marriage; the intricate emotions of the Kinsman Redeemer relationship. The delicate nature and timing of this event is revealed in an air of suspense and intimacy. Isakkson saw the private nature of "the covering of the nakedness"; here the KJV translates this as, "the spreading of the skirt", (Ruth 3:9). Boaz in his love spread his skirt over Ruth in claiming his bride. Jehovah in his love affair with Israel did the same: "Now when I passed by thee, and looked upon thee, behold, thy time was the time of love; and I spread my skirt over thee and covered thy nakedness; yea, I sware unto thee, and entered into a covenant with thee, saith the Lord God, and thou becamest mine", (Ezek. 16:8). Jehovah God was the Husband of Israel. Boaz, after redeeming Ruth, marries her and brings her into the Hall of Creation-Marriage, the hall of the grandmothers of our Lord and Savior Jesus Christ, (Matt. 1)

Ruth is also a picture of Israel in that she was not forsaken, God loved her with an everlasting love: "I spread my skirt over thee, and covered thy nakedness; yea, I sware unto thee, and entered into a covenant with thee, saith the Lord God, and thou becamest mine." Yes, Jehovah took Israel as His wife: "thou becamest mine."

The Kings of Israel

The next stage of the wife of Jehovah was the Age of the Kings of Israel. Putting the Israeli kings in charge of the creation-marriage was asking the fox to guard the hen-house, nevertheless these kings are in command of the vehicle. Initially all appeared well, as Saul was satisfied with one wife and one concubine. But this was short lived. King David's adultery with Bathsheba would not only lead to the fall of his son, Solomon, but would extend surprisingly to the children of God throughout two millennia of church history. David's sin with Bathsheba has provided an apology for many thousands of marital infidelity cases throughout history. But this is a false apology. This all began when the sons of Samuel departed from walking with the Lord:

> And it came to pass, when Samuel was old, that
> he made his sons judges over Israel. Now the name
> of his first-born was Joel; and the name of his sec-

ond, Abijah; they were judges in Beersheba. And his sons walked not in his ways, but turned aside after lucre and took bribes, and perverted judgment. Then all the elders of Israel gathered themselves together, and came to Samuel unto Ramah, and said unto him, Behold, thou art old, and thy sons walk not in thy ways: now make us a KING to judge us like all the nations. But the thing displeased Samuel, when they said, Give us a king to judge us. And Samuel prayed unto the Lord. *I Sam. 8:1-3*

Although the iniquity of Samuel's sons was only an excuse for the coveting Jewish nation, it nevertheless did open the door for the demand for a king.

Israel was a theocracy. The position of another king, beside the King of Kings, Jehovah, in the theocracy would create one special problem. It was necessary to ensure a temporal sovereignty for the king that would ensure the kings authority among the people. Sovereignty would ensure the king the privilege of being the administrator of the law; the Judge of the land. The problem with this is that the king could not judge himself with the law. By requesting a king the people willed that God provide them with a man that could live—during his lifetime that is—above the sword of the law. The law could not execute the king. Most people and most marriage counselors do not take this into account when applying the outcome of David's sin to the church today. Although Jehovah provided the nation with a lifetime king sovereign, He did not do this for the good of the people, but in response to their murmuring; a thing which He hates.

And the Lord said unto Samuel, Hearken unto the voice of the people in all that they say unto thee; for they have not rejected thee; but they have rejected me, that I should not reign over them. *I Sam. 8:7*

God can be the only sovereign, for the sovereign must be righteous. Jehovah God reigns in Righteousness, and Holiness:

The Lord reigneth, he is clothed with majesty;
the Lord is clothed with strength, wherewith he hath
girded himself: the world also is established, that it
cannot be moved. Thy throne is established of old:
thou art from everlasting. The floods have lifted up, O
Lord, the floods have lifted up their voice; the floods
lift their waves. The Lord on high is mightier than the
noise of many waters, yea, than the mighty waves of
the sea. Thy testimonies are sure: holiness becometh
thine house, O Lord, forever. *Psa. 93*

For a thousand years, Israel experienced the rule of the true sovereign, Jehovah. The special problem of a human king would now affect their understanding of sovereignty. The seasoning of their understanding caused them to believe in a sovereign as a righteous leader. Their faith in the government, a theocracy, was based on the holiness of Jehovah. Israel failed to realize that an earthly sovereign could not meet the standard in which they believed. They simply took their understanding of the Holy Sovereign and applied it to sinful man. This was impossible. Nevertheless, these earthly kings were given a temporal position above the law, and this led to their downfall.

As mentioned, Saul had one wife and a concubine. David on the other hand had eight wives before he entered Jerusalem, however after the victory over this city we are told, "David took him more concubines and wives out of Jerusalem, after he was come from Hebron; and there were yet sons and daughters born to David", (II Sam. 5:13). Keil and Delitzsch count nineteen sons and numerous daughters being born to David.[172] But the real tragedy of David is his desire to take another man's wife, and the violence in manifesting that desire. Adultery. Probably the worlds most infamous recorded act of adultery.

And it came to pass at eventide, that David arose from his bed, and walked upon the roof he saw a woman washing herself, and the woman was very beautiful to look upon. And David sent and inquired

---

[172] Ibid. II Sam. 5:13ff

about the woman. And one said, Is not this Bathsheba, the daughter of Eliam, the wife of Uriah, the Hittite? And David sent messengers, and took her. And she came in unto him, and he lay with her; for she was purified from her uncleanness. And she returned unto her house. *II Sam. 11:2-4*

There appears to be two connected sins here. First, Bathsheba baths her naked body in a location that permitted the king to see her physical beauty. The act of a beautiful woman bathing is perhaps the most difficult temptation for a man to resist—what woman ever bathed in a location where a man could view her naked body? The second sin is that of the king who permitted his eyes to be full of the lusty beauty. David was no Job: "I made a covenant with my eyes. Why then should I think upon a maid?" (Job 31:1). That look formed into lust then conceived the sin of adultery, and deception which brought forth death. The deception, a failed attempt to orchestrate a lie which would have had Uriah raise a son which was not his own—one of the greatest fears of all men—gave David one final evil choice: murder Uriah. It almost appears that Uriah knew that Bathsheba was with child of the king; the reason for his refusal to return to his bed although the king made every arrangement to persuade him. Whatever the reason we know God had intervened in the heart of Uriah to prevent David in his lie. Even if Uriah knew the truth, would he be able to prevail in convicting King David of committing a capital crime; a crime punishable by death. Regardless, God left David the choice to repent. David chose murder.

> And when the wife of Uriah heard that Uriah, her husband, was dead, she mourned for her husband. And when the mourning was past, David sent and fetched her to his house, and she became his wife, and bore him a son. But the thing that David had done displeased the Lord. *II Sam. 11:26, 27*

The marriage of Bathsheba to David is in stinging contrast to the penalty of the law which required the funeral, and burial of both of these partners in adultery. How could this be reconciled with the law? (That is a good question.) Did David conjecture that since polygamy was suffered to exist, and since Bathsheba was now a widow that he had the right to marry her? This is probably exactly what he reasoned; after all Bathsheba was now truly a widow. This would make the marriage legal. He was not convicted of adultery or murder, so he assumed he was legal; and as we have said the king was the state and believed to be beyond the reproach of the law: inculpable.

Nathan put a wrinkle in his rationality, by revealing that his sin was found out. Then David finally reaches into his heart of hearts and musters his last spark of honor. He cries out, "I have sinned against the Lord." Like the publican's cry, "Oh, God be merciful to me a sinner!" And went down to his house justified; here David was told he would not die. He would go on to reveal his confession in Psa. 32, and 51; there can remain no doubt of his full confession.

> Against thee, and thee only, have I sinned, and done this evil in thy sight, that thou mightest be justified when thou speakest, and be clear when thou judgest. Behold, I was shaped in iniquity and in sin did my mother conceive me. Purge me with hyssop, and I shall be clean; wash me, and I shall be whiter than snow. Hide thy face from my sins and blot out all mine iniquities. Create in me a clean heart, O God, and renew a right spirit within me. *Psa. 51:4ff*

> Blessed is the man unto whom the Lord imputeth not iniquity, and in whose spirit there is no guile. I acknowledged my sin unto thee and mine iniquity have I not hidden. I said, I will confess my transgressions unto the Lord, and thou forgavest the iniquity of my sin. *Psa. 32:2ff*

The language of these Psalms reveal that David had knowledge of the vicarious atonement of the Savior, the Lord Jesus Christ. David found repentance and redemption—"Not knowing that the goodness of God leadeth him to repentance." Is it here that David was truly born-again; I believe this is just what took place; David got saved; he was born-again. There is, however, no record of Bathsheba's penitence, nevertheless later we do see her in need of comfort. Their son of adultery would die the death of the law for each of them; not atoning for their souls, but for their lives.

The final element which weighed in David's forgiveness and maintenance must be seen in the covenant of (II Sam. 7:12-16). David was a chosen vessel. He was unconditionally promised a son, upon whom God would establish His kingdom forever. Although David has other sons, he did not have any sons of promise. With the death of his son by adultery, and with the pure confession of David, it appears that God chose to expose his doctrine of Grace on this penitent—A remarkable act of Amazing Grace. The force of Grace is to prove where sin abounds Grace will much more abound. So in other words, God was forgiving, and restoring David on the basis of His unmerited favor, Grace offered through the death of His only begotten Son the Lord and Savior, Jesus Christ. He was forgiving David because David truly repented. On that basis, God wanted to forgive David; and that He did. This is the element which Satan just can't comprehend; just cannot understand. It is beyond his capacity to think of such a thought. He assumes that since his own judgment is everlasting and forever final, that the Lord God must judge all beings according to the standard which was applied to him. Therefore, he believed by trapping the soldiers of Israel to commit fornication and adultery on the Plains of Moab, and by tempting David to commit adultery, Satan could now require God to curse Israel and David forever. But God wanted to forgive David because David believed in the Lord Jesus Christ—read Psalm 22—the only begotten Son of God. This is the total idea of grace; and Satan is Satan because he is ignorant of the Matchless Grace of God. David knew the Son of God:

> The LORD said unto my Lord, Sit thou at my right hand, until I make thine enemies thy footstool. *Psa. 110:1*

> And David comforted Bathsheba, his wife, and
> went in unto her, and lay with her; and she bore a son,
> and he called his name Solomon; and the Lord loved
> him. And he sent word by the hand of Nathan, the
> prophet; and he called his name Jedidiah [beloved of
> the Lord], because of the Lord. *II Sam. 12:24, 25*

Several interesting comments can be gleaned from this text: (1) Bathsheba is distressed by the death of the son of adultery; was she distressed by her sin? (2) God blesses the widow/marriage with the birth of a son, Solomon, [peaceful], (3) Jehovah has a special love for the child and gives him a personal nickname, Jedidiah, (beloved of the Lord), and (4) the special phrase, "because of the Lord." The Lord is telling us that the entire David/Bathsheba restoration was a matter of God doing something for His Beloved Son. He was freely exercising his Grace because of the loving sacrifice of His only begotten Son, our Lord and Savior Jesus Christ.

With this said, let us not loose sight of the total corruption and death which the worlds most published sin of adultery produced. After all the Scripture cannot be broken. Then when lust hath conceived, it bringeth forth sin; and sin, when it is finished, bringeth forth death," (James 1:15). David committed adultery and murder and was forgiven; God did not require the death penalty for the king. But his murder and lust conceived more than his own sin; it also produced sin in his family. Amnon, the elder son of David, saw a chance to explore his lust and follow in his father's footsteps—children always learn the lessons that our own acts teach them. Tamar, Amnon's step-sister, was an especially beautiful virgin, and Amnon had an un-natural lust/love for her. He was literally sick with lust over his sister. With some help from a cousin, Amnon manages to lure Tamar to his bed. Here he viciously rapes the innocent and lovely virgin, Tamar. Shortly thereafter Absalom avenges his sister, he kills Amnon. Absalom continues his rebellion against his father, even threatening the throne. Forming a schism against the king he enters Jerusalem and defiles the king's concubines. Setting up a tent on the top of the king's palace, he enters the tent of his father's concubines in the sight of all Israel. (This is tantamount to claiming himself to be the king.) In the sad end of Absalom, we find him caught by the hair hanging in an oak and struggling to get free when he is found. Joab, the captain of David's army, manages to reach the site in time to thrust three staves through the heart of Absalom. One act of adultery, and now David is faced with three murders, one rape, and the death of a child. Yes, David was forgiven, but when lust is conceived it bringeth forth death. This is the law of sin.

Now just how do we, in the Church Age, interpret David's adultery/murder/remarriage? Consider the following facts: (1) David lived during the period of the Law that divorce/remarriage and polygamy were permitted—Jesus' doctrine of Marriage changed that with His teaching of permanent creation-marriage; (2) David was a sovereign King and, kings believed they are legally inculpable—remember what King Louis the XIV said: "The State Is Me"; L'etat c'est moi; although this did not permit any king's violence; and (3) Technically, Bathsheba was now a widow and free to take another husband. (4) Thus, David's future intercourse with Bathsheba was not a continuous act of adultery. (5) God forgave David—this side of death—for his murder. Think this through.

The real question facing modern man as we will see later is: Since marriage is permanent until death do us part, can a man have more than one living wife this-side-of-death, during the Christian age of monogamy? The age of Grace will reveal some interesting facts supporting creation-marriage. "For the precept of divorce was given by Moses, but Grace and Truth (permanency-marriage) came by Jesus Christ," (Jn. 1:17). The day of Grace and Truth would be radically different from the age of law. The Church has a superior priest, and a superior doctrine. The Church by permitting remarriage this-side-of-death is dancing to the wrong pipe and drummer. Modern divorce and remarriage is either continuous illegal adultery or what has been dressed as a false legal-adultery—double-speak. Augustine referred to this continuous adultery as "Adulterous-Marriage."[173] Adulterous-

---

[173] Augustine, Adulterous Marriages, (trans. C.T. Huegelmeyer) Fathers of the Church, (M.M. Maryknoll NY, 1955)

Marriage is what this paper refers to as legal-adultery—which, of course is being satirical. Sarcastic!

> But King Solomon loved many foreign women; in addition to the daughters of Pharaoh, women of the Moabites, Ammonites, Edomites, Sidonians, and Hittites, of the nations concerning which the Lord said unto the children of Israel, Ye shall not go in to them, neither shall they come in unto you; for surely they will turn away your heart after their gods. Solomon clave unto these in love. And he had seven hundred wives, princesses, and three hundred concubines; and his wives turned away his heart. *I Kings 11:1-3*

"Tel pere tel fils" (like father like son). David's life of polygamy and adultery would bear fruit in the beloved son, Solomon. Although many of these wives and concubines were probably common gifts, peace offerings, of foreign kings, nevertheless many of them were bedded by Solomon. We are clearly told that Solomon sinned:

> Did not Solomon, king of Israel, sin by these things? Yet among many nations was there not a king like him, who was beloved of his God, and God made him king over all Israel; nevertheless, even him did foreign women cause to sin. *Neh. 13:26*

Solomon places a heavy stress on the doctrine of creation-marriage, with what might be termed as, a man drunk with marriage. But marriage was ordained in the act of creation therefore even this outrageous indulgence of polygamy could not destroy that which God had foreordained.

After Solomon, the kings of Israel and Judah would slowly diminish in glory and power until they would be totally defeated by the heathen. Then, would follow six hundred years of Israeli history without a king; but, the story does not end there. Jehovah, her Husband, did not forsake her but delivered her with shouts of a king:

On the next day much people that were come
to the feast, when they heard that Jesus was coming
to Jerusalem, took branches of palm trees, and went
forth to meet him, and cried, Hosanna: Blessed is the
King of Israel that cometh in the name of the Lord.
John 12:12, 13

Was God a Divorcé?

The Triumphal Entry of Jesus into Jerusalem on Palm Sunday
was God's assurance that His Beloved Wife was not forsaken. Jehovah
was forever married to Israel, His Beloved. They formed an indissoluble bond: Permanency-Marriage. Her Maker was her Husband.

God married Israel on the foothills of Mount Sinai. In her youth
she was a slave in the kingdom of Pharaoh, where her infant sons were
persecuted. One of those infants, Moses, led the children of Israel to
the altar where she married Jehovah; she became one with Him—a
type of creation-marriage. Later Israel's conduct as a wife became
disgraceful, and illegal, as we have noted above. The law set certain
conditions on the marriage relationship: (1) Adultery was a capital
crime, and (2) certain acts could result in divorce with a prohibition
to any future reconciliation of the original marriage. Israel committed
adultery and those certain acts; yet, Jehovah never put her away. His
perfect love required Him to chasten her, but he never severed His
marriage contract with her.

From King Saul to King Solomon the nation of Israel was united,
but then it divided in a sort of theological war; divided into two
nations: Israel in the north, and Judah in the south. Thirty eight kings
ruled over a period of about 350 years. During this period Jehovah
commissioned Prophets to convey His messages to both the northern
and southern kingdoms; Israel and Judah. Jehovah chided and chas-
tened both kingdoms, permitting their enemies to defeat them and
take them in bondage. Jehovah God often spoke to his wayward Wife
in the language of marriage.

> For thy Maker is thine husband; the Lord of hosts is his name; and thy Redeemer, the Holy One of Israel; The God of the whole earth shall he be called. For the Lord hath called thee like a woman forsaken and grieved in spirit, and a wife of youth [Mal. 2:14], when thou wast refused, saith thy God. For a small moment have I forsaken thee, but with great mercies will I gather thee. *Isa. 54:5-7*

The Queen of Sheba did not believe all she heard of Solomon's splendor, so she decided to visit Jerusalem, and after viewing this glorious kingdom she exclaims: "I believed not the words until I came, and mine eyes had seen it; and, behold, the half was not told me: thy wisdom and prosperity exceedeth the fame which I heard." But this glory was short lived. As this queen was in awe of the kingdom, Solomon was in awe of his wives. Bowing to their every desire; bowing to their gods. Solomon joined in the corruption of the gods of his wives: Ashtoreth, Milcom, Chemosh, and Molech. The worship of the former included licentious ritual prostitution, and to the latter was attributed the debauchery of burning children alive in sacrifice. The apostasy of Solomon provoked the anger of Jehovah:

> And the Lord was angry with Solomon, because his heart was turned from the Lord God of Israel, who had appeared unto him twice...Wherefore the Lord said...I will surely rend the kingdom away from thee and will give it to thy servant. Notwithstanding, in thy days I will not do it, for David thy father's sake: but I will rend it out of the hand of thy son. Howbeit, I will give one tribe to thy son, for David my servant's sake, and for Jerusalem's sake which I have chosen. *I Kings 11:9ff*

Shortly after Solomon's death his kingdom was divided. Rebelling against Rehoboam, Solomon's son the king, the people elected

Jeroboam, the servant of Solomon, to be their king. Rehoboam was able to maintain the city of Jerusalem as his base, while Jeroboam headed north down and away from the promised city. Fearing that by returning up to Jerusalem, Israel would return to Jehovah; Jeroboam desperately invents a cult religion for Israel:

> Whereupon the king (Jeroboam) took counsel, and made two calves of gold, and said unto them, It is too much for you to go up to Jerusalem; behold thy gods, O Israel, which brought thee up out of the land of Egypt. And he set the one in Bethel, and the other put he in Dan. And this thing became a sin; for the people went to worship before the one, even unto Dan. And he made an house of high places, and made priests of the lowest of the people, which were not of the sons of Levi. *I Kings 12:28-32*

This apostasy, the adultery of idolatry, would continue for about two centuries before Israel, the Northern Kingdom, would be brought into captivity and slavery by their enemy, Assyria.

Rehoboam, the son of Solomon was king of Judah, the Southern Kingdom. Although a step above their northern brethren, they lasted 350 years before apostasy, the adultery of idolatry, caused their collapse and captivity, being captured and imprisoned by mighty Babylon. The prophets continually refer to the religious apostasy of Israel and Judah as spiritual adultery and spiritual fornication. Physical adultery was punishable by death. The Lord God was married to the twelve tribes of Israel: "Turn, O backsliding children, saith the Lord; for I am married unto you; and I will take you one of a city, and two of a family, and I will bring you to Zion," (Jer. 3:14). It must be remembered that although Israel and Judah committed many crimes against their marriage with Jehovah, He nevertheless was ever faithful to them. Malachi speaks firmly regarding Jehovah God's commitment to the nation as their Husband:

> For I am the LORD, I change not; therefore ye
> sons of Jacob are not consumed. *Mal. 3:6*

Both Israel and Judah had committed the capital crime of adultery. Both kingdoms could have been annihilated from the earth for their sin, but God makes no mention of their utter destruction. He does however use a few metaphors to describe His anger. The prophets, as with Jesus, were masters at the use of figurative language, metaphors, similes, hyperboles, and other figures of speech. Hebrew poetry is based on comparative thoughts rather than rhyme: "The Lord is my shepherd, I shall not want; Yea, though I walk through the valley of the shadow of death; I will fear no evil." Here in the middle of this viscous apostasy, Jehovah chooses a few appropriate metaphors. None of which threaten Israel, or Judah with total literal separation (divorce as understood by man), or death; to which they deserved.

> They say, if a man put away his wife, and she go
> from him, and become another man's, shall he return
> unto her again? Shall not the land be greatly polluted?
> But thou has played the harlot with many lovers; yet
> return again to me, saith the Lord. *Jer. 3:1*

The illustration here is that Israel was put away (figuratively divorced) by her captivity, and thus, figuratively given a bill of divorce. She had committed adultery with a foreign god, and figuratively, God put her away, i.e. under temporary servitude to her enemy. Then in reference to (Deut 24:1-4) Jehovah annuls the "abomination" and pleads for the return of His harlot wife. We see here strong evidence that the thought (divorce-remarriage) of (Deut. 24:1-4) was not God's will. We read: "they say," indicating that He did not own divorce. But the primary concern of the Jeremiah verse is the fact that God accused the nation of committing adultery, this was certainly not (the some uncleanness) erwat dabar of (Deut. 24:1). It is an illustration of the position of Israel in the eyes of God at this time, a metaphor. A metaphor cannot be translated literally: "It is raining cats and dogs"; when interpreting this metaphor, we must translate the entire context of the metaphor as one. In other words, we cannot say, "It is raining cats and rain." The divorce for adultery metaphor was symbolic language of the captivity of Israel. Captivity was the judgment of Israel for adultery. To add an additional rebuke to those who see a literal application of the (Deut. 24:1-4) text in (Jer. 3:1) God goes on to say, even though you have been defiled by another during our separation, return to me. In (Jer. 3:1) the abomination is annulled. Their reunion was holiness. Why? Because in spite of Israel's adultery and harlotry, and in spite of her symbolic divorce, she was married to Jehovah in creation-marriage.

The sword of the law is absent from this text. The adulterer and adulteress were not executed but were graciously offered a pardon. The text is bursting with mercy, and reason: Jehovah argues that He is married to Israel. He is the faithful Husband. And this marriage is a creation-marriage. Jeremiah labors to portray the first love of Israel, her apostasy, her metaphorical divorce, and her offer of reconciliation:

> Go and cry in the hearing of Jerusalem, saying,
> Thus, saith the Lord, I remember thee, the kindness
> of thy youth, the love of thine espousals, when thou
> went after me in the wilderness, in a land that was not
> sown. Israel was holiness unto the Lord, and the first
> fruits of his increase; all that devour him shall offend;
> evil shall come upon them, saith the Lord. Hear ye the
> word of the lord, O house of Jacob, and all the families
> of the house of Israel. *Jer. 2:2-4*

The allusion here is to the betrothal period when Israel was rescued from the armies of Pharaoh and was romanced by Jehovah God on the foothill of Sinai. She there became His wife.

> Thus saith the Lord, What iniquity have your
> fathers found in me, that they are gone far from me,

and have walked after vanity, and are become vain? Neither said they, Where is the Lord who brought us up out of the land of Egypt, who led us through the wilderness, through a land of deserts and of pits, through a land of drought, and of the shadow of death, through a land that no man passed through, and where no man dwelt? And I brought you into a plentiful country, to eat its fruit and its goodness, but when ye entered, ye defiled my land, and made mine heritage an abomination. The priests said not, Where is the Lord? And they that handle the law knew me not. The rulers also transgressed against me, and the prophets prophesied by Baal, and walked after things that do not profit. *Jer. 2:5-8*

Here the Northern Kingdom is indicted for adultery, i.e., their apostasy into the idolatry of Baalism. The prophesying by Baal was akin to being married to another.

Wherefore, I will yet plead with you, saith the Lord, and with your children's children will I plead. For pass over the coasts of Kittim, and see; and send unto Kedar, and consider diligently, and see if there be such a thing. Hath a nation changed their gods, which are yet no gods? But my people have changed their glory for that which doth not profit. Be appalled, O ye heavens, at this, and be horribly afraid, be ye very desolate, saith the Lord. For my people have committed two evils: they have forsaken me, the fountain of living waters, and hewed out cisterns, broken cisterns, that can hold no water. *Jer. 2:9-13*

The forsaking of God by Israel, the fountain of living waters, and her adultery were acts of marital violence, but her marrying Baal, the hewed out (man-made) cistern, was a second and more violent evil.

This act under the law would have prohibited any further reconciliation. She became the wife of another after a divorce from her first husband. Thus according to the law she was now defiled to her original Husband, Jehovah God:

> Is Israel a servant? Is he a home-born slave? Why is he spoiled? The young lions roared upon him, and yelled, and they made his land waste; his cities are burned without inhabitant. Also, the children of Memphis and Tahpanhes have broken the crown of thy head. Hast thou not procured this unto thyself, in that thou hast forsaken the Lord, thy God, when he led thee by the way? And now what hast thou to do in the way of Egypt, to drink the waters of Sihor? Or what hast thou to do in the way of Assyria, to drink the waters of the river? Thine own wickedness shall correct thee, and thy backslidings shall reprove thee; know, therefore, and see that it is an evil thing and bitter, that thou hast forsaken the Lord, thy God, and that my fear is not in thee, saith the Lord God of hosts. *Jer. 2:14-19*

The desolation of Israel is a direct reference to a type of divorce metaphor. It was a divorce which was self inflicted. God permitted her to exercise her free evil will.

> For of old I have broken thy yoke, and burst thy bands; and thou saidst, I will not transgress, when upon every high hill and under every green tree thou wanderest, playing the harlot. Yet I had planted thee a noble vine, wholly a right seed. How, then art thou turned into the degenerate plant of a strange vine unto me, saith the Lord God. How canst thou say, I am not polluted, I have not gone after Baalim? See thy way in the valley, know what thou hast done; thou

art a swift dromedary traversing her ways, a wild ass used to the wilderness that snuffeth up the wind at her pleasure; in her occasion who can turn her away? All they that seek her will not weary themselves; in her month they shall find her. Withhold thy foot from being unshod and thy throat from thirst; but thou saidst, There is no hope. No; for I have loved strangers, and after them will I go. As the thief is ashamed when he is found, so is the house of Israel ashamed; they, their kings, their princes, and their priests, and their prophets, Saying to a tree, Thou art my father; and to a stone, Thou hast brought me forth; for they have turned their back unto me, and not their face, but in the time of their trouble they will say, Arise, and save us. But where are thy gods that thou hast made? Let them arise, if they trouble; for according to the number of thy cities are thy gods, O Judah. Why will ye plead with me? Ye all have transgressed against me, saith the Lord. In vain have I smitten your children; they received no correction. Your own sword hath devoured your prophets, like a destroying lion. *Jer. 2:20-30*

The nation has been plainly caught in the bed of adultery, and that with her lover, Baalim. Furthermore, she claims that her adulterous marriage is not "polluted." In her imagination her adultery was a holy religious experience. But God tells her, "For though thou wash thee with lye, and take thee much soap, yet thine iniquity is marked before me, saith the Lord God.

O generation see the word of the Lord. Have I been a wilderness unto Israel? A land of darkness? Why do my people say, We are lords; we will come no more unto thee? Can a maid forget her ornaments, or a bride her attire? Yet my people have forgotten me days without number. Why trimmest thou thy way to seek love? Therefore, hast thou also taught the wicked ones thy ways. Also, in thy skirts is found the blood of the souls of the poor innocents; I have not found it by secret search, but upon all these. Yet thou sayest, Because I am innocent, surely his anger shall turn from me. Behold, I will plead with thee, because thou sayest, I have not sinned. Why gaddest thou about so much to change thy way? Thou also wast ashamed of Assyria. Yea, thou shalt go forth from him, and thine hands upon thine head; for the Lord hath rejected thy confidences, and thou shalt not prosper in them. *Jer. 2:31-37*

Her apostasy was preceded by fornication, she trimmed her ways to "seek love." She left her wedding gown behind.

They say, If a man put away his wife, and she go from him, and become another man's, shall he return unto her again? Shall not that land be greatly polluted? But thou hast played the harlot with many lovers; yet return again to me, saith the Lord. Lift up thine eyes unto the high places and see where thou hast not been lain with. In the ways hast thou sat for them, as the Arabian in the wilderness; and thou hast polluted the land with thy harlotry and with thy wickedness. Therefore, the showers have been withheld, and there hath been no latter rain; and thou refusedst to be ashamed. Wilt thou not from this time cry unto me, My Father, thou art the guide of my youth? [see Mal. 2:14 "wife of thy youth"] Will he reserve his anger forever? Will he keep it to the end? Behold, thou hast spoken and done evil things as thou couldest. *Jer. 3:1-5*

Israel had been metaphorically divorced and remarried. Now God says, "They say", regarding the abomination of (Deut. 24:1-4). It was not his will. The "They" of the verse refers to Moses as the author of the permissive section of the law. For Israel in her marriage to Jehovah, the abomination did not exist (for she was never actually divorced). It did not exist because her marriage was eternal; it was permanent creation-marriage. He was the Guide of her youth; in her youth she was His bride, and now His forever.

> The Lord said also unto me in the days of Josiah, the king, Hast thou seen that which backsliding Israel hath done? She is gone up upon every green tree, and there hath played the harlot. And I said, after she had done all these things, Turn thou unto me. But she returned not. And her treacherous sister, Judah, saw it. And I saw, when for all the causes whereby backsliding Israel committed adultery I had put her away, and given her a bill of divorce, yet her treacherous sister, Judah, feared not, but went and played the harlot also. And it came to pass through the lightness of her harlotry, that she defiled the land, and committed adultery with stones and with trees. And yet for all this her treacherous sister, Judah, hath not turned unto me with her whole heart, but feignedly, saith the Lord. And the Lord said unto me, The backsliding Israel hath justified herself more than treacherous Judah. *Jer. 3:6-11*

Judah, the southern kingdom, is indicted for adultery. The entire nation is equally guilty of capital crimes and of those "certain acts" which caused both kingdom's to be metaphorically divorced, entering into further liaisons that prohibited her return to her husband, Jehovah (Deut. 24:4 the abomination). It is said here that God, "had put her away, and given her a bill of divorce." Her putting away, and bill of divorce was her captivity and destruction by Assyria. These were temporary chastening, not permanent judgments as the law required. Had God actually wrote a bill of divorcement He would have had no further authority over His wife. She would have been permitted to be the wife of another. But she was never so permitted. This is evidence that Jehovah never endorsed (Deut. 24:1-4) as a legal divorce procedure against Israel and Judah.

> Go and proclaim these words toward the north, and say, Return, thou backsliding Israel, saith the LORD; and I will not cause mine anger to fall upon you: for I am merciful, saith the LORD, and I will not keep anger for ever. Only acknowledge thine iniquity, that thou hast transgressed against the LORD thy God, and hast scattered thy ways to the strangers under every green tree, and ye have not obeyed my voice, saith the LORD. Turn, O backsliding children, saith the LORD; for I am married unto you. *Jer. 3:12-14a*

Her acts of adultery and uncleanness reaped neither divorce, execution, nor the abomination of (Deut. 24:1-4). Jehovah, her Husband, pleaded for her return. After her adultery, and uncleanness, Jehovah speaks, "I am married unto you." The metaphor of divorce is only a gentle rebuke to the temporary captivity with which He chastised His beloved wife, Israel. God did not practice divorce at all. God was not a divorcé. He was forever married to Israel: "for I am married unto you."

Some may argue, that since God employs a metaphor of divorce in which he actually offers Israel a "bill of divorce", then divorce is not a sin, because God certainly cannot sin. Please remember, as we explained, divorce was the practice of men; men with hard sinful hearts. Divorce was the invented custom of hardhearted man, an accepted custom generated by the king of his own castle. Jehovah, by employing the custom of divorce as a metaphor, was merely using a teaching tool. As a master of pedagogy, He was taking the people from the known to the unknown. Because God used a teaching metaphor, does not mean that He literally committed the metaphor—I've heard parents say "I wring your neck"; I'm sure they never intended to honor that threat—as we said, Israel had committed spiritual adultery. The metaphor of adultery would be complete only with the death of Israel. God did not subject Israel to the law; He did not exterminate Israel from the face of the earth. Neither did he literally divorce his beloved wife, His companion.

> Turn, O backsliding children, saith the Lord; for I
> am married unto you. *Jer. 3:14*

Mr. Jay E. Adams, in his most unusual style, has come on with the doctrine that God practiced divorce and therefore Christians have the right to practice divorce within the limits of God's use. "If God Himself became involved in divorce proceedings with Israel, it is surely wrong to condemn any and all divorce out of hand."[174] Edward G. Dobson, endorses this thought:

> If the act of divorce is sin, then why would God
> utilize this as an analogy of His relationship to Israel?
> Further, why would God threaten Israel with a bill of
> divorcement? Since God cannot sin, then the answer
> to these questions is that the act of divorce is not an
> act of sin.[175]

It is remarkable that these writers deny God the use of the metaphor, where even secular writers could see the possibility of permitting such use. Don't we all use figures of speech while not endorsing their picture. What parent hasn't said something to the effect to their child, "I'll skin you alive." Do we accuse these parents of threatening to flay their children? Although more conservative, John MacArthur also follows their school of thought:

---

[174] Adams, Jay E. Marriage, Divorce, and Remarriage (Presbyterian and Reformed Pub. Co., Philipsburg, PA 1980) p. 24

[175] Dobson, E.G.; What the Bible Really...p. 43

So even God divorced. And that's important, because God does not do things that aren't right. God doesn't give us living illustrations of His own behavior that we can't follow. That's why it grieves me that people will say: There are no grounds for divorce.[176]

Is MacArthur sure of this? A careful study will reveal that God is not divorced. And that is important. There are no grounds for the divorce of a creation-marriage, which is the foundation of the covenant marriage of God with Israel. MacArthur goes on to accuse God of divorce:

> "Behold, the days come, saith the Lord, that I will make a new covenant with the house of Israel, and with the house of Judah." Do you know what He's going to do? He's going to get married again—to Israel. Verse 32 says, "Not according to the covenant that I made with their father in the day that I took them by the hand to bring them out of the land of Egypt, which, my covenant, they broke, although I was an husband unto them, saith the Lord." Now that affirms that God was no longer their husband, doesn't it? But He will remarry them and make a new covenant.[177]

No, this does not affirm that God was no longer the Husband of Israel. Just read what it says: "which, my covenant they broke, although I was a Husband unto Them." How could Mr. MacArthur say: "Now that affirms that God was no longer their husband:" Therefore I must say, "Now that affirms that Mr. MacArthur is incorrect; doesn't it?" The metaphor does not literally mean that the event was a historical fact. Jehovah told us that "my covenant, they broke, although I was an

---

[176] MacArthur, John Bible Studies on Divorce (Moody Press Chicago, 1985) p. 46

[177] Ibid. p. 46

214

husband unto them, saith the Lord." His use of divorce, putting away, and the bill of divorce were metaphors intended to chasten Israel to re-think their waywardness. The idea that God divorced and remarried Israel after she was the wife of another is to accuse God of committing the sin of the abomination in (Deut. 24:1-4). To defend this conclusion with pseudo scholarship is unfortunate. The idea that God divorced Israel and will remarry her is totally unacceptable. Keil and Delitzsch agree, making the following comment:

> In this view Jerome translates the reception anew of the people being given under the figure of a new marriage. This acceptation is not suitable to the [text], for this, even if taken prophetically it cannot refer to a renewal of marriage which is to take place in the future. The [text] can be referred only to the marriage of Israel at the conclusion of the covenant on Sinai and must be translated accordingly: I am your husband, or: I have wedded you to me. This is demanded by the [text] for the summons to repent cannot give as its motive some future act of God but must point to that covenant relationship founded in the past, which, though suspended for a time, was not wholly broken up.[178]

The use of this metaphor is seen again in the vision of Isaiah, and in the life of the prophet Hosea:

> Thus, saith the Lord: Where is the bill of your mother's divorcement, whom I have put away? Or which of my creditors is it to whom I have sold you? Behold, for your iniquities have ye sold yourselves, and for your transgressions is your mother put away. Isa. 50:1

---

[178] KDOTC, p. 8:90

The only bill of divorce was the captivity of Israel and Judah which of course, God did not write. They could not produce a bill of divorce, because Jehovah never divorced His bride. Did God literally sell Israel to their creditors? No. The nation sold herself, figuratively, to her creditors: Assyria, and Babylon. Did God literally divorce Israel? No. The nation divorced herself from Jehovah through her transgressions. Jehovah God "temporarily" suspended his everlasting covenant with Israel.

Hosea carried the divorce metaphor into a literal illustration, and that of his own married life:

> The beginning of the word of the Lord by Hosea. And the Lord said to Hosea, Go, take unto thee a wife of harlotry and children of harlotry; for the land hath committed great harlotry, departing from the Lord. So, he went and took Gomer... who conceived and bore him a son, Jezreel for yet a little while, and I will avenge the blood of Jezreel upon the house of Jehu and will cause to cease the kingdom of the house of Israel. And she conceived again, and bore a daughter, Lohruhamah... Now when she had weaned Loruhamah, she conceived, and bore a son, Loammi.
> *Hosea 1:1-9*

The prophet was to make the divorce metaphor a literal visual aid. Before the days of photography, Jehovah's prophets often used their lives as pictures when preaching God's message. Some may argue whether the marriage of the prophet with an adulterous woman, which is twice commanded by God, is to be regarded as a marriage that was actually consummated, or merely as an internal occurrence, or as a parabolic representation,[179] but this writer believes that the powerful force of a prophet who literally lives with a wife of harlotry serves as the perfect picture of Israel, the harlot wife of Jehovah. This is an overwhelming picture of the truth of God's unthinkable marriage to

---

[179] KDOTC, p. Hosea 1:1

Israel; as was Hosea's marriage to Gomer. The simple language of the text supports the actual consummation view which seems a fitting message from Jehovah to his sinful wife. Further the children of that marriage certainly appear to be literally born, and are given names which suggest judgment for the purpose of conveying God's message: Jezreel, (scattered), the judgment of the northern kingdom; Loruhamah, (unpitied), no mercy to the northern kingdom; Loammi, (not my people), you are not my people, and I will not be your God.

The one unmistakable theme throughout the book of Hosea is that this adulterous wife in not judged, divorced, or put to death. She is not totally destroyed. She is not stoned to death. But she is wooed as a virgin. Chapter one begins by portraying Israel in the wife of the prophet as a harlot, and her offspring as children of judgment. Remarkably it ends with a beautiful scene of complete restoration:

> Yet, the number of the children of Israel shall be like the sand of the sea, which cannot be measured nor numbered; and it shall come to pass that, in the place where it was said unto them, Ye are not my people, there it shall be said unto them, Ye are the sons of the living God. Then shall the children of Judah and the children of Israel be gathered together, and appoint themselves one head, and they shall come up out of the land; for great shall be the day of Jezreel.
> *Hosea 1:10, 11*

It must be pointed out that although the judgment of Israel would be severe, as noted in the meaning of the names of Hosea's children, there is also an unconditional promise of complete and full restoration for both the northern kingdom, Israel, and the southern kingdom, Judah. The putting away in the divorce metaphor was figurative for a temporary chastisement of Ephraim, the northern kingdom, and her adulterous sister Judah. It certainly was not the finality of legal marital divorce as practiced by the ancients, the west, and the church today. Alexander MacLaren makes these fitting comments regarding the chastening of Israel found in Hosea:

I must begin by explaining what, in my judgment, this text does not mean. First, it is not what it is often taken to be, a threatening of God's abandoning of the idolatrous nation…the very fact Hosea was prophesying to call Ephraim from his sin showed that God had not let Ephraim alone, but was wooing him by His prophet, and seeking to win him back by the words of his mouth. God was doing all that He could do, rising early and sending His messenger and calling to Ephraim: 'Turn ye! Turn ye! Why will ye die?' For Hosea, in the very act of pleading with Israel on God's behalf, to have declared that God had abandoned it, and ceased to plead, would have been a palpable absurdity and contradiction.[180]

Chapter two begins with Hosea speaking to Gomer of divorce and chastisement. As we shall see this was only a metaphoric divorce, a temporary punishment.

Plead with your mother, plead; for she is not my wife, neither am I her husband. Let her, therefore, put away her harlotry out of her sight, and her adulteries from between her breasts. Hosea 2:2

In (v. 19) the prophet then begins to drift into a direct discourse with Israel, as is customary of biblical prophecy. Jehovah becomes completely personified in the spirit of the prophet, and Jehovah speaks to His nation. In a spirit of jealousy God, declaring that although the nation had apostatized to the point of calling Jehovah, Baali, they would be restored and call him Ishi, my husband. And then he drifts into a beautiful song which Jehovah sings to His lady, speaking to her with the language of love:

---

[180] MacLaren, A. Expositions of the Scriptures, (Baker Books, Grand Rapids, MI) Hosea 4:17

And I will betroth [woo as a virgin] thee unto me forever; yea, I will betroth thee unto me in righteousness, and in justice, and in loving-kindness, and in mercies. I will even betroth thee unto me in faithfulness; and thou shalt know the Lord. And it shall come to pass in that day, I will hear, saith the Lord, I will hear the heavens, and they shall hear the earth; And the earth shall hear the grain, and the wine, and the oil; and they shall hear Jezreel. And I will sow her unto me in the earth; and I will have mercy upon her that had not obtained mercy; and I will say to them who were not my people, Thou art my people, and they shall say, Thou art my God. *Hosea 2:19ff*

The chastening, putting away of Ephraim, was certainly not divorce. Keil and Delitzsch agree:

But as God the Lord has no pleasure in the death of the sinner, but that he should turn and live, He would not exterminate the rebellious tribes [Israel] of the people of His possession from the earth, or put them away forever from His face, but would humble them deeply by severe and long-continued chastisement... Consequently, even in the book of Hosea, promises go side by side with threatening's and announcements of punishment, and that not merely as the general hope of better days, kept continually before the corrected nation by the all-pitying love of Jehovah, which forgives even faithlessness, and seeks out that which has gone astray, but in the form of a very distinct announcement of the eventual restoration of the nation, when corrected by punishment, and returning in sorrow and repentance to the Lord it's God, and to David it's king (ch. iii.5)—an announcement founded upon the inviolable character of the divine covenant of grace, and rising up to the thought that the Lord will also redeem from hell and save from death, yea, will destroy both death and hell (ch. xiii.14). Because Jehovah had married Israel in His covenant of grace, but Israel, like an unfaithful wife, had broken the covenant with its God, and gone a whoring after idols, God, by virtue of the holiness of His love, must punish its unfaithfulness and apostasy. His love, however, would not destroy, but would save that which was lost. This love bursts out in the flame of holy wrath, which burns in all the threatening and reproachful addresses of Hosea.[181]

In chapter three Hosea is asked to take the wife back and to love her in spite of the fact that she had committed adultery:

Then said the Lord unto me, Go yet, love a woman beloved of her friend, yet and adulteress, according to the love of the Lord toward the children of Israel, who look to other gods and love cakes of raisins. *Hos. 3:1*

Initially Hosea secretly supplies Gomer will all her needs. She unwittingly believes she is being sponsored by her lovers. Then Hosea removes his support, leaving her to be caught in a society without any wealth but the flesh of her life. She is reduced to a slave and is auctioned for a price. As Jehovah remained the husband of Israel even though she committed adultery, so Hosea purchases her from the auction block and restores Gomer to the full status of a beloved wife:

So, I bought [redeemed] her for myself for fifteen pieces of silver, and for an homer of barley, and an half homer of barley. And I said unto her, Thou shalt abide for me many days; thou shalt not play the harlot, and thou shalt not be for another man; so will I also be for thee. *Hos. 3:2-3*

---

[181] KDOTC, Hosea, introduction p. 22

The book then drifts back to a full dissertation between Jehovah and Israel. The tender and amiable language of the book speaks of the love Jehovah has for his adulterous wife. A wife who did not deserve His affection, but as Keil and Delitzsch comment, "by pointing out the unfaithfulness which Israel has displayed towards its God from the very earliest times, the prophet shows that it has deserved nothing but destruction from off the face of the earth."[182] But to the contrary, God's love faileth not:

> I will ransom them from the power of the grave; I will redeem them from death. O death, I will be thy plagues; O grave, I will be thy destruction; repentance shall be hidden from my eyes. *Hosea 13:14*
>
> I will heal their backsliding, I will love them freely; for mine anger is turned away from him. I will be as the dew unto Israel; he shall grow like the lily, and cast forth his roots like Lebanon. His branches shall spread, and his beauty shall be like the olive tree, and his fragrance like Lebanon. *Hosea 14:4-6*

Hosea did not practice divorce. God did not practice divorce. It does appear that Hosea put Gomer away (metaphorically) in the beginning of chapter two: "Say ye unto your brethren, Ammi; and to your sisters, Ruhamah. Plead with your mother, plead; for she is not my wife, neither am I her husband." In chapter three however he immediately takes her back on the command of God: "Then saith the Lord unto me, go yet, love a woman beloved of her friend, yet an adulteress, according to the love of the Lord toward the children of Israel...So, I bought [redeemed] her for myself for fifteen pieces of silver." God's divorce scenario certainly did not match the scenario of (Deut. 24), and it did not match the judgment of (Deut. 22:22), i.e., death for adultery. But putting that aside for a moment and conceding that the metaphor met the divorce criteria, we can say that: Yes, Hosea was metaphorically divorced. And metaphorically it rains cats and

---

[182] Ibid. Hosea, intro. p. 25

dogs. But please dear reader don't teach anyone that the use of a metaphor means that cats and dogs fall from the sky, or that you are going to report the woman down the street to the police because she said she was going to "skin her children alive." As a loving mother metaphorically skins her children alive, so God metaphorically divorced his beloved wife. But to accuse Him of committing literal divorce is to accuse the loving mother of murder because she metaphorically skinned her children alive. Hosea was not a divorcé. God was not a divorcé. "For the Lord, the God of Israel, saith that he hateth putting away [divorce]" (Mal. 2:16). Metaphors are figures of speech and are used to permit the speaker the liberty to drive home his thought by creating a picture of the idea. God is not a divorcé, and it does not rain cats and dogs.

Ezra, Nehemiah, and Malachi

As we continue our journey with Israel, we will conclude this chapter with the regathering of Israel from captivity of Assyria and Babylon. Note that this is not the Restoration of Israel predicted by the prophets which is yet to be fulfilled. Let us proceed to the books of Ezra, Nehemiah, and Malachi where the doctrine of Jewish Creation-Marriage was God's vehicle to deliver the child to be born in the manger in Bethlehem. As we said earlier, the vehicle of the Messiah was in the hands of the administrators of Jewish marriage. The contemporaneousness of Ezra, the scribe, Nehemiah, the governor, and Malachi, the prophet, is without question. Ezra and Nehemiah are co-workers in their ministry, causing the ancients to refer to their writings as a single volume: Ezra-Nehemiah. Some scholars even believe that Ezra was Malachi, nevertheless this reveals the context linking the messages of these men.[183]

---

[183] Ibid. Malachi, intro. "The Targumist, Johnathan,...has given the statement that Ezra the scribe is the prophetic author of our book, as a conjecture founded upon the spirit and contents of the prophecy. The notion that Malachi is only an official name is therefore met with in many fathers, and has been vigorously defended in the most recent times by Hengsterberg,

These three writers were equally perplexed with the conduct of the Jewish remnant returning to Jerusalem. While in Babylon the children of Israel learned a custom of the heathen—divorce with remarriage, and Jewish-Gentile mixed-marriage—this was forbidden under the Law of Moses. Thus, the mixed-marriage of Israel was a direct threat to the deliverance of the Messiah, the seed of David. In God's wisdom He saw a Jewish child as the only hope for the world. Consequently, when these prophets found divorce, remarriage, and heathen-remarriage in the ranks of Israel, they began barking. Ezra pulled out his hair, while Nehemiah pulled out the hair of the offenders, and Malachi warns the guilty that God will "cut off" those who divorced their Jewish wives and married the daughters of the heathen. Some see the marriage account of Ezra and Malachi as one, nevertheless there is ample evidence that they describe two separate accounts of marital apostasy in Israel. But the one cohesive element here is Jewish-marital corruption. On the one hand Jewish men were found to have married heathen women and some had illegitimate (half-Jewish) children by them; and on the other hand, some had divorced their Jewish wives and had taken up home-making with heathen wives.

While Ezra was in prayer, distressed about the problem of the mixed marriages, some of which produced offspring, Shecaniah offered a remarkable solution, "Now, therefore, let us make a cove-nant with our God to put away all the wives, and such as are born of them, according to the counsel of my lord, and of those who tremble at the commandment of our God; and let it be done according to the law." The Jewish Publication Societies translation of the Holy Scriptures according to the Masoretic Text translates the phrase "according to the counsel of my lord", as "according to the counsel of my LORD", indicating that Shecaniah was, for the moment at least, a prophet. Kiel and Delitzsch agree making this statement regarding the phrase:

---

who follows the lead of Vitringa, whilst Ewald lays it down as an estab-lished truth."

Instead of, according to the counsel of my Lord, De Wette, Bertheau, and others, following the paraphrase in the LXX. and 1 Esdras, read, according to the counsel of my lord, i.e., of Ezra. But this paraphrase being of no critical authority, there is no sufficient reason for the alteration. For Shecaniah to call Ezra my lord sounds strange, since usually this title was only given by servants to their master, or subjects to their sovereign, and Shecaniah afterwards addresses him simply as thou. Besides, Ezra had given no advice at all in this matter, and still less had he come to any resolution about it with the God-fearing members of the community.[184]

The solution included the putting away of both the strange women and their children. Keil and Delitzsch comment, "Separation from women who already have children is far more grievous than parting with childless wives."[185] The repentance suggested by Shecaniah was referred to as evangelical repentance or true repentance by the puritan preacher, John Colquhoun[186] (1748-1827), that all repentance must depart from all ungodliness, or it is not repentance; consequently, repentance needs no adjectives.

The putting away of these women and their children appears to be a simple matter of divorce, after all the act of "putting away" refers to divorce. The comment made by Shecaniah, "and of those who tremble at the commandment of our God, and let it be done according to the law," means that the act is proscribed in the law. But you may ask where? He cannot be referencing (Deut. 24), for as we explained there is no commandment to divorce there. The only commandment he could be referring to is (Deut. 7:1-11):

---

[184] KDOTC; Ezra 10:3

[185] Ibid. Ezra 10:44

[186] Colqhoun, J. Repentance; (Banner of Truth Trust, London; 1826, 1965)

> When the Lord thy God shall bring thee into
> the land where thou goest to possess it, and hath cast
> out many nations before thee, the Hittites, and the
> Girgashites, and the Amorites, and the Canaanites, and
> the Perizzites, and the Hivites, and the Jebusites, seven
> nations greater and mightier than thou, and when the
> Lord thy God shall deliver them before thee, thou
> shalt smite them, and utterly destroy them; thou shalt
> make no covenant with them, nor show mercy unto
> them. Neither shalt thou make marriages with them;
> thy daughter thou shalt not give unto his son, nor his
> daughter shalt thou take unto thy son. For they will
> turn away thy son from following me, that they may
> serve other gods; so will the anger of the Lord be kin-
> dled against you, and destroy thee suddenly. *Deut. 7:1-4*

Israel was to "utterly destroy" their heathen neighbors, being forbidden to make any covenant with them especially a marriage covenant. Some have reasonably concluded that if the only relationship
the Israelite's were permitted to have with these seven heathen nations
was that of annihilator, then all other relationships were void; consequently, the heathen marriages of Ezra would be considered "unreal
marriages." Heth and Wenham note, "As early as 1890, George
Rawlinson observed:"

> It is quite clear that [Ezra] read the Law as
> absolutely prohibitive of mixed marriages (Ezra ix.
> 10-14)—i.e. as not only forbidding their inception,
> but their continuance. Strictly speaking, he probably
> looked upon them as unreal marriages, and so as no
> better than ordinary illicit connections. <u>For the evils
> which flow from such unions, those who make them,
> and not those who break them, are responsible.</u>[187]

---

[187] Heth and Wenham; Jesus and Divorce; p. 163 note 27 quote G. Rawlinson:
Ezra and Nehemiah: Their Lives and Times (NY; Randolph, 1890) 42 Cr.

Keep that idea in mind regarding unreal-marriages—those who make them, and not those who break them, are responsible for the evils of such unions. These writers go on to explain the meaning of the Hebrew words employed by Ezra:

> In Ezra's eyes this was not a question of breaking up legitimate marriages but of nullifying those which were contrary to the law. This is further suggested by the two Hebrew words Ezra chose to describe these 'marriages'(nasa and yasab) and the 'divorce' terminology he employs. Ezra was a scribe skilled in the law of Moses (Ezra 7:6). He studied, practiced and taught it in Israel (v. 10). Yet he employs out-of-the-ordinary terminology to describe the 'marrying' ('taking') and the 'divorcing' ('sending away') of these women. Furthermore, how could these Israelites have made a covenant with God (Ezra 10:3) to put away their legal 'wives' if it is true that Scripture portrays marriage as a covenant made between husband and wife in the presence of God? Ezra's prayer seems to indicate further that 'intermarriage' had not yet actually taken place (cf. Ezra 9:2 with 9:14).

John MacArthur agrees, "There's a sense here in which God doesn't even recognize these marriages."[188] The concept of "unreal marriages" sounds a note with Agustine's "adulterous marriages,"[189] which we will address later. As for now, "unreal marriages" are a distinct possibility, and if so, Rawlinson is correct, "For the evils which flow from such unions, those who make them, and not those who

---

The Oxford Annotated Bible with Apocrypha (ed. H.G. May and B.M. Metzger; NY; Oxford Univ. Press, 1965) 584 n. at Ezra 10:2)

[188] MacArthur, John, Bible Studies on Divorce, (Moody Press Chicago, 1985) p. 44

[189] Augustine, Adulterous Marriages, (trans. C.T. Huegelmeyer) Fathers of the Church, (M.M. Maryknoll NY, 1955)

break them, are responsible." It must be noted that although the separation of the wives with children is especially difficult, it nevertheless was the fruit of true repentance.

The concept of "unreal marriges" is simple, i.e. a marriage within the forbidden degrees, consanguineous, would be "unreal"; or a marriage to a person who was to be annihilated would have been an "unreal" marriage, or an abomination. Augustine refers to marriages built on adultery as unreal: adulterous marriages, e.g. (remarriage of a divorced spouse this-side-of death.) In each case the shame of sin belongs to him who unites such marriages not to him who puts them asunder. These "unreal-marriages" simply are not joined together by God, and they should be put asunder. Since these "unreal" marriages were never marriages their disunion cannot legally meet the definition of divorce; however, the term, legal divorce, in the discussion of remarriage after divorce in our day would be appropriate. But to justify the act of divorce on the basis of the Ezra text is wrong. Technically, there was no divorce in Ezra, it was legal abandonment, legal separation. In that case, this is true of those caught in a divorce/remarriage today. Divorce in such a union is technically only a legal separation, since divorce is not possible for an unreal marriage; and this paper identifies all divorce/remarriage contracts as unreal-marriages or adulterous-marriages. But to legally activate a total break with a divorce/remarriage contract the parties would have to sue for a legal divorce since the state has no other way to dissolve the divorce/remarriage contract. So, the new divorce is actually only a permanent legal separation; a dissolution of their unreal-marriage contract.

Ezra's prayer is answered and the Israelites including some priests actually separate from their foreign wives and children. Lanely, referencing Wright, places Ezra in Jerusalem with the mixed marriage problem in 458 B.C.,[190] and he places Nehemiah in Jerusalem facing the same problem in 444 B.C.,[191] just a mere fourteen years later.

---

[190] Laney, Carl J., The Divorce Myth (Minneapolis, MN; Bethany House, 1981) quoting (J. Stafford Wright, The Date of Ezra's Coming to Jerusalem (London; Tyndale Press, 1948 pp. 23-28) p. 361.1.1

[191] ibid p. 39

Laney states, "Unfortunately, the temptation to intermarry continued to plague the restoration community."[192] As mentioned, Nehemiah rather than yank his hair out, chose to yank the hair out of those who defied God's law of separation. It apparently worked, for Nehemiah states that, "I cleansed them from all foreigners." We are not told how he cleansed the defiled lot, perhaps he used the Ezra formula, a logical rather than a legal divorce. It should be noted that the mixed marriages of Nehemiah included defiled foreign children, and since he cleansed them from all foreigners, we can assume that the defiled children were put away with their mothers.

Providing that he is in fact not Ezra,[193] Malachi brings us the final saga of the Israelite propensity toward "unreal" marriage in his writings. Surprisingly, Malachi's account is of particular interest, for it unexpectedly reads like a NT text. It is for this reason that some object to the traditional understanding of the text:

> Have we not all one father? Hath not one God created us? Why do we deal treacherously, every man against his brother, by profaning the covenant of our fathers? Judah hath dealt treacherously, and an abomination is committed in Israel and in Jerusalem; for Judah hath profaned the holiness of the Lord which he loved, and hath married the daughter of a foreign god. The Lord will cut off the man that doeth this, the master and the scholar, out of the tabernacles of Jacob, and him that offereth an offering unto the Lord of hosts. And this have ye done again, covering the altar of the Lord with tears, with weeping, and with crying out, insomuch that he regardeth not the offering any more, or receiveth it with good will at your hand.
>
> Yet ye say, Why? Because the Lord hath been witness between thee and the wife of thy youth, against

---

[192] ibid p. 39

[193] KDOTC, Introduction to Malachi; p. v10:423

whom thou hast dealt treacherously; yet is she thy companion, and the wife of thy covenant. And did not he make one? Yet had he the residue of the spirit. And why one? That he might seek a godly seed. Therefore, take heed to your spirit, and let none, deal treacherously against the wife of his youth. For the Lord, the God of Israel, saith that he hateth putting away; for one covereth violence with his garment, saith the Lord of hosts; therefore, take heed to your spirit, that ye deal not treacherously. *Mal. 2:10-16*

Able Isaksson, for one, labors to explain this text metaphorically or what is referred to as the cultic interpretation. Here Israel's marriage to the daughter of a foreign god is explained by Isaksson to be a symbolic description of Israel's embracement of idolatry. He makes a point of the obscurity of the text and that he believes v.15 is corrupt.[194] But regardless of this one obscure text the entire treatise of Malachi has a literal format referring directly to Jacob, Easu, Levi, God's covenant with Israel, God's immutability, the sudden coming of the Forerunner, John the Baptist, the people robbing God of tithes, John's rebuke of adulterers, and his prediction of the coming Day of the Lord.

Most commentators agree that in this text for a Jewish man to act "treacherously" meant that he divorced the wife of his youth, and married a younger foreign woman. This traitorous act of no longer cleaving to their wives of their youth, was being committed by many Israelites, priests included, and is fiercely attacked by Malachi. He explains the reason for his anger. God had chosen the nation to be a holy nation; a nation which would be a blessing to all other peoples; a nation that was the Wife of Jehovah, in holy covenant. The chosen covenant nation which would be the progenitors of the holy seed, the Infant Son of God in Bethlehem. By departing from the wives of their youth and marrying foreign women the nation was breaking their covenant marriage with Jehovah, falling into idolatry, and cor-

---

[194] Isaksson, A. Marriage and Ministry; p. 27

rupting Jewish creation marriage, the ultimate hope of mankind; that would bring forth the victorious "seed of the woman" Gen. 3:15 the Messiah, Jesus the Savior of mankind.

Isaksson disbelieves that Israel understood monogamous marriage at this time, but the text betrays his belief. Even though he believes the text to be corrupt he has severe problems with the question in v.15, "And did he not make one?" Most commentators see this as a reference to (Gen. 2:24), "Therefore shall a man leave his father and his mother and shall cleave unto his wife; and they shall be one flesh." This combined with v.16, "For the Lord, the God of Israel saith that he hateth putting away (divorce)," drive home the truth of monogamy, the single pair.

An interesting comment regarding the question of: "Whom hath God joined together?", is answered here; He hath joined together all "real" marriages. In v.14 we are told that God was a witness between the marriage which these Jews had contracted with the wives of their youth; these earlier wives were their true wives. Their first marriage was a covenant between the Jewish man and a Jewish woman and witnessed by God. Keil and Delitzsch make this comment regarding the sacredness of the marriage ceremony:

> The words, "because Jehovah was a witness between thee and the wife of thy youth," cannot be understood as Ges., Umbreit, and Koehler assume, in accordance with ch.iii.5, as signifying that Jehovah had interposed between them as an avenging witness...but they refer to the fact that the marriage took place before the face of God, or with looking up to God; and the objection that nothing is known of any religious benediction at the marriage, or of any mutual vow of fidelity, is merely an argumentum a silentio, which proves nothing. If the marriage was a brith' Elohim (a covenant of God), as described in Prov. ii.17 [Who forsaketh the guide of her youth, and forgetteth the covenant of her God], it was also concluded before the face of God, and God was a wit-

ness to the marriage. With the expression "wife of thy youth" the prophet appeals to the heart of the husband, pointing to the love of his youth with which the marriage had been entered into; and so also in the circumstantial clause, through which he brings to the light the faithless treatment of the wife in putting her away; "Yet she was thy companion, who shared thy joy and sorrow, and the wife of thy covenant, with whom thou didst make a covenant for life."[195]

The exasperating thing about these blessed marriages of their youth was that the Jewish men mentioned had dealt treacherously with their first wives by divorcing them. The pleasing thing about their new mix-marriage wives was the fact that God saw these Jewish men as still married to their covenanted wives of their youth, "yet is she thy companion, and the wife of thy covenant." Thus the new mixed-marriages were not recognized by the Lord God. Thus to legally separate (divorce) these new mixed-marriage wives and to return to the wives of their youth was the will of God for these men. The marriages with the mixed-marriage wives were "unreal marriages" or "adulterous-marriages" as spoken of by Augustine.

The next statement of the text presents a most startling element to those who hold a divorce view, "for the Lord, the God of Israel, saith: "He hateth putting away." At the mention of the God of Israel hating divorce, the commentators start a flurry of quick deflections and scurry for a divorce cover. But what has been said is said, "The God of Israel hates divorce!" Throughout this treatise we have laid the explanation for this cry. Slowly, layer by layer the flesh has been removed from the breast of God and now His heart is fully revealed to the eyes of the world. God cries out, "I love creation-marriage, I hate divorce." As a mother Grizzly bear closing in to revenge an assault on her cubs, the God of these Israelite divorced women was raging with fury to establish justice. The treacherous act of divorcing these women caused the altar of Israel to catch the tears and the voices of these

---

[195] KDOTC, Mal. 2:13-16

weeping women. Their cries caused God to condemn their Jewish husbands, "I will cut off (kill) the man that doeth this, the master and the scholar." God continues His rant, He accuses these men of wearing blood stained garments, "for one covereth violence with his garment." His cries will not stop until He intercedes, He will send a special messenger (the Baptist) to correct the problem of "adulterous and unreal marriages", divorce and remarriage (John would be literally decapitated in defense of the doctrine of creation-marriage)! The nation had fallen into the decay of sin causing it to threaten the only hope of mankind, creation-marriage, and the gift of the babe wrapped in swaddling clothes in Bethlehem's manger. God would now intercede:

> Ye have wearied the Lord with your words. Yet ye say, In, what way have we wearied him? When ye say, Everyone, that doeth evil is good in the sight of the Lord, and he delighted in them; or, Where, is the God of justice? Behold, I will send my messenger, and he shall prepare the way before me; and the Lord, whom ye seek, shall suddenly come to his temple, even the messenger of the covenant, whom ye delight in; behold, he shall come, saith the Lord of hosts. But who may abide the day of his coming? And who shall stand when he appeareth? For he is like a refiner's fire, and like fullers' soap. And he shall sit like a refiner and purifier of silver; and he shall purify the sons of Levi, and purge them like gold and silver, that they may offer unto the Lord an offering in righteousness. Then shall the offering of Judah and Jerusalem be pleasant unto the Lord, as in the days of old, and as in former years. And I will come near to you to judgment; and I will be a swift witness against the sorcerers, and against the adulterers, and against false swearers, and against those that oppress the hireling in his wages, the widow, and the fatherless, and

that turn aside the sojourner from his right, and fear
not me, saith the Lord of hosts. For I am the Lord, I
change not; therefore ye sons of Jacob are not consumed. *Mal. 2:17-3:6*

God was angry with the practice of divorce. He hateth putting
away. He will answer their query, "Where is the God of Justice?" He
will send His messenger, who shall prepare the way before Him, and
then He, the Lord, shall suddenly come. The prophet could not see
the Day of Grace for the Day of the Lord. Nevertheless, God's anger
would reveal itself universally. He was angry with all men, everywhere.
Then He sent John the Baptist to make his path straight. One of the
primary ways of the Lord was creation-marriage. John the Baptist
was sent to make the way of creation-marriage straight. His sermon:
"Repent for the kingdom of heaven is at hand." Here Malachi cries
against adultery. His cries were provoked by those who dealt treacherously divorcing the wives of their youth. Malachi calls on his hearers
to repent; to return to the ordinance of the Lord, the ordinance of
creation-marriage: "Even from the days of your fathers ye are gone
away from mine ordinances and have not kept them. Return unto me
[Repent], and I will return unto you, saith the Lord of hosts."

God sent John the Baptist to restore, among other things, creation-marriage In his effort to do just that he was required to place
his bloodied head and tongue on a platter of silver which was his final
sermon against divorce, and "unreal-remarriage": the incest of Herod.

The marriage covenant is a natural symbol of God's covenants,
especially His covenant with the nation He married, Israel. For a man
to break his marriage covenant is diametrically opposed to the nature
of God. Jehovah God would never break his covenant with Jacob:
"For I am the Lord, I change not; therefore, ye sons of Jacob are not

consumed. God was not a divorcé? A thousand times, NO!

Israel the Wife of Jehovah – Her Restoration!

No, Israel was never divorced, but just the opposite—Israel the
wife of Jehovah God has been promised the greatest restoration of

any nation, of any marriage. Jehovah God said that Israel would not only be restored but that all nations will come to her in Jerusalem to worship the Lord God Jehovah, and His Son our Lord and Savior Jesus Christ.

> Who shall not fear thee, O Lord, and glorify thy name? for thou only art holy: for all nations shall come and worship before thee; for thy judgments are made manifest. *Rev. 15:4*

In his comment of this verse, John Walvoord in his commentary on the book of Revelation states:

> The futuristic context of this ascription of praise is indicated in the question in verse 4, "Who shall not fear thee, O Lord, and glorify thy name?" Though the nations neither fear God nor glorify Him in their mad unbelief during the great tribulation, the day is to come soon when they will both fear Him and be forced to acknowledge Him as God...The prospect of all nations worshiping the Lord, a familiar theme of the prophets, is brought out in the next statement: "For thou only art holy: for all nations shall come and worship before thee" (cf. Ps. 2:2-4; 22:27; 24:110; 66:1-4: 72:8-11: 86:9: Isa. 2:2-4: Isa. 9:6, 7: 66:18-23: Dan. 7:14: Zeph. 2:11; Zech. 14:6; Rom. 9 - 11; Rev. 15:4.)[196]
> Isa 2:2 And it shall come to pass in the last days, that the mountain of the LORD'S house shall be established in the top of the mountains, and shall be exalted above the hills; and all nations shall flow unto it.

---

[196] Walvoord, John F. The Revelation of Jesus Christ (Moody Press, Chicago 1966) Rev. 15:4

Isa 2:3 And many people shall go and say, Come ye, and let us go up to the mountain of the LORD, to the house of the God of Jacob; and he will teach us of his ways, and we will walk in his paths: for out of Zion shall go forth the law, and the word of the LORD from Jerusalem.

Isa 2:4 And he shall judge among the nations, and shall rebuke many people: and they shall beat their swords into plowshares, and their spears into pruninghooks: nation shall not lift up sword against nation, neither shall they learn war any more.

Psa 22:27 All the ends of the world shall remember and turn unto the LORD: and all the kindreds of the nations shall worship before thee.

Rom 11:1 I say then, Hath God cast away his people? God forbid. For I also am an Israelite, of the seed of Abraham, of the tribe of Benjamin.

Rom 11:2 God hath not cast away his people which he foreknew.

Rom 11:25 For I would not, brethren, that ye should be ignorant of this mystery, lest ye should be wise in your own conceits; that blindness in part is happened to Israel, until the fulness of the Gentiles be come in.

Rom 11:26 And so all Israel shall be saved: as it is written, There shall come out of Sion the Deliverer, and shall turn away ungodliness from Jacob:

Rom 11:27 For this is my covenant unto them, when I shall take away their sins.

Yes, the beloved Wife of Jehovah shall be fully restored as the King of Kings, the Lord Jesus Christ, the Son of David, the Son of God shall a second time enter the City of Jerusalem, and Israel will worship Him along with ALL the nations of the earth. No! God is not a Divorcé. Troubled marriages do not need divorce; they need Grace and Restoration.

CHAPTER SIX

What is Jesus' Doctrine of Marraige, Divorce, and Remarriage?

It is a delight to consider the theme of marriage in the N.T. As with all our knowledge of the truths of Scripture the N.T. completes the written revelation of God. Like the O.T. where marriage is used typically for Jehovah's marriage to Israel, so the N.T. speaks of the union of Christ and His Church as the ultimate indissoluble marriage; raising marriage as the final eternal state, while fully defending its original meaning—again this treatise does not teach sacramental marriage; the act by which grace is acquired, i.e., a Roman Catholic Doctrine. In the doctrine of salvation by Grace we learn that our eternal security is directly proportional to our union with Christ; the Scriptures refer to this union as a marriage. Our Salvation is by Grace through Faith, not of Works, lest any man should boast; it is permanent, inseparable, and indissoluble; just as Creation-Marriage. Divorce is non-existent and incomprehensible to creation-marriage; therefore, remarriage after divorce is even more non-existent, and more incomprehensible—If that is possible!

Position of This Paper Regarding the NT Divorce Texts

This paper takes the position that the texts of Mark, Luke, and Paul regarding divorce are harmonious, clear and direct; they are not obscure, or ambiguous, and thus are foundational to Jesus' teaching on MDR (marriage divorce remarriage).

The use of the word "obscure" in this paper means the text in question is hermeneutically obscure, or obscure in permitting a clear interpretation. This word, obscure, in this case does not mean they are obscure because of their Greek MS manuscript evidence; that is a different subject. I am not criticizing the Greek MS (manuscript) evidence.

Obscure Text Rule: *The Principle of preference for the clearest interpretation*

In his volume, Protestant Biblical Interpretation, Bernard Ramm defines the hermeneutical principle known as the Principle of preference for the clearest interpretation:

> Frequently the interpreter is confronted with two or more equally probable interpretations as far as grammatical rules permit. One is a strain on our credulity; the other is not. One meaning is rather obvious, the other recondite. The rule is: choose the clear over the obscure, and the more rational over the more credulous. Or, in the words of Horne, "Of any particular passage, the most simple—or that which most readily suggests itself to an attentive and intelligent reader, possessing competent knowledge—is in all probability the genuine sense or meaning."[197]

Therefore, prior to the exposition of Matthew's divorce texts I will introduce its study with a preface or summary of the position of this paper; I do this in order to maintain the truth under discussion. I believe this is necessary since the texts of Matthew will cause extensive controversies, and it will, otherwise, be difficult to maintain a clear vision of the position of this paper regarding Jesus' Doctrine of Marriage Divorce Remarriage.

Matthew's texts introduce five serious problems. I see these as obscure texts (texts of thought) into the N.T. discussion of divorce. These five problems or enigmas create ideas that are contrary to the common sense of Scripture, and to the common sense of man. They are so antithetical (contrary) to the discussion that this paper considers them: Matthew's five OBSCURE TEXTS; and they will be

---

[197] Ramm, Bernard; Protestant Biblical Interpretation (W.A. Wilde, Boston 1956) p. 120

treated as such under the rules of hermeneutics. The interpretation of an obscure text is determined by first comparing all clear Scripture that relates to the obscure text. Scripture must interpret Scripture. This was the position of the Reformers who opposed Rome—Rome was not the exclusive interpreter of Scripture. They said, "Scripture must interpret Scripture." Thus, this paper will do just that, and this paper will not build any doctrine on any obscure text. Period!

This paper takes the position that the other writers: Mark, Luke, and Paul will lead the way, and that Mark will be honored by offering the summary of this paper's position. This writer believes that Mark is the earliest written Gospel; I believe there is solid scholarship to support this position. Historically the Church and its exegetes have dishonored Mark, by minimizing his contribution, by putting him on the back burner. This was accomplished by setting Matthew up at the front table. (It is true that the first may be last and the last first.)

The Divorce Text (Mark 10:1–16)

Mar 10:1 And he arose from thence, and cometh into the coasts of Judaea by the farther side of Jordan: and the people resort unto him again; and, as he was wont, he taught them again.

Mar 10:2 And the Pharisees came to him, and asked him, Is it lawful for a man to put away his wife? tempting him.

Mar 10:3 And he answered and said unto them, What did Moses command you?

Mar 10:4 And they said, Moses suffered to write a bill of divorcement, and to put her away.

Mar 10:5 And Jesus answered and said unto them, For the hardness of your heart he wrote you this precept.

Mar 10:6 But from the beginning of the creation God made them male and female.

Mar 10:7 For this cause shall a man leave his father and mother, and cleave to his wife;

Mar 10:8 And they twain shall be one flesh: so, then they are no more twain, but one flesh.

Mar 10:9 What therefore God hath joined together, let not man put asunder.

Mar 10:10 And in the house his disciples asked him again of the same matter.

Mar 10:11 And he saith unto them, Whosoever, shall put away his wife, and marry another, committeth adultery against her.

Mar 10:12 And if a woman shall put away her husband, and be married to another, she committeth adultery.

Mar 10:13 And they brought young children to him, that he should touch them: and his disciples rebuked those that brought them.

Mar 10:14 But when Jesus saw it, he was much displeased, and said unto them, Suffer the little children to come unto me, and forbid them not: for of such is the kingdom of God.

Mar 10:15 Verily I say unto you, Whosoever, shall not receive the kingdom of God as a little child, he shall not enter therein.

Mar 10:16 And he took them up in his arms, put his hands upon them, and blessed them.

Some may say: "That is not fair! Starting a N.T. dissertation of MDR (Marriage Divorce Remarriage) with the Gospel According To Mark." I might say to the gainsayer that since when is the Word of God divided? Does Matthew have a higher authority then Mark? Is Mark a lesser disciple? The scholarship supporting this choice is far from novel—after all Jesus said: "The last shall be first." Timothy states: All scripture is given by inspiration of God, and is profitable for doctrine, for reproof, for correction, for instruction in righteousness: That the man of God may be perfect, thoroughly furnished unto all good works (2Ti 3:16-17). I will give all the N.T. writers, surrounding this doctrine, their full time and space as well.

Let us exposit this marvelous sermon with loving care. It is a precious revelation:

> Mar 10:1 And he arose from thence, and cometh into the coasts of Judaea by the farther side of Jordan [Perea]: and the people resort unto him again; and, as he was wont, he taught them again.

This is a simple declaration of what is going on in this place: the coast of Judaea (identified as Perea). Jesus was teaching, to what appears to be, a good representation of the general local population: "the people resort to Him again." Perhaps the young children in v. 13 were in this party; they certainly could have been.

> Mar 10:2 And the Pharisees came to him, and asked him, Is it lawful for a man to put away his wife? tempting him.

Here we learn that the Pharisees had separated themselves from the crowd and were interested in making a public scene of their own in front of the crowd. The text reveals their motive: they deliberately desired to make a public spectacle of Jesus in an attempt to confound the Savior. They see the social issue of divorce as their opportunity. So they proceed with a simple question: "Is it lawful for a man to put away his wife?"

Jesus answered them with His own question:

> Mar 10:3 And he answered and said unto them, What, did Moses command you?

This is a great reply: remember, they asked Him: "Is it LAWFUL? Jesus' answer: What LAW are you referring to? "What commandment?" The Pharisees were caught. Jesus immediately shattered their argument, and as a ready hunter he could now move in for the kill. That simply! As I preached over and over to this point: "In the Law of Moses there was NO COMMANDMENT regarding divorce." Divorce was the immoral invention of man. Immoral Man owned the doctrine of divorce: it was merely an accepted immoral custom, tolerated, (suffered) because of hardhearted men.

The Pharisees were perplexed, and they needed to answer this simple question immediately. In order to retain the crowd, they had to speak the truth; and they did.

> Mar 10:4 And they said, Moses suffered to write
> a bill of divorcement and put her away.

Here, the answer of the Pharisees is profound. Yes, Moses SUFFERED to write a bill of divorcement, to put her away. This answer is so profound that it really needs no further comment. Jesus had the Pharisees in checkmate! Notice, they gave up the ghost. Yes, they stopped breathing—they had no further breath to speak words against the Master. Jesus, the Master, would masterly finish them off; and please note that we will hear no more words from these Pharisees. Jesus would go on to finish teaching the crowd His doctrine of creation-marriage. In the end the only voices we will hear on this subject are those of His disciples (in the house privately): asking him to repeat what they heard, and Jesus would CLEARLY repeat His doctrine of creation-marriage in vs. 11-12.

> Mar 10:5 And Jesus answered and said unto them, For the hardness of your heart he wrote you this precept.
> Mar 10:6 But from the beginning of the creation God made them male and female.
> Mar 10:7 For this cause shall a man leave his father and mother, and cleave to his wife;
> Mar 10:8 And they twain shall be one flesh: so then they are no more twain, but one flesh.

Mar 10:9 What therefore God hath joined together, let not man put asunder.

Jesus teaches the doctrine of creation-marriage; plain and simple. That is almost proof that Jesus is God. That which man has made so complicated; God has made so simple. So here in vs. 6-9 we have all the words of the doctrine of Creation-Marriage; which I have fully explained except for v. 9, the prohibition regarding creation-marriage—that prohibition is that man is NOT permitted to divorce his wife; and therefore, he also cannot remarry. Later, in the house Jesus clarifies that the word "man" is in reference to mankind: thus, to both the husband and the wife.

The word that men and women do not understand about v.9, "let NOT" man put asunder" is the word "NOT." Like the man said: What don't you know about NO? Mark uses this same word NOT in Mk. 10:19 five times:

Mar. 10:19 Thou knowest the commandments, Do not commit adultery, Do not kill, Do not steal, Do not bear false witness, Defraud not,

Yes: What don't you know about NO. "Let NOT man put asunder!"

David Instone-Brewer, commenting on "let not man put asunder", goes on to say: "None of these [let not phrases] carry the suggestion that it is impossible to disobey the command or plea. Therefore, when Jesus said, "let not man put asunder," Jesus was telling believers that they should not break up marriages, but He was not telling them that a breakup was impossible."[198] In my understanding of "let not", I see a parallel with: Thou shalt not kill! Thou shalt not commit adultery! Thou shalt not steal! Thou shalt not use the name of the Lord thy God in vain! Of course, it is not impossible to kill, or it is not impos-

---

[198] Instone-Brewer, David; Divorce and Remarriage in the Bible; (Eerdmans, Grand Rapids, MI) p. 283

243

sible to commit adultery: that is always the result of violence (it is not impossible) it is just forbidden by Jehovah God.

Marriage, to Jesus was literally a band, or bond of God and those enemies of God who oppose this band of God and His Son are marked in Psa. 2 where they take counsel together and cry out in unison against the Lord and against His Anointed Son:

> They take counsel together, against the LORD, and against his Anointed, saying: Let, us break their bands asunder, and cast away their cords from us. *Psa. 2:3*

The act of endorsing divorce is a critical act of moving against God and His Son. That endorsement or act of man does not mean that the marriage union is dissolved; it only means that man stands in violation of God's Law of Creation. They twain shall be one flesh is God's act of creation, and man cannot in any way dissolve that union, save by a false edict which will not hold up in the Courts of God's Final Judgment. Jesus simply said: if you divorce; then when you remarry you will be committing adultery. I believe the only way adultery can occur in this saying is if the original marriage is totally in existence, and totally alive. It has not been put asunder, because it CANNOT be put asunder. It is a permanent organic union. Period! Yes, in the same manner when God said: Thou shalt not kill; He did not imply that it is impossible to kill. So, it is with, thou shalt not put asunder, in that sense those commands are comparable.

Thus, the idea that it is not impossible to put asunder is a dangerous statement and is comparable to the events in the Garden: God said: "But of the tree of knowledge of good and evil, thou Shall Not Eat of it: for in the day that thou eatest thereof thou shalt surely die." And the serpent said, "Ye shall not surely die: for God knoweth in the day ye EAT thereof, then your eyes shall be opened…and she took of the fruit thereof and did eat"; and since that day every man that was ever born has died or will die. Let not man put asunder, and thou shalt not kill have that same word "not," and: What don't you know about

NO! The reason man cannot put asunder is because: "They twain shall be one flesh, so they are NO MORE twain but ONE; until death do them part.

Now, dear reader, take note that here in the Gospel of Mark something very special is revealed. In verse nine Jesus has completely taught his doctrine of MDR (Marriage Divorce Remarriage). Completely! It appears He then dismissed the crowd and He and His disciples resort to a house for a rest. The crowd dispersed with only those last words in their minds: "What God hath joined together let not man put asunder!" Jesus' doctrine regarding divorce was complete with those words: "let not man put asunder." To Jesus, His teaching was complete. The next words in Mark regarding this matter ONLY belong to the disciples. That is profound. That fully answered the Pharisees question: "Is it lawful for a man to put away his wife?" Jesus' answer was: NO!

> Mar 10:10 And in the house his disciples asked
> him again of the same matter.

The disciples and Jesus retire to a house after teaching the crowd ALL they need to know about His doctrine of MDR (marriage divorce remarriage). However, the disciples here are a bit out of sorts; in this scene they appear to be humbly troubled about what they heard. Yes, Jesus teaching regarding MDR is very troubling (then as now) to even the disciples of Jesus. Very, very simply they quietly asked Him of the same: the translator added the word "matter." Here in Mark we find the disciples repeating the exact words of the Pharisees. Exactly! Then we hear Jesus' concluding words:

> Mar 10:11 And he saith unto them, Whosoever
> shall put away his wife, and marry another, commit-
> teth adultery against her.
> Mar 10:12 And if a woman shall put away her
> husband, and be married to another, she committeth
> adultery.

Jesus forever seals His marvelous doctrine of creation-marriage with this astounding Revelation, it is so much like Jesus, as when He said, "I am the way the truth and the life." With words like these we know that Jesus is God. Need I say more.

Before I leave this logion, I believe the text here has a very possible connection Mk. 10:13-16 the children. Perhaps it is a deliberate link that Jesus intended to connect children to the issue of MDR (marriage divorce remarriage).

> Mar 10:13 And they brought young children to him, that he should touch them: and his disciples rebuked those that brought them.
>
> Mar 10:14 But when Jesus saw it, he was much displeased, and said unto them, Suffer the little children to come unto me, and forbid them not: for of such is the kingdom of God.
>
> Mar 10:15 Verily I say unto you, Whosoever shall not receive the kingdom of God as a little child, he shall not enter therein.
>
> Mar 10:16 And he took them up in his arms, put his hands upon them, and blessed them.

"And they brought young children to him, that he should touch them;" this text appears to place children, young children, in the midst of the MDR issue; they certainly fit. For the sake of all the children of divorce permit me to bring them into our conversation, right here. If you note the dedication of this book is to that little Amy, that little Tommy, and brave little ten year old Zahra,[199] God rest her soul. Children that long or have longed to be with their biological parents; and by all of God's love and righteousness deserve

---

[199] Gould/Williamson, StepMonster, (Hickory Daily Record, Hickory, NC) The story of a brave little girl; a tragic story of Zahra, the beautiful little ten year old girl, who deserved the very best of life, but was in fact given the very worst. God rest her soul.

and have the absolute right to have it so. Yes, divorce places a heavy burden on our little children. Jesus warns us not to forbid the little children to come unto Him so He can TOUCH and bless them; and that unless we receive the kingdom of God as little children, we shall NOT enter therein.

So where do we go from here? All has been said by the Master the God of all Creation, the Savior of all mankind. Well, from here I will compare Jesus' doctrine with ALL other N.T. words that may have any firm relation to Mark 10:2-12. I will start with Mat. 1:1 and go through to Rev.22:21.

Matthew and MDR: Marriage Divorce Remarriage

The Book of Matthew has raised more questions, and complications to understand marriage, then any other volume in the history of man. That alone should send up some hermeneutical red flags. Matthew immediately introduces us to a unique custom that regulated marriage during the Jewish Betrothal period and the act of fornication. Technically this rule is extra-biblical: it does not have any authority from the Law of Moses. So here, in his first chapter Matthew, while he sets his pen to the revelation of the mystery of the incarnation of Christ: Matthew introduces us to a peculiar unique obscure custom regarding an act of fornication (premarital intercourse, betrothal fornication) and its required penalty, the act of divorce which existed (as a social extra-biblical custom in Israel at the time of the birth of Christ). So dear reader, I cannot be accused of forcing this issue of fornication into Matthew, for he himself initiates this obscure custom.

Matthew 1:18-19

Now the birth of Jesus Christ was on this wise: When as his mother Mary was espoused to Joseph, before they came together, she was found with child of the Holy Ghost. Then Joseph her husband, being a

just man, and not willing to make her a public example, was minded to put her away privily. *Matt. 1:18, 19*

As Matthew begins his account of the virgin birth he strikes at a
very perplexing moment in the life of Joseph. Unknown to Joseph, the
virgin birth at that moment undoubtedly created in his mind the crisis
of shame; for Joseph felt the conviction and need to bring a judicial
judgment against his betrothed spouse, Mary. Matthew specifically
notes that the birth of Jesus Christ was on this wise: "When as his
mother Mary was espoused to Joseph, before they came together, she
was found with child." (Just a note here: the word found in the Law
often referred to being found in a manner of having one's sin exposed.)
We can narrow this down to the fact that Joseph either noticed or was
informed that Mary was pregnant. Of course, Mary knew that the
Holy Ghost came upon her, and the power of the Highest overshad-
owed her, and that behold she conceived in her womb, and would
bring forth a son. But as we see here, Joseph apparently did not have
this knowledge. The Scripture is silent as to Mary's thoughts or words
at this moment, however Joseph is being moved by thoughts and
emotions that are devastating—It should be noted here that Mary
was one who "pondered" the deep things of God in her heart. She
waited for God the Holy Spirit to inform Joseph. This faithful pon-
dering woman is a tribute to the life of faith; she certainly was a hero
of the faith.

This revelation to the reader must be considered vital to the doctrine of Christ and the subject of creation-marriage. We are clearly
told that Joseph was a just man. This of course means that Joseph was
slow to anger, and was willing to investigate the matter, and come to
a reasonable decision as to his action. His immediate thought was
that Mary had committed a special act of fornication. This idea is
certainly supplied with Joseph's first assessment, i.e. he thought Mary
had committed an act of fornication and it required that he "put her
away," that is divorce her as per the Jewish custom at that time. The
revelation here is that Joseph was living under a Jewish betrothal-mat-
rimonial custom, that legally regarded Mary his espoused fiancée, in

equal status as his legal wife. In this case her being with child out of wedlock, before they came together to consummate the marriage, constituted an illegal act of premarital sexual intercourse, a special act of fornication. To Joseph this was a sin. The specific definition of fornication in this case is reserved to the Jewish betrothed couple. In the event that an espoused fiancée was found to have committed fornication the espoused fiancé (the male) was expected to put the woman away publicly, i.e. divorce her in the public square. Matthew obviously understood the options of his cultural setting. He is specific and clear in his revelation. Here in chapter one and verse eighteen Matthew introduces the subject of divorce. This is remarkable to Matthew that will be of hermeneutical importance to the exegete. Keep this in mind as we study divorce in the N.T. Edersheim makes the following comment:

> According, their betrothal must have been of the simplest, and the dowry settled the smallest possible. Whichever of the two modes of betrothal may have been adopted: in the presence of witnesses—either by solemn word of mouth, in due prescribed formality, with the added pledge of a piece of money, however small, or of money's worth for use; or else by writing (the so-called Shitre Erusin)—there would be no sumptuous feast to follow; and the ceremony would conclude with some such benediction as that afterwards in use: 'Blessed art Thou, O Lord our God, King of the World, Who hath sanctified us by His commandments, and enjoined us about incest, and forbidden the betrothed, but allowed us those wedded by Chuppah (the marriage-baldachino) and betrothal. Blessed art Thou, Who sanctifiest Israel by Chuppah and betrothal'—the whole being perhaps concluded by a benediction over the statutory cup of wine, which was tasted in turn by the betrothed. From that moment Mary was the betrothed wife of Joseph; their

relationship as sacred, as if they had already been wedded. Any breach of it would be treated as adultery; nor
could the band be dissolved except, as after marriage,
by regular divorce.[200]

Take note of this interesting benediction which makes a peculiar
mention of incest (another act of fornication): "Blessed art Thou, O
Lord our God, King of the World, Who hath sanctified us by His
commandments, and enjoined [warned] us about incest, and forbidden the betrothed." Incest was a concern of the N.T. marriage codes; as
we shall see shortly. Th is divorce exception for betrothal fornication
is called the Betrothal View of Divorce. This exception for a violation
of brtrothal-fornication certainly qualifies as a possible interpretation
of the exception clause of Matthew's understanding of "except for
fornication."

Joseph was rightly perplexed and troubled. He knew the Law of
Moses prohibited betrothal fornication, in spite of the local custom of
Betrothal Divorce. The Law of Moses directly addressed what Joseph
perceived as Mary's sin:

> Deu 22:23 If a damsel that is a virgin be betrothed
> unto an husband, and a man find her in the city, and
> lie with her;
> Deu 22:24 Then ye shall bring them both out
> unto the gate of that city, and ye shall stone them with
> stones that they die; the damsel, because she cried not,
> being in the city; and the man, because he hath hum-
> bled his neighbour's wife: so thou shalt put away evil
> from among you.

In the context of this law there is an exception if the virgin did
loudly cry out, or if her cries were unheard, she qualified for a special
exemption of the law. But if she could not prove innocence she was to

---

[200] Edersheim, Life and Times, p. Book II:126

be stoned to death along with her male violator. No mention is made of this law in Matthew's account.

How does this measure up to what we have studied thus far in the doctrine of N.T. MDR. Thus far we have the revelation of Mk.10:2-12 where Jesus simple states: "They twain shall be one flesh, and What God hath joined together let not man put asunder." That is all we have. But now, we have an unusual extrabiblical custom that appears obscure: Betrothal Fornication Divorce.

John the Baptist: MDR (Mt 3 & 14; Mk. 6; Lk 9)

Jesus and Divorce is the title of the treatise of Heth and Wenham regarding the teaching of the N.T. and divorce. A correct understanding of divorce in the N.T. must rely on Jesus' teaching on the subject. In this volume, Heth and Wenham defend the "Early Church View" of divorce and remarriage, concluding that Jesus taught a no-remarriage-this-side-of-death doctrine of divorce; where separation of bed and board (a type of divorce is exercised) yet the marriage is not dissolved; thus the possibility of its restoration is possible during the life of its partners. To understand Jesus and divorce we must first spend some time with John the Baptist, whom Jesus ordained.

Prior to Jesus' Sermon on the Mount and divorce: John the Baptist preached a fiery marriage message. Remember Malachi preached that sermon: "For the LORD, the God of Israel saith that He hateth putting away (divorce). Malachi's prophecy declared that John would be sent to prepare the way of the Lord. Then Malachi goes on to say that John would be a swift witness against sinners, and he specifically mentions adulterers (Mal. 3:5). John certainly fulfilled this prophecy as we follow his ministry. As a matter of fact it appears that his public discourse on adultery-incest was his greatest sermon. Matthew chooses to reveal the fullness of John's sermon in chapter fourteen of his Gospel.

The O.T. closes with this promise, "Behold, I will send my messenger, and he shall prepare the way before me,"(Mal. 3:1a). Creation-marriage has its place in the Lord's way, and the Messenger, John, preparing the Lord's way defended creation marriage with his life. Literally! Malachi has his own dissertation on marriage, divorce, and remarriage as we have previously observed (a position that has N.T. ideas imbedded within Mal. 2:11-17). Luke commences the life of the Baptist with this statement,"There was, in the days of Herod, the king of Judea, a certain priest named Zacharias," (Lk.1:5a). Zacharias was the father of John the Baptist. Herod and his family played a signifi-cant role in the lives of Jesus and the Baptist. The Herod mentioned here (Lk. 1) is Herod the Great, Herod I. Edersheim reports that Herod the Great had ten wives and many sons. His wife Malthake, a Samaritan, was the mother of Herod Archelaus, and Herod Antipas. Another wife, Cleopatra of Jerusalem, bore Herod Philip.[201] These are the major personages of Herod I who will stage their warfare against creation-marriage, John, and our Lord. Herod the Great was the bloody tyrant who slew the children of Bethlehem after the birth of Jesus. Here in (Matt. 14:1-11) the subjects of our study are Herod Antipas and Herod Philip, sons of the same father. Antipas ordered the bloody decapitation of the Baptist.

Luke goes on to tell us that the priest Zacharias had a wife of the daughters of Aaron, and her name was Elisabeth. They were both righteous before God, walking in all the commandments and ordi-nances of the Lord, blameless (Lk. 1:5, 6). Their marriage was a cre-ation-marriage. Elisabeth was barren. Then, while attending to the altar, an angel appeared to Zacharias telling him that he and his aged wife would bare a son, and call his name John (i.e.) the Baptist. This son would turn the hearts of the fathers toward their children—could it be at that time that the modern divorce-broken-family syndrome had John turning the hearts of divorced fathers and mothers toward their children? While yet in the womb, John leaps for joy at the very presence of Mary who was with child, the child Jesus. From the womb John can prove he loved his Savior. He was a dedicated soldier. He was a devoted preacher. He was John the Baptist, the preacher of repen-tance and the Gospel, the defender of creation-marriage. His message

---

[201] ibid. Bk. II:126

of repentance was simple, "Repent for the Kingdom of Heaven is at hand."To John, repentance was the first step in making the way of the Lord straight. To John repentance was the first step in dealing with any and all the sins of the people. All the marriage sins of his day were relegated to that first step, repentance. If John were to address the marriage sins of the world today he would again preach repentance. The first word John preached was "Repent Mat. 3:2." The first word Jesus preached was "Repent Mat. 4:17." Today this must also be the first step for everyone involved in a marriage sin. This is the only way of Salvation by Grace. Sola Gratia. Now let us return to the preaching of the Baptist and the power of his last sermon.

At that time Herod the tetrarch heard of the fame of Jesus, And said unto his servants, This is John the Baptist; he is risen from the dead; and therefore mighty works do shew forth themselves in him. For Herod had laid hold on John, and bound him, and put him in prison for Herodias' sake, his brother Philip's wife. For John said unto him, It is not lawful for thee to have her. And when he would have put him to death, he feared the multitude, because they counted him as a prophet. But when Herod's birthday was kept, the daughter of Herodias danced before them, and pleased Herod. Whereupon he promised with an oath to give her whatsoever she would ask. And she, being before instructed of her mother, said, Give me here John the Baptist's head in a charger. And the king was sorry: nevertheless, for the oath's sake, and them which sat with him at meat, he commanded it to be given her. And he sent, and beheaded John in the prison. And his head was brought in a charger and given to the damsel: and she brought it to her mother. *Matt. 14:1-11*

John's last and greatest sermon was aimed at the marriage sin of the political ruler of his time, Herod Antipas. We must not loose site of the fact that John, and Jesus were one in their doctrine and teaching. Jesus testified to this when he was preaching his landmark sermon, Ye Must Be Born-Again, to the Pharisee, Nicodemus: "Verily, verily, I say unto thee, We speak that we do know, and testify that we have seen; and ye receive not our witness" (Jn.3:11). John was the sharp sword witness of his Lord, and his last sermon cut to the heart

253

of Herod Antipas and Herodias. Antipas' half-brother by his father, Herod Philip was previously married to Herodias. She became disenchanted with Philip because he was disinherited by his father Herod the Great. The following is a excerpt from the N.T. commentator R.C.H. Lenski:

> This Philip was disinherited through the treachery of his mother and lived privately in Rome with Herodias and their daughter Salome. Herod Antipas was a son of Herod the Great and the Samaritan Malthake and thus a half-uncle of Herodias, and was married to the daughter of Aretas, King of Arabia Petrea. While he was on a visit to Rome, Antipas and Herodias eloped, and the wife of Antipas, not waiting to be divorced, returned to her father, and a war followed between Aretas and Herod Antipas.
>
> Matt. 14:4 "For John said unto him, It is not lawful for thee to have her." Herod's crime [his marriage] was a public outrage. The woman Herodias had first married her own father's brother and then had run away and lived with the half-brother of her husband, who thus was also her half-uncle and already had a wife. Two marriages were disrupted, and the new union was not a marriage. It was plain adultery and within the forbidden degrees of consanguinity [incest] Josephus charges Herodias with the intention of confounding her country's institutions. No wonder John raised his voice although Herod was his ruler. "To have her"i.e., to have as a wife.[202]

The editor and translator of The Works of Flavius Josephus, William Whiston makes the following comment regarding the Baptist's accusation of Herod:

---

[202] Lenski, NTC Matt. 14:3-4

Nor was it, as I agree with Grotius and others of the learned, Philip the tetrarch, but this HerodPhilip, whose wife Herod [Antipas] the tetrarch had married, and in that her first husband's lifetime, and when her first husband has issue by her; for which adulterous and incestuous marriage John the Baptist justly reproved Herod [Antipas] the tetrarch; and for which reproof Salome, the daughter of Herodias by her first husband Herod Philip, who was still alive, occasioned him to be unjustly beheaded.[203]

So now we have Matthew describing another case of "special fornication" regarding marriage, i.e. incest-marriage. This is remarkable to say the least. Matthew reports two cases of porneia (fornication) in marriage and both cases required divorce to conclude them. John's sermon was so cutting that the only alternative for the King and his illegal wife was to repent or silence the tongue of John the Baptist; and what better way to silence his tongue then to decapitate the preacher; cutting off his head with his tongue in his mouth. What a successful preacher was this John the Baptist—like Churchill declared to his heckler, Hitler, who mocked the skinny little island nation that looked like a chicken with its neck: Churchill retorted: "Some chicken, Some neck"—we can likewise say, Some preacher, Some tongue. John the Baptist was a defender of creation-marriage; he literally defended the doctrine with his bloody head on a platter offered to the primary recipient of his sermon, Herodias. I find it an interesting point that this man John was a man whose sermons would drive him to advance upon every sin of all men. His assault was relentless. But regardless of his ubiquitous attack one particular sin, divorce-remarriage, would fail to yield to him without a death-to-death fight. John was called upon to confront this sin head-on—no pun intended.

---

[203] Josephus, Flavius; trans. William Whiston, Works of Flavius Josephus; (Baker Book House, Grand Rapids, Mi 1974) v. IV p. 19; Antiq. XVIII 5.1

John was consumed with conviction. His eyes blared. His mind was set for the attack. He formulated the exact phrase he needed and cried out, "It is not lawful for thee to have her." "It is not lawful for thee to have her.""It is not lawful for thee to have her." John's last sermon was his best. He was a seasoned preacher. Fearless! He calculated his offensive thrust. His aim was perfect. He fires his shot heard round the world: Herod commits incest! Herod commits incest! Herod commits incest! He divided Herod's soul and spirit, and Herodias' bone and marrow. Herod was wounded, but Herodias was mortally wounded. She was now heart dead—dead hardened. Breathing a fiery rage, she now has one burning desire, the death of the Baptist. John called for Herod to repudiate Herodias. He was crying out to Herod, "It is unlawful to have her"—Put her away!—"It is unlawful to have her"—Divorce her!

This is Matthew's second record of a special case of fornication that disrupts certain marriages. Both uses of fornication in this case resemble the complicated case of the forbidden special remarriage violation, the Fornication-Abomination of Deut. 24:1-4.

> But what went ye out for to see? A prophet? yea, I say unto you, and more than a prophet. For this is he, of whom it is written, Behold, I send my messenger before thy face, which shall prepare thy way before thee. Verily I say unto you, Among them that are born of women there hath not risen a greater than John the Baptist: *Matt. 11:9 ff*

Yes, Herod it is unlawful for you to have your brother Philip's wife. John had two verses in mind: Lev. 18:16 Thou shalt not uncover the nakedness of thy brother's wife: it is thy brother's nakedness, and Lev.20:21 And if a man shall take his brother's wife, it is an unclean thing: he hath uncovered his brother's nakedness. Both of these verses speak of incest, sexual intercourse within the forbidden degrees i.e. sexual intercourse between blood relatives, consanguineous marriage if you will—another special case of porneia, fornication. An unreal-marriage! As we contemplate these two exceptions, we must admit that they are both kind of obscure in the MDR discussion and seem to complicate Jesus' clear-cut sermon in Mark 10:2-12: "Let not man put asunder!"

Before we leave the last sermon, and martyrdom of the Baptist we must note the geography of this event, some exegetes believe that it is relative to the N.T. view of divorce known as the Incest View. Edersheim makes the following comment regarding the geographic location of John's last public preaching:

> There is no necessity for supposing that John and the disciples of Jesus baptized at, or quite close to, the same place. On the contrary, such immediate juxtaposition seems, for obvious reasons, unlikely. Jesus was within the boundaries of the province of Judea, while John baptized at Aenon (the springs), near Salim. The latter site has not been identified. But the oldest tradition, which places it a few miles to the south of Bethshean (Scythopolis), on the border of Samaria and Galilee, has this in its favour, that it locates the scene of John's last public work close to the seat of Herod Antipas, into whose power the Baptist was so soon to be delivered.[204]

Another element in the martyrdom of John noted by Edersheim was the intrigue of the Pharisees and the influence they exerted on Herod Antipas. The Pharisees certainly knew the threat John posed to Herod Antipas and Herodias; did the Pharisees actually help create the crisis that led to John's death? Edersheim believes that is just what happened.

> Besides, the Pharisees may have used Antipas as their tool, and worked upon his wretched supersti-

---

[204] Edersheim, Life and Times, Bk. III p. 383

tion to effect their own purposes. And this is what we suppose to have been the case. The reference to the Pharisaic spying and to their comparisons between the influence of Jesus and John, which led to the withdrawal of Christ into Galilee, seems to imply that the Pharisees had something to do with the imprisonment of John. Their connection with Herod appears even more clearly in the attempt to induce Christ's departure from Galilee, on pretext of Herod's machinations. It will be remembered that the Lord unmasked their hypocrisy by bidding them go back to Herod, showing that He fully knew that real danger threatened Him, not from the Tetrarch, but from the leaders of the party [Pharisaic] in Jerusalem (Lk.13:31-33). Our inference therefore is that Pharisaic intrigue had a very large share in giving effect to Herod's fear of the Baptist and of his reproofs.[205]

The next question we face is that after John's death, were the Pharisees trying to likewise have Jesus incarcerated in the prison of Antipas? When we open (Mk. 10; Matt.19) Jesus is found again in the coasts of Judea beyond Jordan, Perea. It was here that the Pharisees tempt Jesus to discuss the subject of divorce. They knew that Jesus and John preached the same message concerning creation-marriage. Were they trying to get Jesus to make a public statement on divorce in order to excite the wrath of Herod and Herodias? Edersheim makes this fitting comment:

> Accordingly, when these Pharisees again encountered Jesus, now on his journey to Judea, they resumed the subject precisely where it had been broken off when they had last met Him, only now

---

[205] Ibid. Bk. III p. 658

with the object of 'tempting Him.' Perhaps it may also have been in the hope that, by getting Christ to commit Himself against divorce in Perea—the territory of Herod—they might enlist against Him, as formerly against the Baptist, the implacable hatred of Herodias.[206]

Edersheim is focused. Yes, the Pharisaic intrigue played a role in the life of John and Jesus. The Pharisees were certainly aware of Herod Antipas' authority and control over John and Jesus; and as he points out Jesus knew His real threat was not Herod but the Pharisees and the leaders at Jerusalem. Edersheim does us a fine service here. Luke points this out:

> The same day there came certain of the Pharisees, saying unto him, Get thee out, and depart hence: for Herod will kill thee.
>
> And he said unto them, Go ye, and tell that fox, Behold, I cast out devils, and I do cures to day and tomorrow, and the third day I shall be perfected.
>
> Nevertheless I must walk to day, and tomorrow, and the day following: for it cannot be that a prophet perish out of Jerusalem.
>
> O Jerusalem, Jerusalem, which killest the prophets, and stonest them that are sent unto thee; how often would I have gathered thy children together, as a hen doth gather her brood under her wings, and ye would not!
>
> Behold, your house is left unto you desolate: and verily I say unto you, Ye shall not see me, until the time come when ye shall say, Blessed is he that cometh in the name of the Lord. *Luke 13:31-33*

---

[206] Ibid. Bk. IV p. 332

The Baptists Final Hour

I see it as fitting that we honor John with a short eulogy; I feel it is no burden to the reader to contemplate the tribute Edersheim pays to The Baptist in this finely crafted account of his final hour:

> It was early spring, shortly before the Passover, the anniversary of the date of Herod the Great and of the accession of (his son) Herod Antipas to the Tetrarchy. A fit time for a Belshazzar-feast, when such an one as Herod would gather to a grand banquet his lords, and the military authorities, and the chief men of Galilee. It is evening, and the castle-palace is brilliantly lit up. The noise of music and the shouts of revelry come across the slope into the citadel and fall into the deep dungeon where waits the prisoner of Christ. And now the merriment in the great banqueting-hall has reached its utmost height. The king has nothing further to offer his satiated guests, no fresh excitement. So, let it be the sensuous stimulus of dubious dances, and, to complete it, let the dancer be the fair young daughter of the king's wife, the very descendant of the Asmonaean priest-princes! To viler depth of coarse familiarity even a Herod could not have descended.
>
> She has come, and she has danced, this princely maiden, out of whom all maidenhood and all princeliness have been brazed by a degenerate mother, wretched offspring of the once noble Maccabees. And she has done her best in that wretched exhibition, and pleased Herod and them that sat at meat with him. And now, amidst the general plaudits, she shall have her reward—and the king swears it to her with loud voice, that all around hear it—even to the half of his kingdom. The maiden steals out of the banquet-hall

to ask her mother what it shall be. Can there be doubt or hesitation in the mind of Herodias? If there was one object she had at heart, which these ten months she had in vain sought to attain: it was the death of John the Baptist. She remembered it all only too well—her stormy, reckless past. The daughter of Aristobulus, the ill-fated Asmonaean princess Mariamme (I.), she had been married to her half-uncle, Herod Philip, the son of Herod the Great and of Mariamme (II.), the daughter of the High-Priest (Boethos). At one time it seemed as if Herod Philip would have been sole heir of his father's dominions. But the old tyrant had changed his testament, and Philip was left with great wealth, but as a private person living in Jerusalem. This little suited the woman's ambition. It was when his half-brother, Herod Antipas, came on a visit to him at Jerusalem that an intrigue began between the Tetrarch and his brother's wife. It was agreed that, after the return of Antipas from his impending journey to Rome, he would repudiate his wife, the daughter of Aretas, king of Arabia, and wed Herodias. But Aretas' daughter heard of the plot and having obtained her husband's consent to go to Machaerus, she fled thence to her father. This, of course, led to enmity between Antipas and Aretas. Nevertheless, the adulterous marriage with Herodias followed. In a few sentences the story may be carried to its termination. The woman proved the curse and ruin of Antipas. First came the murder of the Baptist, which sent a shrill of horror through the people, and to which all the later misfortunes of Herod were attributed. Then followed a war with Aretas, in which the Tetrarch was worsted. And, last of all, his wife's ambition led him to Rome to solicit the title of King, lately given to Agrippa, the brother of Herodias. Antipas not only failed, but was

deprived of his dominions, and banished to Lyons in Gaul. The pride of the woman in refusing favours from the Emperor, and her faithfulness to her husband in his fallen fortunes, are the only redeeming points in her history. As for Salome, who was first married to her uncle, Philip the Tetrarch. Legend has it, that her death was retributive, being in consequence of a fall on the ice.

Such was the woman who had these many months sought with the vengefulness and determination of a Jezebel, to rid herself of the hated person, who alone had dared publicly denounce her sin, and whose words held her weak husband in awe. The opportunity had now come for obtaining from the vacillating monarch what her entreaties could never have secured. As the Gospel puts it, 'instigated' by her mother, the damsel hesitated not. We can readily fill in the outlined picture of what followed. It only needed the mother's whispered suggestion, and still flushed from her dance, Salome re-entered the banqueting hall. 'With haste,' as if no time were to be lost, she went up to the king: 'I would that thou forthwith give me in a charger, the head of John the Baptist!' Silence must have fallen on the assembly. Even into their hearts such a demand from the lips of little more than a child must have struck horror. They all knew John to be a righteous and holy man. Wicked as they were, in their superstition, if not religiousness, few, if any of them, would have willingly lent himself to such work. And they all knew, also, why Salome, or rather Herodias, had made this demand. What would Herod do? 'The king was exceedingly sorry.' For months he had striven against this. His conscience, fear of the people, inward horror at the deed, all would have kept him from it. But he had sworn to the maiden who now stood before him, claiming that the pledge be redeemed, and every eye in the assembly was now fixed upon him. Unfaithful to his God, to his conscience, to truth and righteousness; not ashamed of any crime or sin, he would yet be faithful to his half-drunken oath and appear honorable and true before such companions!

It has been but the contest of a moment. 'Straightway' the king gives the order to one of the bodyguards. The maiden hath withdrawn to await the result with her mother. The guardsman has left the banqueting-hall. Out into the cold spring night, up that slope, and into the deep dungeon. As its door opens, the noise of revelry comes with the light of the torch which the man bears. No time for preparation is given, nor needed. A few minutes more, and the gory head of the Baptist is brought to the maiden in a charger, and she gives the ghastly dish to her mother.

It is all over! As the pale morning light streams into the keep, the faithful disciples, who had been told of it, come reverently to bear the headless body to the burying. They go forth forever from that accursed place, which is so soon to become a mass of shapeless ruins. They go to tell it to Jesus, and henceforth to remain with Him. We can imagine what welcome awaited them. But the people ever afterwards cursed the tyrant, and looked for those judgments of God to follow, which were so soon to descend on him. And he himself was ever afterwards restless, wretched, and full of apprehensions. He could scarcely believe that the Baptist was really dead, and when the fame of Jesus reached him, and those around suggested that this was Elijah, a prophet, or as one of them, Herod's mind, amidst its strange perplexities, still reverted to the man whom he had murdered. It was a new anxiety, perhaps, even so, a new hope; and as formerly he had often and gladly heard the Baptist, so now he would fain have seen Jesus. He would see Him; but not now. In that dark night of betrayal, he, who at the bidding of the child of an adulteress, had murdered the Forerunner, might, with the approbation of a Pilate, have rescued Him whose faithful witness John had been. But night was to merge into yet darker night. For it was the time and the power of the Evil One. And yet: Jehovah reigneth.[207]

Could there be any doubt that John would receive the Savior's highest accolade, "Verily I say unto you, among them that are born of women there hath not risen a greater than John the Baptist." We might say that John gave his life for the true doctrine of creation-marriage.

> Now when Jesus had heard that John was cast
> into prison, he departed into Galilee; *Matt. 4:12*

Lenski aptly points out that Jesus' departure into Galilee was not for fear of Herod Antipas, but rather that Jesus retired to Galilee, correctly noting that Galilee was also the territory of Anitpas. Jesus was going to take over where His Witness left off. He would now begin His preaching. Again, His first sermon was one of repentance; for His first word—like the Baptist—was Repent! "Repent for the kingdom of heaven is at hand" (Mt. 4:17). One should not be startled with Herod's remarks when he heard of Jesus and His preaching: At that time Herod the tetrarch heard of the fame of Jesus, And said unto his servants, "This is John the Baptist; he is risen from the dead" (Matt. 14:1, 2). To Herod, Jesus and John were one. They both preached the same sermon on marriage.

---

[207] Ibid. Bk. III p. 671-675

Sermon on the Mount and MDR (Exception Clause #1)

Make a note regarding the context of the Sermon on the Mount (Mt. 5-7). Jesus' teaching regarding the Law of Moses in this sermon places the Law of Moses on the highest possible level—the Philadelphia College of the Bible, my alma mater, in the 1960's had this statement regarding their position on the Sermon on the Mount in their Matthew 114 Class Syllabus: (Keep in mind that PCB is the home of C. I. Scofield; the father of Dispensationalism and the Scofield Reference Bible of 1909). This is the direct quote from that syllabus regarding the Law in the Sermon on the Mount:

> This is where our school's emphasis varies from the traditional emphasis of Christendom. They say that this, the (Sermon on the Mount), is the Christian's code of life. We, PCB, say that, although all Scripture is for us and may be applied to our spiritual welfare, not all Scripture is to us. This sermon is LAW taken to the nth degree—NOT GRACE. (PCB went on to teach that the Sermon on the Mount was the code of the believers in the Millennial Kingdom, and that it did not govern the Church Age.)

I'm not going to prepare an apology for their position. I just want to point out a very important fact about the context of (Mt. 5:31-32 the divorce text); the context, the Sermon on the Mount, presses the Law to its highest possible level (the nth degree). Let us look at a few examples:

> Mat 5:18 For verily I say unto you, Till heaven and earth pass, one jot or one tittle shall in no wise pass from the law, till all be fulfilled.
> Mat 5:19 Whosoever therefore shall break one of these least commandments, and shall teach men so, he shall be called the least in the kingdom of heaven:

Mat 5:20 For I say unto you, That except your righteousness (this must be translated in the obedience to the jot and tittle of the Law) shall exceed the righteousness of the scribes and Pharisees, ye shall in no case enter into the kingdom of heaven.

Mat 5:21 Ye have heard that it was said by them of old time, Thou shalt not kill; and whosoever shall kill shall be in danger of the judgment:

Mat 5:22 But I say unto you, That whosoever is angry with his brother without a cause (it is of interest that this clause, "without a cause", is not supported by the early manuscripts) shall be in danger of the judgment: and whosoever shall say to his brother, Raca, shall be in danger of the council: but whosoever shall say, Thou fool, shall be in danger of hell fire.

Mt. 5:27 Ye have heard that it was said by them of old time, Thou shalt not commit adultery:Mat 5:28 But I say unto you, That whosoever looketh on a woman to lust after her hath committed adultery with her already in his heart.

Mat 5:33 Again, ye have heard that it hath been said by them of old time, Thou shalt not forswear thyself, but shalt perform unto the Lord thine oaths: Mat 5:34 But I say unto you, Swear not at all; neither by heaven; for it is God's throne:

Mat 5:48 Be ye therefore perfect, even as your Father which is in heaven is perfect.

In this sermon Jesus (as PCB suggests) does not reveal Grace but reveals the Law to the nth degree. Jesus gives the Law of Moses an absolute legal interpretation to the nth degree; He refers to those who followed Moses as "Ye have heard that it hath been said by them of old time." Then challenges those He referred to with the words: "But I say unto you." Jesus is about to contradict His predecessors, and He goes on to set the standard higher then any of His audience expected, as well as to us to this day. The six examples here reveal that the law must be obeyed to one jot and one tittle. That means to the dot of the letter (i) to the tittle in the line that makes the letter (t)—actually in the written language of the Law (Hebrew) a jot or tittle was even a smaller matter—that if a man break one of the least commandment he would be the least in the kingdom; unless His followers (legally in the righteousness of obeying the law) exceed the scribes and the Pharisees they shall in no case enter into the kingdom of heaven. If man be angry with his brother and would call him a fool, shall be in danger of hell fire. If a man so much as look upon a woman to lust after her, he hath committed adultery with her already in his heart; this with the threat that the whole body would be cast into hell. Regarding oaths Jesus said: ye have heard that it hath been said by them of old time Thou shalt not forswear thyself: But I say unto you swear not at all. Then we have the final command to be perfect; the sense here is that the person has met the previous instructions to keep the law to the jot and tittle: "Be ye therefore perfect, even as your Father which is in heaven."

The point here that of the contrast Jesus makes with the old teachers of the Law is remarkable, especially when He broadcasts: "But I say unto you." This is in light of these facts is that this is the context of (Matt. 5:31, 32); it makes this absolutely astonishing that Jesus who throughout the entire Sermon on the Mount preaches in a sphere of total black and white, that here—with the use of an exception clause—He suddenly, and unnaturally becomes ambiguous, and obscure with an exception clause for a divorce in marriage. His admonishing is always absolutely to the point. He leaves no question behind. He is clear and unambiguous leaving no doubt in understanding His commands. None! For that fact, throughout the entire N.T. Jesus does not offer any exceptions to His commands: "Ye must be born again!" "Repent for the kingdom of heaven is at hand." I believe I could go on forever with this characteristic of Jesus, except for the saving for the cause of fornication in (Matthew 5:32; 19:9). This is troubling. Thus, Matthew has now added another obscurity to our study. He has Jesus using an exception clause in one of His commandments; which is very rare or perhaps has no other comparison; save for Matthew 19:9 again later. Let us continue:

Mat. 5:31-32 The Short Version of Mat. 19:1-15

> Mt. 5:31 It hath been said, Whosoever shall put away his wife, let him give her a writing of divorcement: Mt. 5:32 But I say unto you, That whosoever shall put away his wife, saving for the cause of fornication, causeth her to commit adultery: and whosoever shall marry her that is divorced committeth adultery.

In the introduction of this book you were introduced to Mr. Edward W. Goodrich (Professor of Greek and Bible Multnomah School of Bible) who said, "If there ever was a place for common sense, it can be found in the rules for interpreting the Bible." I ask the reader to give this some thought. One of the major characteristics about the words: saving for the cause of fornication, is the fact that they are an exception to a rule and clearly attributed to Jesus. This makes this highly unusual for Jesus, who was so profoundly particular and specific with His words, that it is almost impossible to find Him ever using an exception to a rule; especially when he is speaking about something of such great importance.

Not only is His use here of an exception clause difficult to explain, but it is even more complex since He uses the word "fornication" in this clause. Remember; Jesus is the Word. Jesus the Son of God knows words: for Jesus is the Word, and the Word was God; Yes, the Word was God. This being said, we find Jesus using this word in other texts where there is no ambiguity:

> For from within, out of the heart of men, proceed evil thoughts, adulteries, fornications, murders, *Mk. 7:21*

Here, in this context, we find Jesus using both words: fornication and the word adultery in the same sentence; and you can be certain that to Him they have two separate meanings. In the Greek adultery translates (moicheia) and fornication translates (porneia). That is a substantial difference right there; and the fact that Jesus uses both words in the same sentence should be enough to end the madness, and the library of books that the Church has published, regarding the meaning of these two words. Adultery does not mean fornication and fornication does not mean adultery. They are NOT the same!

Adultery is the voluntary sexual intercourse of a married person with a person other than the offender's husband or wife. This is clearly the word Jesus spoke when he referred to adultery. Fornication, regarding marriage, has historically referred to the sexual intercourse between two unmarried persons. In its broader meaning it includes any type of sexual activity outside the sexual act of creation-marriage: incest intercourse, illicit betrothal intercourse, homosexuality, lesbianism, bestiality, masturbation, nudity, partial dress sex-nudity, dressing to sexually allure, viewing pornography (print, video, movies, TV, internet), internet-sex, sexting, phone-sex, sexually-flirting, and et cetera.

One important fact about the word fornication and marriage in the O.T. is that Lev. 18 mentions all the primary acts which meet this definition: incest, homosexuality, bestiality, and certain acts of uncleanness. The violators of any these O.T. acts of fornication were required to face the death penalty. Therefore, none of these acts can be included in Deut. 24:1, or in the word "fornication" in Matthew's exception clauses. That fact my friend is profound. This means that whatever Matthew means by fornication must refer to some act outside the parameters of Lev.18. The Law required the death penalty for any type of fornication of the type involved as a marriage sin. Such sin would have to be some sexual relation with some living being other then, a creation-marriage partner. Remember Jesus was teaching the LAW of Moses to the nth degree in Mt. 5:31, 32; 19:9. Fornication cannot mean adultery to Jesus, who taught the Law to the nth degree. In the law of Moses adultery and fornication both required the death penalty.

Now, dear reader; it seems that all of Christendom is bent on making these two terms porneia (fornication) and moicheia (adultery) synonyms. Here is where I make my stand and say enough is enough: Jesus was addressing marriage. When Jesus used the word fornication in Mt. 5:32; 19:9; He did not mean adultery. Period! The Law of Moses clearly forbid adultery, which commanded the death penalty. Jesus was no violator of the Law; He kept it to the jot and tittle and expected the same of us. The divorce clause in Deut. 24:1 is void of any information regarding adultery: as a matter of fact, the entire regulation Deut. 24:1-4 is void of the idea of adultery. It is even void of the suspicion adultery; which was punishable by the River Ordeal (Num. 5:14-31). But what does the exception clause really say?

The Premium (REWARD) for Adultery or Sexual Immorality

This is a cause for a short parenthesis; therefore, in the middle of expositing Mt. 5:31-32 I have added this parenthetical heading. Matthew's text states here that, saving for the cause of fornication, marriage is permanent. Then, what did Jesus mean by fornication? Matthew, himself by his own confession, gives us two possible choices:

(1) Illicit Betrothal Intercourse Mt. 1:19 Joseph and Mary, or (2) Incest Mt. 14:4 Herod and Herodias. If that is so, Matthew is just saying that the marriages based on illicit sexual intercourse (either betrothal intercourse of incest intercourse) were not real marriages. The fornicator of 1 Cor. 5 had married his step-mother and Paul delivered him to Satan; that marriage was not a real marriage. It was an incestuous-marriage; or no marriage at all, but sin. It had to cease!

However, the Church in violation of common-sense language, or perhaps deceitfully, has broken the rules of hermeneutics by translating porneia as: (adultery or to any sexual immorality, or sexual immorality). I believe that in the context of Mt. 5:32 and 19:9 it is impossible to translate porneia as other than illicit Betrothal intercourse, or consanguineous Incest intercourse; both sins of which the Law required the death penalty. That is the only choice Matthew leaves us.

The person that holds to a non-permanency-marriage doctrine must address another important consideration which is referred to as the Premium of Adultery—this means that the exception clause offers a loop-hole in the otherwise permanency marriage doctrine, that gives an advantage to the spouse who wants to terminate a marriage, i.e. that spouse can simply commit adultery or any marital sexual immorality with the person they want to remarry, thus cause the innocent mate to sue for a divorce on the only (supposed) grounds for divorce (adultery or sexual immorality)—this very idea has entered into the mind of several people that I have personally counseled.

I find it incredible that here in the middle of Jesus' severe denunciation of murder and adultery that the modern interpreter finds adultery, or sexual immorality, to be an advantage to the person who desires to terminate a marriage covenant. If this is the case, then Jesus, did not raise His standard even .00000001 degree above Moses and the Law; and those who interpreted Moses regarding adultery. He actually lowered the Mosaic standard; because Moses required the death penalty for both adultery and marital fornication, or what the exegetes call sexual immorality. But remember, Jesus said: "But, I say unto you", in relation to his higher standard. I ask you dear reader one simple question: "Did Jesus permit, and offer any exception clause for murder, or for any other crime?" Thou shalt not commit adultery; Thou shalt not kill; are the words of God. I'm certain that Jesus never taught such a corrupt doctrine that would offer a man a reward for adultery; a premium. He was teaching men the full meaning of the Law of Moses. He explicitly stated, "Whosoever therefore shall break one of these least commandments, and shall teach men so, he shall be called the least in the kingdom of heaven:" and "Be ye therefore perfect, even as your Father in heaven is perfect." So I am certain that Jesus would not encourage adultery or sexual immorality in marriage; it certainly means something else. Therefore Matthew's exception clauses are obscure texts. To teach otherwise you have Jesus offering a reward to the person who wants to terminate a marriage. That's an Abomination!

Should the Church demand to maintain its stance and endorse divorce for adultery, or sexual immorality, and endorse remarriage then the Church must be warned that to do so: Will have Jesus offering a reward (Premium) to those seeking a divorce: (you can have a divorce for the price of committing adultery or other sexual immorality in marriage). In this case divorce is actually a reward and has been referred to as The Premium (Reward) of Adultery or the Premium (reward) of Any Sexual Immorality in marriage. The Church has been accused of offering this premium for centuries, and yet has been able to maintain their dogma. I do not believe this is Christ's Doctrine of marriage. This is an Abomination!

Mat. 5:32b The Harmony Problem

Mat 5:32(a) But I say unto you, That whosoever shall put away his wife, (saving for the cause of fornication) causeth her to commit adultery:

Mat 5:32(b) and whosoever shall marry her that is divorced (add saving for…again) committeth adultery.

Stuart Tyson points out here that the only way to harmonize (5:32b) with (5:32a) is to add the clause, save for the cause of fornication, after the word divorced in 5:32b: and whosoever shall marry her that is divorced save for the cause of fornication committeth adultery. In other words, the texts in the KJV has every man marrying a divorced woman as committing adultery. Matthew is approving a divorce in Mt. 5:32a and then disapproving of the remarriage of the innocent new husband in 5:32b. The only way the new husband could be free to marry the divorced woman is if you add the (saving for phrase) after "divorced" in 5:32b. Therefore, this verse is obscure in that without the fornication clause in (b) it clearly contradicts the Scripture. We will hear more from Tyson shortly.

Also, here Matthew states that the divorced wife cannot remarry because whosoever marries her will be committing adultery. This is tantamount of saying: The reason the man who marries a divorced woman commits adultery is because the woman is still married to her original husband. Thus, the text states that the original marriage has not been dissolved. So, that is a contradiction to the divorce granted in Mt. 5:32a. So here, we find yet another obscure element in Matthew's divorce texts. So just add another element to this Obscure Divorce Text View of Mat. 5 and 19; we are not done yet.

Now for just a mental reference let us read Mark 10:11-12 on this point;

> Mar 10:11-12 Whosoever shall put away his wife, and marry another, committeth adultery against her.
>
> Mar 10:12 And if a woman shall put away her husband, and be married to another, she committeth adultery.

Now that is clear and simple: "need I say more?" Jesus always taught with clarity and finality. I post this verse here just to mark the trail of the position of this paper.

Mat. 19:1-15—The Gettysburg of the Divorce War (Exception Clause #2)

We will now address the epic N.T. text of the marriage divorce war that is raging in our land and churches. Again, I will compare this text with Mk. 10:1-16. I will also include a discussion of the battle, and battle field at this junction.

Matt. 19:1-2

> Mat 19:1-2 And it came to pass, that when Jesus had finished these sayings, he departed from Galilee, and came into the coasts of Judaea beyond Jordan; And great multitudes followed him; and he healed them there.

The location here is the same as in Mk. 10:1, the coasts of Judea (Perea). As we pointed out the geography here may be as important as the text itself. As Gettysburg, the city of boots, was located central to the Civil War, so Perea, the geography of (Matt. 19) was central to the Divorce War. Pennsylvania was at the geographical separation of north and south. The site provided both armies to fully vent their ideologies; likewise does this location of Perea.

Where Mk.10 states that Jesus taught the people, Matthew adds that great multitudes followed Jesus and He healed them there. That a great crowd and healing is mentioned here is different, but it is not objectionable (an observation to this study). The fame of Jesus was peaking. The people sit to listen with praise in their hearts; while the Pharisees lay in wait with rage in their hearts to trap their prey, our Lord Jesus Christ. That rage was a cunningly devised plot against the Lord of Glory. Their design was simple. Now that Jesus was in Perea of Judea, they would simply align Jesus with the Forerunner, John, and deliver Him to the fury of Herodias, the Mad-One. Jesus knew their plot and was not fearful to enter it, as we shall see. Edersheim makes this notable comment:

> "Accordingly, when these Pharisees again encoun-
> tered Jesus, now on his journey to Judea, they resumed
> the subject precisely where it had been broken off
> when they had last met Him, only now with the object
> of 'tempting Him.' Perhaps it may also have been in
> the hope that, by getting Christ to commit Himself
> against divorce in Perea (the territory of Herod) they
> might enlist against Him, as formerly against the
> Baptist, the implacable hatred of Herodias.[208]

Edersheim introduces the implacable hatred of Herodias into his interpretation of the Matthew divorce logion. He goes on to state

---

[208] Edersheim, Life and Times, ("So, according to many commentators. See Meyer) Bk. IV: p. 332

that many commentators of his era believed that this was the case, specifically mentioning Meyer as a proponent of this view. Heth and Wenham give honor to the thought:

> It is of interest that Tertullian set Jesus' prohibition of divorce in the context of John's denunciation of Herod's unlawful and adulterous marriage with Herodias (Against Marcion 4.34). J.C. Laney also feels this historical incident is important to consider: John the Baptist's denunciation of the 'unlawful' (Matt. 14:4; Mk. 6:18) union of Herod Antipas with the former wife of his brother Philip fits well with Jesus' confrontation with the Pharisees. Perhaps the test with which the Pharisees confronted Jesus (Matt. 19:3) was related to Herod's situation rather than simply to the rabbinic debate.[209]

(Then again, perhaps it had nothing to do with the rabbinic dabate.) Some honor has been given to the geography of the text, but most draw away in favor of the Hillel-Shammai debate. But is this text a rabbinic debate? Historians tell us that this debate exercised the rabbis at the time of Christ, but did Jesus really address that controversy? Perhaps the geography of the debate weighs the balance in favor of the Herodias view, and the preaching of the Forerunner. Jesus did not immediately answer or remark on the beheading of John, but now He opens the door to Herod's palace and preaches John's message, "It is not lawful for thee to have thy brother's wife," (Mk. 6:18). Is that in fact what Jesus was doing?

Let us now consider this element in the explanation of the dissertation of Jesus regarding divorce. As stated, each of Matthew's divorce statements prohibit divorce and remarriage, except for the exception clause. Consequently, the exception clause has become the crux interpretum (the primary cross, perplexing problem, or puzzle of

---

[209] Heth;Wenham; Jesus and Divorce, p.157, 158

the interpretation) of all Scripture regarding divorce. Creating such a dynamic impact that it seems shelves and shelves of books and tracts have been written to discuss the problem; with positions ranging from its meaning to be adultery to the possibility that it is an interpolation. Certainly, Matthew's exception qualifies as an obscure text. This book has not been entered into without much serious study, and labor, (it was forty years in the making).

With this in mind, the obscure text, we are then forced to choose our hermeneutics. Regardless of your scholarship you must make a choice. If your system believes in the analogy of the faith—this rule states that there is a harmony of Scripture—then you must apply this rule to Matthew's obscure exception clause. Scripture must be used to interpret Scripture. Peter said it this way, "Knowing this first, that no prophecy of the scripture is of any private interpretation," (II Pet. 1:20). The NSRB makes this comment, "Any private interpretation" might read "its own interpretation"; i.e. isolated from what the Scripture states generally elsewhere.[210] It is the exception clause that must be interpreted with the analogy of the Scripture in mind. Since the word porneia has the potential of being interpreted in many ways the understanding of that word must be generated by the context surrounding the word. Perea surrounds the text. John was killed in Perea. There his headless corpse was buried, nevertheless his tongue continued to preach. (Herod thought Jesus' tongue was John's.) Could the Pharisees, again, succeed in arousing the semi-cooled implacable hatred and wrath of Herodias?

John the Baptist was sacrificed on the altar of incest. John's cries were bold against the king of the land. His call was as of a clarion: You Herod are corrupting marriage and I am going to make an example of you. He was willing to do whatever was necessary to make his message known to all mankind. He was even willing to have his throat severed through and have his head with tongue delivered to the king on a silver platter. Now in Perea, Jesus raises the screaming cries of John to

---

[210] NSRB; comment on II Pet. 1:20 p. 1339

Herod and Herodias, Repent, of your sin, for it is not lawful for you to have her. J. Carl Laney agrees:

> The geographical and historical background is crucial to our understanding of this encounter between Christ and the Pharisees. Jesus had concluded His Galilean ministry and was now beginning His journey through Perea to Jerusalem for the Passover and His own crucifixion. Traveling through Perea in the spring of A.D. 33, Jesus was approached by some Pharisees who sought to stump Him with a theological test question. Notice that the Pharisees were not asking the question to learn but only to "test" Jesus. They actually wanted to get Him into trouble.[211]

Heth and Wenham artfully resurrect the scholarship of the early church, showing that until Erasmus (the sixteenth century) the church believed in the permanency of marriage. In their volume they take a no-remarriage-this-side-of-death view, which is constructed on the writings of the early church fathers. Regarding the meaning of the exception clause, Heth and Wenham labor to explain all the present schools of thought on the subject and then say, "Considering the brevity of Jesus' recorded remarks about divorce, the quantity of literature that they have generated is truly remarkable. This survey [their book Jesus and Divorce, my comment] has tried to present the current scholarly theories as fairly as possible, to show their strengths and weaknesses, so that the reader can decide for himself or herself which is the most probable view."

Therefore, if the exception clause did not exist, the Scriptures would overwhelmingly teach us that divorce was absolutely prohibited by the Lord Jesus Christ. Nevertheless, we are not ashamed to address those words: "saving for the cause of fornication, and except it be for fornication." However, it brings to mind those admonitions:

---

[211] Laney, J. Carl; The Divorce Myth p. 53

"As also in all his epistles, speaking in them of these things, in which are some things hard to be understood, which they that are unlearned and unstable wrest, as they do also the other scriptures, unto their own destruction" (II Pet. 3:16). So, keeping this in mind we shall exposit the most wrestled text in the history of Christianity. Let us continue to explore the context of those disputed words: saving for, and except for. It must be noted that John gave his head on a platter for his doctrine of marriage; and John made no exceptions in his doctrine of marriage. (The fact that Matthew's exception clause is perhaps the most wrestled and disputed text in the Bible: then we should at the least delegate it forever as an Obscure Text). This fact is tantamount to the Highest Truth. Let us move on!

Matthew 19:3 "for every cause"

> The Pharisees also came unto him, tempting him, and saying unto him, Is it lawful for a man to put away his wife for every cause? *Matt. 19:3*

This clause, "for every cause" is central to this entire dissertation; and it, alone, will cost this writer some ink; please bear with me. This phrase is only found here in Scriptures: "for every cause;" it is not found in Mk. 10. This fact continues to support the position that the exception clause is obscure. Without this clause the Rabbinic Divorce Debate may have never surfaced as an element in this exegesis. This obscure clause is at direct odds with the entire discussion of Jesus' teaching regarding marriage and divorce. This clause, alone, sets the stage that places Jesus between two rabbinic opinions, and it does not give Jesus any way out. Those two opinions are: (1) that divorce is permitted only for adultery (known as that of Rabbi Shammai; (2) or the view that divorce is permitted for every cause, (known as that of Rabbi Hillel). Jesus has no way out. It is like the question: When did you stop beating your wife? (Just tell me the time; When?) So if we begin the exposition of the Mt. 19:9 exception clause with this debate, as our focal point, we will almost never see the truth of Jesus'

Doctrine of MDR (marriage, divorce, remarriage). The problem here is expanded by the fact that in this text, with its exception clause, Jesus does not rebuke both views of these rabbis. However, in the dissertations of divorce in Luke, Mark, and Paul BOTH rabbis are rebuked, both rabbis are condemned. But as we see here it appears that Jesus endorses Shammai. This certainly does not sound like Jesus—This is obscure. Like I said with Matthew and these rabbis Jesus has no way out, save to rebuke both rabbis which He did in Mark, Luke, and Paul. "For every cause" Obscure!

Now, we began the exposition of Mat.19:1-12 trying to understand the meaning of "fornication." We now have four focal points. (1) The first triggers the Incest View of Divorce by the geography of the text placing Jesus in the danger of Herod and Herodias. (2) The second triggers the Rabbinic Debate, presenting Jesus with only two Rabbinic choices. (3) The third offers the possibility that Jesus was referring to the fornication involved with His birth (Betrothal Fornication). (4) The forth focal point is the Obscure Text View which sees the exception clause as an obscure text that demands that it must be interpreted by the doctrine of the whole Bible that is revealed in Mark, Luke, and Paul which will bring us into a view that reinstates Mark 10:1-12 and the final doctrine of Christ on MDR is that divorce is prohibited completely. Thus, we now have four views from which to approach this text; that in itself favors the position that Matthew's texts are Obscure.

The Rabbinic Debate: Shammai Verses Hillel

Nevertheless, we will examine this Rabbinic Debate: but be assured this debate issue does not have a clean enough record to stand alone. The reason is that this clause: "for every cause" is, in itself another OBSCURE TEXT, and in that it refers to an extra-biblical doctrine (The Rabbinic Debate Doctrine) which is found no-where in the Bible; save for this clause. This obscure clause should not have the power to diminish Mark who many believe was a scribe of the Apostle Peter—So who will you trust: some obscure clause, or will you trust the Apostle Peter, speaking through Mark, and Luke the beloved physician, and the Apostle Paul; who see Jesus teaching creation-marriage, indissoluble and inseparable.

With that being said, let us go on to the Rabbinic Divorce Debate: and remember this writer unfortunately must use more ink to explain a view which in itself is obscure. So this simple clause (for every cause) has raised the theological controversy of Rabbi Shammai and Rabbi Hillel. Was the real purpose of the question to draw the Lord Jesus into the jaws of Herod and Herodias? Well, if it was so, Jesus could have been forced to say what He said in Mk. 10:11, 12 thus agreeing with John causing the distain of Herodias. John attacked the incestuous marriage of Herod. The Herod-Herodias snare is a reasonable interpretation of the trap of this incident. If so; Why would the Pharisees draw Jesus into a debate where both rabbis agreed: that divorce was acceptable? Both Rabbi Shammai and Hillel agreed 100% that divorce was permitted. The Pharisees knew that Jesus did not agree with either one of these rabbis. They knew that Jesus, as John, taught a revolutionary doctrine of marriage—revolutionary to their own liberalism—however the doctrine of Jesus and John was nothing more than the old fashion doctrine of permanency creation-marriage. Some scholars put Jesus on the side of Shammai; but this is wrong since Shammai did not teach permanency; he taught that divorce and remarriage was permitted in the event of adultery. Rabbi Hillel taught that divorce and remarriage was permitted for any reason. Alfred Edersheim, a Jewish convert to Christ and Bible commentator of the 19th Century wrote:

> The Jewish Law unquestionably allowed divorce on almost any grounds; the difference being, not as to what was lawful, but on what grounds a man should set the Law in motion and make use of the absolute liberty which it accorded him. Hence, it is a serious mistake on the part of commentators [Christian] to set the teaching of Christ on this subject by the side of that of Shammai. [divorce for adultery]

But the School of Hillel [divorce for every cause] proceeded on different principles. It took the words, 'matter of shame' (erwat dabar) in the widest possible sense and declared it sufficient ground for divorce if a woman had spoiled her husband's dinner. Rabbi Akiba thought, that the words, 'if she find no favour in his eyes,' implied that it was sufficient if a man had found another woman more attractive than his wife. All agreed that moral blame made divorce a duty, and that in such cases a woman should not be taken back; according to the Mishnah, if they transgressed against the Law of Moses or of Israel. The former is explained as implying a breach of the laws of tithing, of setting apart the first of the dough, and of purification. The latter is explained as referring to such offences as that of going in public with uncovered head, of spinning in the public streets, or entering into talk with men, to which others add, that of brawling, or of disrespectfully speaking of her husband's parents in his presence. A troublesome, or quarrelsome wife might certainly be sent away; and ill repute, or childlessness (during ten years) were also regarded as valid grounds of divorce.[212]

On the other hand, the conservative rabbi, Shammai, set unchastity or adultery as the only legal ground to secure a divorce; for which Moses of course required the stoning to death of both guilty partners. Both doctrines of these rabbis were extra-biblical. Jesus taught the Law to the nth degree: He certainly could not avoid calling for the death penalty for adultery.

But the real problem with putting Jesus in the middle of this controversy is like I said: "it puts Jesus in a position, where there is no way out." This is so, because both Rabbis in the end believed in divorce.

---

[212] Edersheim, Life and Times, Bk. IV p. 334

But, by asking Jesus to choose between these two opinions: Jesus has no way out—however the question that Mark 10 conveyed: ("Is it Lawful for a man to put away his wife"?) affords the free element for Jesus to take a critical response to both sides of the debate: which is expected of Him in such cases.

The modern understanding of the exception clause in (Matt. 5:32 and 19:9) does not harmonize with the context of the Sermon on the Mount, and this disparity has led some, to even go as far as, to suspect the Greek MS (manuscript) text. Stuart L. Tyson wrote a little book, The teaching of our Lord as to the Indissolubility of Marriage, where he sternly defends the doctrine of permanency-marriage. He argues to defend the teaching of Jesus regarding creation marriage. He understands Jesus to teach the absolute permanency of marriage this side of death; and this fact causes him to struggle with the exception clause in both (Matt. 5:32; 19:9). His sincere and rigorous effort to harmonize the divorce texts with the teaching of Jesus drives him to suspect those very texts (he suspects both the language hermeneutically and the Greek MMS manuscripts in this regard.) Donald W. Shaner quotes Tyson:

> Tyson does not see how the statements of Matthew attributed to Jesus (5:32; 19:9) can be brought into accord with the previously mentioned biblical authors [Mark, Luke, and Paul]... if Christ really uttered these words [the exception clause], so far from elevating the conception of marriage, He has not raised it one whit higher than the level of Moses, whereas the very purpose of His previous words [Matt. 5] is to contrast His teaching with that of Moses!" And to Mark's question, "Is it lawful for a man to divorce his wife?" requiring a direct Yes or No. Matthew adds "for every cause?" presupposing his acceptance of the Deuteronomic Law but asking him to decide for either the strict or liberal view of certain Rabbis. Jesus, by including the exception of

adultery, seems to accept the view of Shammai, rather than abrogating the Mosaic law (the death penalty). If so, it is difficult to understand the disciples' protest (vs. 10), since it was merely a reaffirmation of a Jewish doctrine accepted by a large segment of the population. The only conclusion is that the exception clause is an interpolation due to a Jewish-Christian compiler or editor.

In Matt. 5:32 Jesus also simply confirms the Old Testament teaching; this is contradictory to the structure of the verse which has Christ saying, "But I say unto you," in contrast to the Mosaic law in the preceding verse. The second half of the verse, "and whosoever shall marry her that hath been put away committeth adultery," is almost verbatim with the last portion of Luke 16:18. The anarthrous participle apolelymenhn, occurring in both Gospels, denotes "... any woman divorced for any cause whatever." Luke is consistent, but the only way to harmonize Matthew is to place the exception clause also in the second half of the verse 32, or to eliminate it from the first.[213]

Tyson wrote this in 1909 when marriage was relatively sound in our country. He had so much difficulty with the exception clauses of Matthew that he believed that Jesus, whose teaching of marriage was ablaze with the doctrine of permanency, certainly could not have spoken them. He accurately states: "If Christ really uttered these words [the exception clause], so far from elevating the conception of marriage, He has not raised it one whit higher than the level of Moses, whereas the very purpose of His previous words [Matt. 5] is to contrast His teaching with that of Moses!"

I am very surprised that today most scholars, pastors, students, and confessed Bible believers seem to have no difficulty with the

---

[213] Shanner, D.W.; A Christian View; p. 11-12

apparent blatant contradiction of the Matthean divorce texts and Jesus' teaching on permanency-marriage. Tyson was not a fundamentalist—he was a southern Episcopalian—nevertheless even in 1909 this gentleman was having serious trouble thinking through these texts. It is just remarkable today that from student to scholar our generation does not at least admit to the difficulty and contradiction of the modern interpretation that the exception clause permits a man to put asunder that which God has joined together. Matthew's exception clause texts are absolutely obscure texts, and if our generation does not make that admission then this writer suspects not the Matthean MS Greek text: rather, I suspect the honesty of our Bible believing pastors, scholars, and students—I adamantly suspect our generation of prophets. Suspect!

Matthew 19:4-6

> And he answered and said unto them, Have ye not read, that he which made them at the beginning made them male and female, And said, For this cause shall a man leave father and mother, and shall cleave to his wife: and they twain shall be one flesh? Wherefore they are no more twain, but one flesh. What therefore God hath joined together, let not man put asunder. *Matt. 19:4-6*

At this point in Mark we have Jesus answering the Pharisees with His question: "What did Moses command you?" Here in Matthew we have a totally different scenario: Jesus asks a rhetorical question: "Have ye not read," then He goes on to teach the lesson of creation-marriage from Gen. 1-3; along with the final commandment: "let man not put asunder." But here, in Mt. 19:4-6 we miss Jesus' powerful rebuke of Mk. 10.3 when He demands to know from them: To what O.T. divorce commandment they are referring? In Mark, Jesus handed them a death blow (He checkmated them); their answer caused them to cease speaking: "Moses suffered to write a bill of divorcement." This is critically important to this study. This change in Matthew is critical and adds to Matthew's obscure language here in Matthew 19:1-12.

Regardless, here again the doctrine of Permanency-Creation Marriage is affirmed by Jesus. The marriage bond is permanent. Man cannot divide that which is indivisible. The words above declare that Jesus believed and taught the doctrine of permanency creation marriage and that is indisputable. Therefore, before any interpreter teaches that Jesus did not teach permanency, they must be absolutely sure they can prove their claim. For this reason, the Early Church View understood the exception clause to permit a separation of the marriage partners without any right to remarry; "no-remarriage-this-side-of-death." It is called: Divorce a mensa et thoro: a divorce from table and bed, or from bed and board. This was a partial or qualified divorce, by which the parties are separated and forbidden to live or cohabit together, without affecting the marriage itself (Blacks Law Dictionary). Grace is predominate in divorce a mensa et thoro since the marriage here is completely redeemable: love or grace is extended with the possibility of a complete restoration of the marriage. Another monumental consequence of the twain becoming one flesh, and Jesus' prohibition of remarriage is the truth that Jesus taught, that marriage is monogamous, a permanent organic union; thereby he absolutely repudiated polygamy; as well as condemning all sexual acts of men, outside the marriage bond.

Matthew 19:7-9 The Crux Interpretum of the Entire Debate

> Mat 19:7 They say unto him, Why, did Moses then command to give a writing of divorcement, and to put her away?
>
> Mat 19:8 He saith unto them, Moses because of the hardness of your hearts suffered you to put away your wives: but from the beginning it was not so.
>
> Mat 19:9 And I say unto you, Whosoever shall put away his wife, except it be for fornication, and

shall marry another,committeth adultery: and whoso
marrieth her which is put away doth commit adultery.

Dear reader, please note here that 19:7 Matthew displays an
entirely different scenario then the Gospel of Mark. Here we have
the Pharisees continuing to rebuke Jesus, where in Mark they were
silent and defeated. This is very different. Here we have the Pharisees
in charge of the word "COMMAND". Where in Mark Jesus said:
"What did Moses command you"; they were the one that used the
word suffer: Moses suffered to write a bill of divorcement. In Mark
they conceded that there was no commandment. Here we have the
Pharisees saying: Why then did Moses command to give a writing of
divorcement? This is profoundly disturbing to this author. This is the
most critical pericope of the MDR debate, and it is full of obscurities.
Not only have the Pharisees regained life here but as soon as Jesus
finishes with Mt. 19:9 we appear to have the disciples publicly com-
plaining to the Lord about his message. There were no complaints
recorded in (Mt.5:32; or Mk. 10) but here we have the disciples with
a public grievance against Jesus; and it appears the Pharisees are still
standing. I also find this troubling.

Mt. 19:9, as noted, has opened the flood-gates to so called
Christian divorce and remarriage. Here in the same pericope with
the most-simple marriage phrase known to mankind: "The twain
shall be ONE flesh: so then they are no more twain, but one flesh;
and What therefore God hath joined together, let not man put asunder;" we have what appears to be an open gate to the broad road that
leads to destruction. Mt. 19:9 has now been interpreted by many in
the Church to mean: Man may put asunder any marriage he pleases.
I'm literally startled by this madness. The church today does not even
bother with sexual immorality; it appears everything goes. "For any
cause" is the doctrine of many in the church of Jesus today. Thus this
practice of the Bible believing churches is ludicrous at best.

Heth and Wenham realized that pastors and laymen would not
have the time or the resources to examine the extensive literature
surrounding the divorce debate therefore they completed that task
and have established a standard explanation of all the early church

literature in their volume: Jesus and Divorce. Establishing the Early Church View[214]as their position, where they go on to examine the Church Fathers; "namely those Christian theologians who wrote in the first five centuries of the Christian era."[215] The most remarkable discovery of Heth and Wenham is that the Early Church Fathers had a remarkable common belief regarding MDR. One influencing observation is that the early father's shared unanimity in their understanding of the divorce texts. These authors then summarize the fathers as teaching a MDR doctrine of no-remarriage-this-side-of-death.[216]

Their comprehensive study—it possibly could be described as the most comprehensive study of this subject that was ever written—contends that in the first five centuries all Greek writers, and all Latin writers, except one, agree that remarriage following divorce for any reason is adulterous. The marriage bond was seen to unite both parties until the death of one of them. When a marriage partner was guilty of unchastity, usually understood to mean adultery, the other was expected to separate—separation without divorce—without the right to remarry. Even in the case of I Corinthians 7:15, the so-called Pauline privilege, which later Catholics interpreted to permit a believer deserted by an unbeliever to remarry, the early church

---

[214] Heth and Wenham; Jesus and Divorce: The reader should refer to this work as the modern foundation of the divorce debate. Heth and Wenham lay out all the elements of the ancient and modern controversy on the divorce texts. They side with the primary concepts of the Early Church View, which is a "no-remarriage-this-side-of-death."

[215] Ibid. p. 19

[216] Ibid. p. 21; Heth and Wenham acknowledge that the early church father's had the advantage of living and learning in an era where the ancient languages were their common tongue. Therefore, their understanding of the (Mt. 5:32; 19:9) texts may have been more clear to them. After stating that there were long debates among the fathers about some doctrines, but regarding divorce and remarriage this was not so: "In contrast, on the subject of divorce and remarriage there was practically no dispute in the early church: for the first five centuries there was virtual unanimity on this issue from one end of the Roman empire to the other.

fathers said that the deserted Christian had no right to remarry.[217] Heth and Wenham commence the third chapter of their dissertation with this sentence:

> The early Christian writer's interpretation of the divorce texts remained the standard view of the church in the West until the sixteenth century when Erasmus suggested a different view that was adopted by Protestant theologians.[218]

It is of utmost importance that one understands that Erasmus was a man who shunned sound doctrine in spite of the serious warnings of the Apostle: "For the time will come when they will not endure sound doctrine; but after their own lusts shall they heap to themselves teachers, having itching ears; And they shall turn away their ears from the truth, and shall be turned unto fables" (2 Ti. 4:3, 4). Again Heth and Wenham quote V.N. Olsen who writes in his study of the interpretation of the New Testament divorce texts from Erasmus to Milton:

> In his interpretation of the New Testament logia on divorce Erasmus reveals himself as a Christian theologian who seeks to solve an ethical problem within Church and society by finding a solution [to permit divorce with remarriage, my comment] based on Scripture and centered in Christ. No ecclesiastical institution should stand between the needy [i.e., the divorced needy who wish to remarry, my comment] and the Good Samaritan [Erasmus]. Erasmus appears not as an academic theorist but as a Christian pragmatist who is devoted to his Master in service for his fellow men.[219]

---

[217] Ibid. p. 22

[218] Ibid. p. 73

[219] Ibid. p. 73

The overwhelming thrust of Heth and Wenham is to reveal that the Erasmian view "flatly contradicts the patristic interpretation." This is a very important observation. Has the Erasmian view been dogmatized by the spirit of compromise? Modern Protestant scholars embrace the Erasmian view as the Roman church embraces the doctrine of the papacy and the mass. Heth and Wenham go on to exposit the teaching of the following Fathers: Hermas, Justin Martyr, Athenagoras, Theophilus of Antioch, Irenaeus, Clement of Alexandria, Origen, and Tertullian. They go on to list the others who agree to the doctrine no-remarriage-this-side-of-death, Basil of Ancyra, Basil of Caesarea, Gregory Nazianzus, Apollinaris of Laodicea, Theodore of Mopsuestia, John Chrosostom, Theodoret, Epiphanius, Ambrose, Innocent I, Pelagius, Jerome, Leo the Great, and Augustine. "In all, twenty-five individual writers and two early councils forbid remarriage after divorce."[220] They also point out that the early church fathers debated many doctrines but regarding no-re-marriage-this-side-of death there was no debate; they all agreed. In general, the early church fathers take the following position: (1) the heart of their doctrine saw marriage as organically indissoluble—permanent; (2) if infidelity interrupts the marriage bond the faithful partner could separate from the infidel—the innocent to wait for the infidel to repent, but the innocent partner could not remarry (3) remarriage was only permitted to the widow or widower, and then sometimes reluctantly; (4) the remarriage of a separated partner to another, while their original marriage partner was alive, was considered adultery; (5) they understood the "exception clause" to apply only to the first part of the conditional clause, and that it did not apply to remarriage; (6) the repentance of the guilty partner was the only hope of the innocent partner to establish any marriage relationship, and that repentance was taken seriously:

> Whoever has committed adultery will be excluded
> from the sacraments for fifteen years: he must weep

---

[220] Ibid. p. 38

for four years [outside the door of the church during the service], then he must listen for five years [in the vestibule], be prostrated [among the full congregation] for two years without receiving communion.[221]

Some of these penalties seem exceptionally harsh to our age partly because discipline has virtually disappeared in many parts of the modern church. Excommunication, however, was a regular feature of the New Testament church for various sins (cf. Matt. 18:15-18; II Cor. 2:5-11; II Thess. 3:14) including sexual offences (1 Cor. 5:1-13). We do not know how long such a sentence would have lasted, though presumably it could not have been revoked until the offender showed signs of repentance (cf. 2 Cor. 7:7-13; 2 Tim. 2:24-6).[222]

Matthew 5:32; 19:9: The Exception Clauses

But I say unto you that whosoever shall put away his wife, saving for the cause of fornication, causeth her to commit adultery; and whosoever shall marry her that is divorced committeth adultery. *Matthew 5:32*

And I say unto you, Whosoever shall put away his wife, except it be for fornication, and shall marry another, committeth adultery; and whosoever marrieth her who is put away doth commit adultery. *Matthew 19:9*

As noted, the exception clause is common only to Matthew; therefore, I see it as one comment, i.e. one witness. The three other N.T. writers who discuss the subject of marriage and divorce—Mark, Luke, and Paul—preach the doctrine of permanency-marriage with

---

[221] Ibid. p. 42 Heth and Wenham quoting Stromata

[222] Ibid. p. 44

no divorce-remarriage option. (Later, I will fully discuss 1 Cor. 7 which I believe supports that statement.) This in itself, beside the fact that the tremendous weight of the literature that 19:9 has spawned, qualify Matthew's texts to be tagged an obscure text. With this in mind—noting that we have earlier eliminated (Deut. 24:1-4) as a possible reference to the unclean/thing (fornication)—we must ask ourselves the following question; since no other author permits us to cross reference Matthew, does Matthew himself interpret his own words of the obscure text? As the honest student proposes this question to Matthew, he will find that Matthew offers a possible answer. It appears that Matthew, himself, actually gives us two causes that can be interpreted as fornication. Two separate meanings of porneia that could explain his obscure text. We will exposit the definitions as they appear chronologically. They have been given the theological titles of: (1) The Betrothal View, (2) The Unlawful Marriage or The Incest View.

Betrothal View: Fornication

I have fully explained this view at the beginning of this chapter in my exposition of (Matthew 1:18, 19). Joseph, while engaged to Mary, found her with child. On the surface this appeared to Joseph as an illegitimate child. His exact thought was that Mary had committed an act of premarital sex, i.e. she committed a special act of fornication. His immediate reaction was to put her away, divorce her. This required a public act of repudiation—divorce was public—and Joseph could not bring himself to commit such a public act. So he decided to privately divorce Mary. The Scripture clearly tells us that Joseph was a "just man." He had the perfect legal right to put his betrothed (engaged wife) away; it was the accepted legal custom at that specific time in Jewish history. At that moment he thought she had committed betrothal fornication. This is one of Matthew's own answers to the question as to the meaning of fornication. Therefore, if we rewrite the text in question it would read:

But I say unto you, That whosoever shall put away his wife, saving for the cause of betrothal fornication, causeth her to commit adultery: and whosoever shall marry her that is divorced committeth adultery. *Matthew 5:32*

And I say unto you, Whosoever shall put away his wife, except it be for betrothal fornication, and shall marry another, committeth adultery: and whoso marrieth her which is put away, doth commit adultery. *Matthew 19:9*

The Unlawful Marriage Incest View: Fornication

The Book of Leviticus is the ruling text of this view. As mentioned under the discussion of John the Baptist we found John in his sermon accused Herod of committing incest, i.e. being unlawfully wedded to Herodias according to Levitical law. Thus, the Unlawful Marriage View may be referred to as the Incest View. In Chapter Three of this dissertation we have explored the abominable custom of the Egyptians—Incest. We noted from (Lev.18:1-18) that Jehovah God specifically threatened the death penalty to any Israelite who committed the abominations of the Egyptians. Marriage within the forbidden degrees of (Lev. 18:1-18) was absolutely prohibited. Lev. 18:16 specifically prohibits a man to marry his brother's wife; this was the very act that John accused Herod Antipas of committing. World governments today have similar definitions of incest and prohibit marriage within the forbidden degrees. This being the case we now might interpret Matthew to read:

But I say unto you, That whosoever shall put away his wife, saving for the cause of incest, causeth her to commit adultery: and whosoever shall marry her that is divorced, committeth adultery. (*Mt. 5:32*)

And I say unto you, Whosoever shall put away his wife, except it be for incest, and shall marry another,

committeth adultery: and whoso marrieth her which
is put away, doth commit adultery. (*Mt. 19:9*)

The primary argument against both these views from divorce
scholars is that both of them are remote interpretations of the word
porneia. So be it, I say, Matthew has spoken, the obscure text, and
no other biblical writer has; and beside that it appears Matthew has
explained himself. Therefore, we can conclude that remarriage this
side of death is adultery. This is exactly what Augustine referred to as
"Adulterous-Marriage."

Mt. 5:32; 19:9 Augustine: Adulterous-Marriages; Obscure Texts

Late in his career, Augustine, after a lifetime of experience
regarding Biblical issues wrote extensively about MDR. He wrote a
two-part book, Adulterous Marriages, in which he adamantly took
the position that remarriage after divorce for any cause was adultery.
The two-part book is occasioned by a debate he had with a fellow
Christian, Pollentius, who disagreed with him. His opponent argued
that remarriage was permissible for certain reasons: Augustine argued
that remarriage was adultery, and if that union occurred it was simply
what he called: "Adulterous-Marriage." For his defense he stated that
the exception clauses of Matthew should not be the foundation text
for the MDR doctrine of the church.

Augustine said;

> But, if Matthew the Evangelist has made the ques-
> tion difficult to comprehend, because he mentioned
> the one case and was silent concerning the other, have
> not the other Evangelists treated the same matter so
> comprehensively that both sides of the problem can
> be understood? Mark wrote the following: "Whoever
> puts away his wife and marries another, commits
> adultery against her; and if the wife puts away her

husband and marries another, she commits adultery." And Luke wrote: "Everyone who puts away his wife and marries another commits adultery; and he who marries a woman who has been put away from her husband, commits adultery.

Therefore, who are we to say that there is one who commits adultery in taking another woman after he puts away his wife, and there is another who, in doing this does not commit adultery, when the Gospel says that everyone who performs such an act commits adultery?

But what is insufficiently understood in Matthew's account can be understood from the words of the other Evangelists.

All that pertains to this question is not expressed in the Gospel of Matthew, but the portion contained therein is expressed in such a way that from it may be inferred the whole, that both Mark and Luke have preferred to state, in explanation, as it were, so that the sense might be understood in full.

And, therefore, what Matthew has put down somewhat OBSCURELY, because the whole has been signified by the part, has been explained by those who expressed the whole in a general way, just as we read in Mark: "Whoever puts away his wife and marries another commits adultery," and in Luke: "Everyone who puts away his wife and marries another commits adultery." For, they have not said that some who marry others after putting away their wives commit adultery, and some do not; but they have said: "Whoever puts away," that is, absolutely everyone without exception, who puts away his wife and marries another commits adultery.

However, the Apostle forbids it by counsel of charity, because it impedes the salvation of unbelievers, not only because the parties offended are most harmfully scandalized, but also because it is most difficult to free them from the ties of an Adulterous-Marriage, in the event they have fallen into such marriages, while the ones who put them away are still living.

To Augustine separation in the case of adultery was legally permitted, but not divorce; he referred to this as a legal-separation. Legal separation was permitted, but divorce was forbidden; thus even with separation of this nature, remarriage was also forbidden. Legal separation was often associated with excommunication. Its purpose was to have the Church deal with the sinning spouse by bringing them to repentance and forgiveness; all this by the "Blood of the Covenant," or by the Gospel with repentance and restoration. Now, one more quote here:

"A woman is bound [in marriage] as long as her husband is alive," that is, to speak more plainly, as long as he is physically alive. The husband, being subject to the same law, is likewise bound as long as his wife is physically alive. Wherefore, if he wishes to dismiss and adulteress, he is not to marry another, lest he himself commit what he reproaches in her. And so with the wife. If she puts away her adulterous husband, she is not to enjoin herself to another husband. She is bound as long as her husband lives. She is not freed from the law of her husband, unless he be dead, so that she will not be guilty of adultery if she has been with another man.

So, here we see that Augustine almost speaks like this author speaks, or I speak like him. Regardless, it is simple: Mark, Luke, and Paul must lead in the content of Jesus' Doctrine of Marriage, Divorce and Remarriage. Augustine clearly identified Matt. 5:32 and 19:9 as OBSCURE TEXTS and therefore Augustine refused to build any doctrine on such texts: especially Jesus' Doctrine of MDR.

Matthew 19:10-12

> His disciples say unto him, If the case of the man
> be so with his wife, it is not good to marry.
> But he said unto them, All men cannot receive
> this saying, save they to whom it is given.
> For there are some eunuchs, which were   so
> born from their mother's womb: and there are some
> eunuchs, which were made eunuchs of men: and there
> be eunuchs, which have made themselves eunuchs
> for the kingdom of heaven's sake. He that is able to
> receive it, let him receive it. *Matt. 19:10-12*

I find this outburst of the disciples almost hostile—the outburst in itself confirms that the disciples understood Jesus to teach that marriage is indissoluble and permanent—I believe it was driven by their personal opinion that they believed that marriage certainly was not permanent; that all men, even a disciple, had the right to put away a wife and remarry, i.e. at least for some causes. But they now understood Jesus to absolutely forbid divorce, and remarriage. Jesus was also absolutely declaring that marriage is permanent until death do-you-part. One must note that all of Jesus' disciples strenuously objected; almost to the point of threatening a departure with Christ over this issue. "If the case of a man be so, it is not good to marry." The disciples were divided against Him; but, Jesus quickly puts them in their place.

He gives them the door. Go from me if ye will, he cries. "All men cannot receive this saying, save them to whom it is given." Please note that all the disciples are silent. They now had to evaluate their hearts. They certainly knew that the arguing Pharisees were not among the given. So in plain English they shut up, in fear of perhaps being counted among the unsaved ones. They must have pondered what they perceived as His awful words "What therefore God hath joined together let not man put asunder."Their silence is louder than a shrilling scream.This is a far cry from the reaction of the disciples described in Mark 10:10 and just adds to the obscurity of Matthew.

Matthew 19:13-15

> Then were there brought unto him little children,
> that he should put his hands on them, and pray: and
> the disciples rebuked them. But Jesus said, Suffer little
> children, and forbid them not, to come unto me: for of
> such is the kingdom of heaven. And he laid his hands
> on them, and departed thence. *Matt. 19:13-15*

Some may object to including the little children in the marriage-divorce logion; but I say it is fitting and should be included. What is the bottom line of the divorce controversy? Is it not the children; the orphans of divorced-broken families. Don't these orphans have any rights? Well, Jesus said that they sure do have rights. "Suffer little children, and forbid them not, to come unto me: for of such is the kingdom of heaven. And he laid his hands on them and departed thence." Yes, He laid his hand on them. He touched them. Marriages are to be built on Christ. What God hath joined together. The most powerful evangelistic tool in the hand of God is a saved mother and father; and I might add a saved grandmother and grandfather. The heart of a true believing parent prays fervently for its child; presenting the Gospel with great care so as to ensure that their child truly gets every opportunity to get saved; to have his or her own experience of repentance and faith in the Lord Jesus Christ. This is difficult to provide to the child of a broken-family.

In the dedication of this book you will read that I have honored the faithful spouse who is awaiting the return of a departed sinful spouse; in all actuality dying for the beloved departed one. I believe that is what it means to give your life for your wife—to wear yourself out till death if necessary, for your departed spouse. These faithful men and women are offering the Grace of God to their unfaithful and abusive mates to the Glory of God, waiting lovingly for their reconciliation in this lifetime if possible. The second person I honored are the children of divorce; especially that little Amy, and Tommy, also brave little Zahra who wish they could live, or be alive, with their creation-marriage biological father and mother, and have all his or her love; not being required to share it with alien children, or an alien parent. These children have rights to.

Luke 16:18 Luke and MDR

> Whosoever putteth away his wife, and marrieth another, committeth adultery; and whosoever marrieth her that is put away from her husband, committeth adultery. *Lk. 16:18*

Many believe this text appears just randomly here in Luke's Gospel; but I disagree. I believe it is directly tied into the context of a discussion of certain legal problems that Jesus was addressing in His preaching at this time, especially to the self-righteous Pharisees. R.C.H. Lenski agrees; regarding the question of the randomness of this text: he writes:

> Jesus is not throwing together heterogeneous and non-pertinent thoughts when he now scores the Jewish practice of dissolving marriage ad libitum. Among the "open sinners" who drew near to Jesus were harlots (Lk. 15:1, 2), and some of these may have been in the present audience. But did these holy Pharisees keep the Seventh Commandment any better when they drove one wife after another away and took a new one as often as they pleased? So this statement is decidedly pertinent.
>
> It is in order, too, because the parable and its exposition (v. 16:1-13) dealt with mammon, and the scorn of the Pharisees was aroused by what Jesus said on that subject (v. 14). Jesus therefore brings in this other flagrant sin of the Pharisees and exhibits likewise how they manipulate the Word of God in order to permit its open violation, their most famous teachers showing them the way. But, here, too, no single letter of the

word can be abrogated, God will judge also these sins according to that authoritative Word, never according to the Pharisaic perversions of that Word. By bringing in this different group of open sins Jesus makes the Pharisees understand that he could go on and on by enumerating still other sins. To understand the wickedness of their love of money they must understand this same wickedness in its workings also in other directions [marriage sin of adultery and divorce: my comment]. Jesus rips away their defenses and drives hard at their conscience.[223]

Please note that Lenski sees the context of Lk.16:18 as part of a pericope that begins with Lk.15:1, 2 where Jesus was dining with publicans and sinners. Some murmuring Pharisees approached this gathering; Jesus begins preaching, and He continues through to Lk. 16:31. He notes that Jesus' sermon was particularly pointed at the interpretation of the law: Luk 16:17 "And it is easier for heaven and earth to pass, than one tittle of the law to fail." He was preaching the need to be saved in the parables of the lost sheep, the lost coin, and the lost son. Then he again called for repentance. He continues with the parable of the unjust steward, which dealt with Mammon or God, arousing the scorn of the Pharisees. Then Jesus immediately deals with one of the most secret of sins: adultery; and finishes with the parable of the rich man and Lazarus. Yes, I agree with Lenski that Lk.16:18 is not a random heterogeneous non-pertinent thought; rather it is a deliberate statement of the Son of God.

So again, here in Lk. 16:18 we have, without the exception clause, the absolute prohibition of divorce and remarriage. Jesus was adamant, He forbid divorce. Jesus absolutely taught that marriage is permanent. Thus, to this point in our study, we can say, that Luke agrees with Mark.

---

[223] Lenski, R.C.H. The Interpretation of St. Luke (Augsburg Pub. House, Minn. MN) p. 842

John 4:6-32 Jesus and the Samaritan Harlot

The position of this paper sees the woman of Samaria as a harlot. Cooper P. Abrams III in his commentary on John 4 and the Samaritan women agrees:

> The woman saith unto him, Sir, give me this water, that I thirst not, neither come hither to draw. Jesus saith unto her, Go, call thy husband, and come hither. *John 4:15, 16*

The woman responds with her earthly understanding. She asked Jesus to give her this water that everlastingly satisfied thirst. Jesus' reply to her certainly was unusual, because He asked her to go and get her husband. In order to receive salvation a person must first understand that they are a sinner. The woman had unknowingly asked for salvation when she had asked for the "living water." Jesus used the question to reveal the spiritual need in her life. She needed to see her real need that she might subsequently desire to be saved. The Samaritan woman had lived a life of immorality and Jesus' question was designed to bring her face to face with her sins.

> The woman answered and said, I have no husband. Jesus said unto her, Thou, hast well said, I have no husband: For thou hast had five husbands; and he whom thou now hast is not thy husband: in that saidst thou truly. The woman saith unto him, Sir, I perceive that thou art a prophet. (*John 4:17-20*)

The woman honestly replied that she did not have a husband because she had never been married. The Greek word "aner" is translated each time in this text, "husband." However, it is used also to mean "an individual, a man, a fellow or a Sir." Like many Greek words the context interprets the correct meaning or use of the word. She correctly said she did not have a husband, which would be a man she was legally married to. Jesus replied that she had stated the truth, because you have had five "men" (not legal husbands) and the one you are now living with is not your husband. The position of this paper is that her answer implies that she was never married. Therefore, the woman answered and said: I never had a husband. Jesus said unto her, Thou, hast well said, I have no husband: For thou hast had five men; and he whom thou now hast is not thy husband: in that saidst thou truly. The context tells us that the woman had not had five legal husbands, but had lived with five men, or fellows [a secret harlot: my comment].

> The woman saith unto Him, Sir, I perceive thou art a prophet. (*Jn. 4:19*)

I believe that her sudden revelation that Jesus was the Prophet is evidence that her secrets were now revealed. Jesus knew the deepest secrets of her life; she was stunned, she literally falls down and now worships Him in her heart. Listen to her further words:

> The woman saith unto him, I know that Messias cometh, which is called Christ: when he is come, he will tell us all things. (*John 4:25*)
> Jesus saith unto her, I that speak unto thee am he. (*John 4:26*)
> Come, see a man, which told me all things that ever I did: is not this the Christ? Then they went out of the city and came unto him. (*Jn. 4:29*)

The woman speaks: "He will tell us all things." Jesus confirms her lead: "I that speak unto thee am He." Jesus made this emphatic statement that He was the Messiah; interestingly He makes it first to a Samaritan woman and not to the Jews. Jesus made this same statement again after He healed the blind man as recorded in John 9:37. Jesus' going to the Samaritan woman shows God's purpose for this Gospel. God inspired John to proclaim in detail the fact that Jesus was the Messiah, the promised One of Israel. Here Jesus, Himself, expresses this truth plainly so there can be no misunderstanding about who He was. It is important to consider that Jesus was replying to the Samaritan woman who said she believed the Messiah would come and would tell all things. Jesus is therefore reaching out to her with the truth, so she might believe and be saved. It appears that is exactly what happened: this woman repented and believed in Christ. She then goes immediately to her home and witnesses to her neighbors: "Come, see a man, which told me all things ever I did: is not this the Christ." She publicly confesses that Jesus revealed everything ever I did (this is a direct reference to her secret life as a harlot.)

> And upon this came his disciples, and marvelled that he talked with the woman: yet no man said, What seekest thou? or, Why talkest thou with her?
> The woman then left her waterpot, and went her way into the city, and saith to the men, Come, see a man, which told me all things that ever I did: is not this the Christ? Then they went out of the city and came unto him. *John 4:27-30*

The woman, who had come to get water, was so taken by Jesus, and His statements, that she left immediately in apparent haste leaving behind her water pot. The woman rushes to the city and compels the men of the village to come with her and see a man who had told her everything she had done. She tells them He has supernatural powers and proclaims to them that He must be the Christ.[224]

I agree with Pastor Abrams, that the Greek word is explained by it context and "aner" in each case here means that none of the men this woman had a relationship with was ever her husband. She was a harlot that desperately needed to come face to face with her sin and repent

---

[224] Abrams III, Cooper P. Commentary on the Gospel of John (bible-truth. org/ JohnChapter4.html)

and get saved; and she did just that. I believe that key elements in support of the position that she was a secret harlot is her absolute astonishment: "Sir I perceive that thou art a prophet" and the additional comments: and "When Messias cometh, He will tell us all things;" and, "Come, see a man, which told me all things that ever I did: is not this the Christ?" The words: "all things that ever I did" exclaim more then the idea that Jesus knew she had five husbands; this was something more startling. When Jesus told her, He knew she had five secret promiscuous affairs; she was stunned. Only God knows the secrets of our hearts. She was a secret harlot. Revealed! This story, improperly interpreted, has led many: pastors and saints to put asunder (by law) marriages what God hath joined together.

John 7:53-8:11 The Woman Taken In Adultery

They say unto him, Master, this woman was taken in adultery, in the very act. Now Moses in the law commanded us, that such should be stoned: but what sayest thou? This they said, tempting him, that they might have to accuse him. But Jesus stooped down, and with his finger wrote on the ground, as though he heard them not. So, when they continued asking him, he lifted up himself, and said unto them, He that is without sin among you, let him first cast a stone at her. And again, he stooped down, and wrote on the ground. And they which heard it, being convicted by their own conscience, went out one by one, beginning at the eldest, even unto the last: and Jesus was left alone, and the woman standing in the midst. When Jesus had lifted up himself, and saw none but the woman, he said unto her, Woman, where are those thine accusers? hath no man condemned thee? She said, No man, Lord. And Jesus said unto her: Neither, do I condemn thee: go, and sin no more. *John 8:4-11*

In the 1907 Scofield Reference Bible we have a note here regarding C.I. Scofield's position on the Textual Criticism of this text. He points out that (Jn. 7:53 – 8:11) "is not found in the most ancient MSS." R.C.H Lenski in his Commentary of John states: "7:53–8:11 is not an integral part of John's Gospel." I just mention these textual criticisms since some see this text as completely obscure. My interest here is not the Greek text but the doctrine taught here regarding marriage.

Because of this text many folks out there say that adultery is not a serious sin since Jesus forgave the woman taken in adultery. I don't see that here. What I see is that the lawyers brought a case against this woman: "this woman was taken in adultery, in the very act." My position on this story is that for adultery the Law required: Lev 20:10 and Deut. 22:22 the death penalty: "And the man that committeth adultery with another man's wife, even he that committeth adultery with his neighbour's wife, the adulterer and the adulteress shall surely be put to death."

Since the man, the adulterer, in John 8 is absent from the court; Jesus throws the case out of court. They just did not have a case without the man. Case dismissed. I don't believe this is a case of adultery at all. It is a case of legal malpractice. I just will not teach a lesson on adultery here; although the text is textually obscure. It is also hermeneutically obscure in its relation to adultery.

We Be Not Born of Fornication Jn. 8:41

Ye do the deeds of your father. Then said they to him, We be not born of fornication; we have one Father, even God. *Jn. 8:41*

There are two views to the interpretation of this text (Jn. 8:41): (1) The first view sees the use of the word "fornication" by the Pharisees as a response to Jesus' insinuation in verse 38: "I speak that which I have seen of my Father: and you do that which ye have seen of your father." In that exchange Jesus implies that they seek to kill him because their father is not God but someone of an evil nature. Later

Jesus completes the thought in v.44 "Ye are of your father the devil." In v.41 the Pharisees try to certify that they are true Jews who have the genealogy to prove it; they are not born of fornication (idol worship, or children of Ishmael, or of such origin) but Abraham is literally our Father. Jesus rebuked them with if ye were Abraham's seed you would not seek to kill Me. Therefore, this view sees Jesus as insinuating that the Pharisees are born of fornication, i.e. that was the understanding of Jesus' previous charge.

(2) The second view believes that the Pharisees are angered by Jesus' insinuation that they are not true sons of Abraham therefore they attack Jesus' integrity—an attempt to assassinate His character—and therefore indirectly accuse Him of being born of fornication; apparently having knowledge of Jesus' birth to the virgin Mary.

I believe view (1) is the correct view. However, if one holds to the Betrothal view of "fornication" in Mt. 5:32 and 19:9 this second view would give you additional support for your understanding of betrothal-fornication in the exception clause.

Acts Chapters 15 and 21 Incest View; Unlawful Marriage View

> Wherefore my sentence is, that we trouble not them, which from among the Gentiles are turned to God: But that we write unto them, that they abstain from pollutions of idols, and from fornication, and from things strangled, and from blood. *Acts 15:19, 20*
>
> That ye abstain from meats offered to idols, and from blood, and from things strangled, and from fornication: from which if ye keep yourselves, ye shall do well. Fare ye well. *Acts 15:29*
>
> As touching the Gentiles which believe, we have written and concluded that they observe no such thing, save only that they keep themselves from things offered to idols, and from blood, and from strangled, and from fornication. *Acts 21:25*

As we continue into the N.T. some scholars find the above texts to be the next major reference in the incest view of porneia. As we explore these texts, known as the Jerusalem Decree, we notice some of the nomenclature of the priesthood. We should not be surprised to find that scholars see these texts as a clear reference to (Lev. 17, 18). Although Heth and Wenham do not embrace the Unlawful Marriage Incest View, or the Rabbinic Betrothal View they nevertheless give it some respect.

> Leaving the idea of mixed marriages—Jews with heathen, Heth and Wenham go on with this consideration: [my comment.] This is not impossible, but another view may offer greater possibilities of being the correct one [a reference to the Incest View, my comment]. In the light of the almost unanimous scholarly consensus that "porneia" in Acts 15:20, 29 and 21:25 denotes intercourse with close of kin [within the forbidden degrees—incest, my comment], that no great problem exists in lining up a moral regulation with several ceremonial restrictions, and that the four things prohibited by the decree [pollutions from idols, from fornication, from things strangled, and from blood - my comment] are the same four prohibited by the holiness Code of Leviticus 17-18 for both Israelites and strangers among them, it seems that the rabbinic [incest] variation of the unlawful marriage view has a better chance of being the correct one. On this view, Gentiles who had 'married' within the categories forbidden by Leviticus 18:6-18, upon becoming Christians, found themselves in a double-bind: caught by Jesus' absolute prohibition of divorce. Matthew solves their dilemma by inserting the clauses which indicated such unions were in fact non-marriages. They did not fall under Jesus' abso-

lute prohibition of divorce where a valid marriage is concerned.[225]

I see this commentary as a remarkable discussion that certainly places the Unlawful Marriage Incest View interpretation of the exception clauses as viable.

Romans 7:1-3 a Case for Permanency

> Know ye not, brethren, (for I speak to them that know the law,) how that the law hath dominion over a man as long as he liveth?
> For the woman which hath an husband is bound by the law to her husband so long as he liveth; but if the husband be dead, she is loosed from the law of her husband.
> So then if, while her husband liveth, she be married to another man, she shall be called an adulteress: but if her husband be dead, she is free from that law; so that she is no adulteress, though she be married to another man. *Rom. 7:1-3*

Our conscience is pricked with these words. They are so clear. The thought of permanency is so profound and so simple. This verse has created great difficulty for the "not permanency" camp. It clearly teaches permanency, causing the "not permanency" camp to cry, "But, But, But." The "permanency camp" realizes that this text is an illustration to explain a Christian's relation to the Law. As a widow is free from the law of her husband and free to remarry, so the Christian is no longer bound by the Law, but is free to marry another, i.e. Christ. The "dissolution camp" cries that this text is just an illustration, it is not a divorce text.

---

[225] Heth, Wehham: Jesus and Divorce, p. 154

The opponents of permanency-marriage cry out that Rom. 7:1-3 is not an MDR text. I totally disagree. In his reply to Pollentius, regarding MDR Augustine writes:

> What the Lord says as Master, therefore—that is, not in the nature of counsel on the part of one advising, but in the nature of a command on the part of one who is Master—cannot lawfully be left undone and is therefore inexpedient. So, the Lord commands: The woman is not to depart from the man, but if she departs (legal separation), for one reason, at any rate that makes the departure lawful, to remain unmarried or be reconciled to her husband (*1 Cor. 7:10, 11*). For the married woman is bound by the Law, while her husband is alive, and, while her husband is alive, she shall be called an adulteress, if she lives with another man (*Rom. 7:2, 3*), because the married woman is bound as long as her husband lives (*1 Cor. 7:39*). Wherefore, If the wife puts away her husband and marries another, she commits adultery (*Mk. 10:12*), and He who marries a woman who has been put away by her husband commits adultery (*Lk.16:18*)[226]

So, as you can see, Augustine works Rom. 7:1-3 along with Mark 10, Lk. 16, and I Cor. 7:10, 11, and 39 as if they are absolute cross references without any obscurity. I take the position that Rom. 7:1-3 is absolutely a MDR text. Yes, it does provide some illustration for Paul, but nevertheless, the illustrator, Paul, chose to dissolve marriage only by death, and that point must be addressed. From this verse it can be argued that Paul personally believed in a "permanency-marriage" doctrine; and as we shall see Paul believed in absolute permanency, as did Christ. This is a difficult thought to those looking for license to divorce; so as for the "dissolution" camp we see them laboring to con-

---

[226] Augustine, Adulterous Marriages, (trans. C.T. Huegelmeyer) Fathers of the Church, (M.M. Maryknoll NY, 1955) p. 93

vert Paul to their false doctrine. They cry that the Jews according to the law practiced divorce and remarriage as expounded in (Deut. 24:1-4), but this text was thoroughly discussed in Chapter 4 of this book—dear reader please keep in mind that Jesus rejected the Deuteronomy text and relegated it to a mere concession of Moses. Can any reader be sure that Paul wrote this text with the understanding that he was only making a general illustration of binding and loosening elements of the law? I believe that Paul's other writings combined with this text, will prove that creation-marriage, permanency marriage, was his view of a sound doctrine of MDR. The next text in our discovery is found in I Corinthians.

I Corinthians 5:1-5 Fornication Means Incest

> It is reported commonly that there is fornication among you, and such fornication as is not so much as named among the Gentiles, that one should have his father's wife.
>
> And ye are puffed up, and have not rather mourned, that he that hath done this deed might be taken away from among you.
>
> For I verily, as absent in body, but present in spirit, have judged already, as though I were present, concerning him that hath so done this deed,
>
> In the name of our Lord Jesus Christ, when ye are gathered together, and my spirit, with the power of our Lord Jesus Christ,
>
> To deliver such an one unto Satan for the destruction of the flesh, that the spirit may be saved in the day of the Lord Jesus. *I Cor. 5:1-5*

The Unlawful Marriage school, the incest view, has the right to claim this as a proof text in support of their understanding of porneia. The Corinthian church obviously did not get the message of Acts 15 and 21; reasoning that since they were NOT under the law, they were free from all aspects of the law. The interpretation of porneia in this context is not disputed. A man in the church had married his father's wife—the man's stepmother. It is only probable to assume that his father was dead. This was a clear violation of the Jerusalem Decree where fornication (incestuous marriage) was forbidden. Paul is alarmed. His distress is exasperated by the fact that the entire church had not only approved the unlawful marriage, but they were glorying in it, i.e. they were puffed up (literally proud of it). Consequently, Paul lashes out with his most severe N.T. censure, "In the name of our Lord Jesus Christ, when ye are gathered together, and my spirit, with the power of our Lord Jesus Christ, to deliver such an one unto Satan for the destruction of the flesh, that the spirit may be saved in the day of the Lord Jesus."

The professed believer, the fornicator, violated Leviticus 18:8, the nakedness of thy father's wife shalt thou not uncover: it is thy father's nakedness. Paul's doctrine is without question; he saw this marriage as a fornication-marriage that must be put away. This was an unlawful marriage, and Paul screamed it must be put away (divorce was immediate). So here in Corinth divorce was permitted for the exception, incest. Let us continue to follow Paul as he continues teaching his doctrine of creation-marriage.

I Corinthian 6:15-18 Permanency and the Body of Christ

> Know ye not that your bodies are the members of Christ? shall I then take the members of Christ, and make them the members of an harlot? God forbid.
>
> What? know ye not that he which is joined to an harlot is one body? for two, saith he, shall be one flesh.
>
> But he that is joined unto the Lord is one spirit. Flee fornication. Every sin that a man doeth is without the body; but he that committeth fornication sinneth against his own body. *I Cor. 6:15-18*

This text suggests that the Corinthian church was perhaps as corrupt as any church in history. Heth and Wenham commenting on I

Corinthians 7:2 (Nevertheless to avoid fornication), see a reference to I Corinthians six here: "As Fee suggests, the 'because of immoralities' (nevertheless, to avoid fornication, KJV) in verse 7:2 is probably a direct reference back to 6:12-20 where men, in all probability married, were going to the house of prostitutes (and possibly even at the suggestion of their ascetic wives?).[227] A doctrine existed in the Corinthian Church that permitted their men to have free sexual relations with the many prostitutes of that city. Paul cries out against this immorality, declaring that the believer's body—contrary to the Corinthian opinion—experienced salvation in Christ equally as his spirit. The body is for the Lord, and the Lord for the body. The body will experience redemption (resurrection). A believer's body is a member of Christ's body; it is a temple. By having sexual union with harlots, a believer was taking the members of Christ and uniting them to the harlot. In (I Cor. 6:18) Paul exhorts them to flee this kind of fornication. The union of Christ's body with a harlot is absolutely forbidden, because he that is joined to a harlot is one with a harlot, "For two, saith he, shall be one flesh." We should be one spirit and one flesh with Christ. Fornication is a sin against oneself. Fornication should not be committed in the temple of God, and your body is the temple of God the Holy Spirit. You no longer own your body, it has been bought (redeemed) by another. Bought with a price, the precious blood of the Lamb of God, our Lord and Savior Jesus Christ, who taketh away the sin of the world.

The Erasmian's draw an unusual conclusion from this text. Removing this text from the context of the Corinthian practice of a free permission to visit the brothel, they conclude that when a married person unites with a harlot something besides fornication has taken place. With the act of fornication their creation-marriage died, because their act created a new union. They reason that since fornication required them to unite with another, this could only be accomplished by dissolving the original union. This idea should be stricken from the record—to believe this is to deny the power of the Gospel

---

[227] Heth, Wenham; Jesus and Divorce p. 146 quoting Fee

that unites the believer to Christ forever. The text does not honor the thought of dissolution of any marriage. It is shear conjecture. Note that in spite of their sin, Paul indicates that all is well. He reaches in to salvage them, wholly. For this they have been chided and called on to repent; being offered complete Christian restoration: for after he chided them, he proclaims that they have been "bought with a price," bought means they are redeemed.

Contrary to the Erasmian's who see the dissolution of marriage in this text, the text clearly supports the permanency of marriage even in the event of fornication, i.e., in this case their unions with harlots. Paul clearly extends complete salvation to these sinning Corinthians. "You are bought with a price; therefore, glorify God in your body and in your spirit, which are God's." There is absolutely no mention of these men losing their wives (their earthly marriages), or salvation (their heavenly marriage to Christ) in this text. Their wives are for some reason unusually silent. Was it in fact that because they were ascetic, they were refraining from conjugal reciprocation. Did they believe abstinence was holiness? Well, chapter seven seems to answer that question in the affirmative. Nevertheless, chapter six is a victory for the permanency camp.

I Corinthians 7: Marriage Is Indissoluble

Here in I Cor. 7 we will find another field in this battleground of the "not permanency" camp. These forty verses are intertwined into a strong rope anchoring the text to the doctrine of permanency. There is but one possible thread that seems to give some hope to the "not permanency" group: verse 15. But before we discuss that verse let us examine each preceding verse of this chapter:

> Now concerning the things whereof ye wrote
> unto me: It is good for a man not to touch a woman.
> *I Cor. 7:1*

Paul here refers to a specific question about MDR from their earlier letter to him—remember the discussion at the conclusion to (I

Cor. 6)—by stating his primary position on marriage: "It is good for a man not to touch a woman." Paul's voluntary celibacy is his primary platform, and verses (7, 8, 25, 26, 40) reflect on that. He appears to directly reference (Matthew 19:11, 12) the eunuch reference: "All men cannot receive this saying, except they to whom it is given." Paul was one who made himself a eunuch for the kingdom's sake. He was able to receive the saying of Jesus. Gordon Fee understands that the "to touch" is a reference to sexuality in marriage. The word in classical Greek literature, and in the Greek O.T., is a figurative expression for sexual intercourse. The question the church obviously presented: Is it good for a man to abstain from sexual relations with a woman.[228] Therefore the real question of the text is not fornication—here referring to premarital sex—but is a question of marriage. In other words, Paul is saying that although he advises that men practice celibacy, nevertheless, because of strong sexual passions that they evidence, "it is better to marry then to burn,"(v. 9).

> Nevertheless, to avoid fornication, let every man have his own wife, and let every woman have her own husband. *I Cor. 7:2*

Here he simply permits marriage and enforces conjugal liberty in monogamous marriage: "own wife and own husband." This implies full conjugal rights and a right to full sexual satisfaction of the marriage bed. Paul's is forced to explain:

> Let the husband render unto the wife due benevolence: and likewise also the wife unto the husband.
>
> The wife hath not power of her own body, but the husband: and likewise also the husband hath not power of his own body, but the wife.
>
> Defraud ye not one the other, except it be with consent for a time, that ye may give yourselves to fast-

---

[228] Ibid. p. 145 quoting Fe

ing and prayer; and come together again, that Satan tempt you not for your incontinency. *1 Cor. 7:3-5*

Paul, a single man, has a marvelous grasp of marital relations, and a full understanding of copulation. Full sexual satisfaction of the marriage partners is their right. He clearly teaches that sexual satisfaction is in the power of each other partner. Impotence may not be the problem of the partner diagnosed with the malady. Paul goes as far as to make sexual satisfaction a moral right; he admonishes the partners not to defraud one another. The only room Paul provides for avoiding a partner is a period of fasting created by the burden to pray. Certainly, one cannot fast for a long period of time. But if a partner determines to fast the abstinence from conjugal rights is permitted during the fast. Fasting in the Scriptures meant to go without eating, not a mere abstinence of certain foods; it was the abstinence of all food—I believe that the act of fasting is only dictated by the urgency to pray; in other words the only reason a man or woman fasts is because they are too busy praying—the period of fasting here was obviously a relatively short period, other-wise, Paul states that there is no room for asceticism in marriage.

Paul moves away from the married for a moment, and now addresses the unmarried and widows:

> But I speak this by permission, and not of commandment.
> For I would that all men were even as I myself. But every man hath his proper gift of God, one after this manner, and another after that.
> I say therefore to the unmarried and widows, It is good for them if they abide even as I.
> But if they cannot contain, let them marry: for it is better to marry than to burn. *I Cor. 7:6-9*

Paul, in this parenthetical note, states that what he is about to say is not a commandment; but as you will see shortly, he will speak by commandment in (v.10, 11). Paul obviously sees celibacy as a voluntary, or as a special gift from God. He then gives his personal testimony, that he is one who has been given special grace, he is celibate, but he goes on to permit others to marry. This is a marriage text. Paul stresses his personal belief that celibacy is his preference for all men. He then defines the eligible for marriage as the unmarried and the widows. Note here that Paul specifically sees unmarried people as never-been-married-people, or those with a dead partner. But Paul does not stop there. He recommends marriage over burning in sexual desire; for if burning is not cooled, it will foster fornication. Paul will now reverse his role as a guidance counselor and speak as a prophet of the living God:

> And unto the married I command, yet not I, but
> the Lord, Let not the wife depart from her husband:
> But and if she depart, let her remain unmarried, or
> be reconciled to her husband: and let not the husband
> put away his wife. *I Cor. 7:10, 11*

Gordon Fee comments: "This is the only command in the entire chapter. While Paul displays ambivalence toward whether widowers and widows should get married (vv. 8-9), he consistently rejects the notion that the married may dissolve their marriages."[229] Fee continues: Jesus in effect interpreted the seventh commandment to mean NO divorce;[230] and Paul in keeping with his own personal view expressed elsewhere that for the believer's marriage is permanent, from its inception until the decease of one of its partners (1 Cor. 7:39 and Rom. 7:1-3).

This text solidly embraces permanency. Note: This is not Paul's command, it is the actual command of the Lord Jesus Christ. Paul explicitly tells us this: "And unto the married I command, yet not I, but

---

[229] Fee, Gordon D. NICNT The First Epistle to the Corinthians (Eerdmans, Grand Rapids, 1987 p. 291

[230] Ibid. p. 293

the Lord." (Fee again reports that, "This is one of the rare instances in Paul's extant letters when he appeals directly to the teaching of Jesus.")[231] Paul makes no exceptions for divorce. He interprets Jesus' Gospel texts of Mark and Luke perfectly; he is in perfect agreement with the Lord Jesus Christ. I see this text as a clear repudiation of remarriage after divorce or during the life of a living partner, regardless of any condition—Absolutely without Exception. Even if as some writers believe, that depart refers to divorce—which I see as conjecture—then there is again an unmistakable command not to remarry.[232] I believe the word depart here means to separate without divorce; regardless, the idea of permanency-marriage is the focus of this text. The husband is commanded by God not to put away (divorce) his wife. It is as if Paul is exclaiming Jesus' permanency doctrine that he preached to the Pharisees and His disciples: "They twain shall be one flesh; and What therefore God hath joined together, let not man put asunder." Paul certainly knew and understood what Jesus taught as Paul himself now teaches the same doctrine of permanency-creation-marriage here in Corinth.

The other important doctrine here is the doctrine of reconciliation, which must remain a permanent option for this N.T. marriage scenario; reconciliation speaks of Salvation by Grace Alone. Therefore, we can conclude that Jesus, Mark, Luke, and Paul are in complete agreement, the only obscure text belongs to Matthew, and as I have labored throughout this entire dissertation to show that Matthew is also in full agreement—providing that Matthew referred to fornication, as a reference either to Betrothal Fornication, or Marriage Incest as I have noted.

One additional observation: If one teaches that marriage is dissoluble and that a remarriage is possible and permitted, then that teacher is not permitting the door of reconciliation to remain open. This can only be done by employing the Law (with the fantasy that the offender is dead). If this is the case that teacher has forsaken the

---

[231] Ibid. p. 291

[232] Heth, Wenham; Jesus and Divorce; p. 137

Gospel of Grace, for the Works of the Law. (Think about it!) The only way one can permit divorce and remarriage is to preach the Law, and to forsake Grace.

As Lincoln said: Let us go on to the city of boots; the battle of Gettysburg draweth nigh; (the last decisive battle of this war).

> But to the rest speak I, not the Lord: If any brother hath a wife that believeth not, and she be pleased to dwell with him, let him not put her away.
>
> And the woman which hath an husband that believeth not, and if he be pleased to dwell with her, let her not leave him.
>
> For the unbelieving husband is sanctified by the wife, and the unbelieving wife is sanctified by the husband: else were your children unclean; but now are they holy. *I Cor. 7:12-14*

The question of the mixed marriage, the believer with the unbeliever surfaced in Corinth. Paul only instructs the believer. His primary instruction is that the believer should not put away the unbeliever. He does indicate that if the unbeliever is pleased to remain in the union, then that union is holy, or sanctified. The believer is commanded to stay with the marriage; it is the unbeliever who is not commanded. The unbeliever appears to have the right to control the outcome. Paul gives the unbeliever the right of choice. If the unbeliever is pleased to remain, then he/she may do as he/she pleases. The choice is entirely with the unbeliever. The believer must permit the unbeliever the choice. Mixed marriages are holy in these circumstances; thus, the children are not unclean but holy:

I Cor. 7:15: the Pauline Privilege: Yes, or No?

> But if the unbelieving depart, let him depart. A brother or a sister is not under bondage in such cases: but God hath called us to peace. *I Cor. 7:15*

Gordon Fee has with pen and ink made this profound statement:

> This statement is the source of the notorious "Pauline Privilege," in which the text is understood to mean that the believer is free to remarry. BUT despite a long tradition that has so interpreted it, several converging data indicate that Paul is essentially repeating his first sentence: that the believer is not bound to maintain the marriage if the pagan partner opts out.
>
> (1) Remarriage is not an issue at all: indeed, it seems to be quite the opposite. In a context in which people are arguing for the right to dissolve marriage, Paul would scarcely be addressing the issue of remarriage, and certainly not in such circuitous fashion. (2) The verb "to be under bondage" is not his ordinary one for the "binding" character of marriage (cf. 7:39; Rom. 7:2); that means that Paul does not intend to say one is not "bound to the marriage."[233]

The believer must permit the unbeliever the choice. The unbeliever has the freedom to make the choice; and since the unbeliever has the free choice to depart, the believer then has the responsibility to permit that departure, peacefully. As we said earlier, marriage has always invoked the man's sense of sovereignty and ownership, his sense of authority. A believer might even argue that the unbeliever does not have the right to depart based on Jesus command, "Let not man put asunder," and "They twain shall be one flesh." Although this is so, it is nevertheless true, that God permits man the right to choose, even if the choice is sinful or leads to his destruction—However in this case the departure does not dissolve the marriage—as Fee reported: "while Paul displays ambivalence toward whether widowers and widows should get married (vv. 8-9), he consistently rejects the notion that the married may dissolve their marriages;" the unbeliever thus,

---

[233] Fee, Gordon NICNT I Cor. p. 302-303

cannot dissolve the marriage. They can depart legally, but no divorce court can dissolve their creation marriage.

The Scriptures are clear in teaching that the believer is not under bondage to force the unbeliever to stay. He/she must not thwart that free choice. The unbeliever must be permitted to leave in peace. In God-speed if you will. The believer is not bound to force the unbeliever to remain, however the believer is bound to permit the unbeliever to leave in peace with the hope of a future restoration; always restoration and reconciliation, the mark of Salvation by Grace; the only Christian Gospel. The Christian must extend to the unbeliever the invitation to return to the marriage bond and must remain unmarried as taught in (v. 10, 11) thus permitting the indissoluble union to physically reunite again should repentance and salvation take hold of the departed one. To the believer this is the true essence of love. As with the Grace of God, He waits for the return of all unbelievers and for wayward believers. God keeps the door of His heart ready to open; all we have to do is come and knock. We as pastors must teach our dear people to do the same for the lost husband or wife. The believing partner must keep the door of his/her heart ready to open and must keep the literal door of his/her home ready to open it's door to the departed spouse. Hope must not be abandoned; hope that the lost partner will find true repentance and faith upon their return and be saved. What better words can be said then these:

> For what knowest thou, O wife, whether thou shalt save thy husband? Or how knowest thou, O man whether thou shalt save thy wife? *I Cor. 7:16*

Gordon Fee, again has a fitting comment regarding the indissolubility of marriage in this case:

> What is not allowed is remarriage, both because for him that presupposes the teaching of Jesus that such is adultery and because in the Christian commu-

nity reconciliation is the norm. If the Christian husband and wife cannot be reconciled to one another, then how can they expect to become models of reconciliation before a fractured and broken world?[234]

The extension of love to the departed is intended to bring the loved one to salvation, "whether thou shalt save thy husband, or thy wife." I find this statement very interesting since the salvation of the departed loved one is now the target of the believer's love. He/she must pray for the departed loved one to be saved. The question this verse raises is: When do we stop? When do we stop praying for them to return to the Lord, and to us? This verse indicates that the believer permitted the unbeliever to leave in peace, and with the condition that when they return it implies the hope that they will also accept Christ as their own personal Savior, and thus be saved—this all involves the repentance, forgiveness, and restoration of this returning sinner. You never stop praying for your loved ones until your, or their dying day. Therefore, this verse states that unless the unbelieving spouse returns there is to be no remarriage for the believer this-side-of-death. Again, this verse speaks for permanency; even if that partner is never heard from again, or even if the believer has no knowledge of whether they are dead or alive. This is the complete translation of Ephesians 5:25: Husbands love your wives, even as Christ also loved the church, and gave himself for it—that verse could just as well read: Wives love your husbands, even as Christ also loved the church, and gave himself for it.

I agree and say, NO to the Pauline Privilege. No, it is not God's will for His MDR; it's false doctrine. Period! As in the Civil War and Gettysburg, verse 15-16 of I Cor. 7 marks the last pivotal battle of the Biblical Marriage Divorce War. It is the last significant battle and permanency-marriage is the victor. From here we will go on to exposit the few remaining pertinent texts of our topic. The conclusion draweth nigh.

---

[234] Ibid. p. 296

In verses (17-24) Paul introduces a parenthetical statement regarding the need for men to be content with their personal calling. He simply exhorts: The believer is to stay as one was when called.

1 Cor. 7:25-40 One Completely Related Section: About Virgins

The one most remarkable fact concerning this section of Scripture is that it also has all the characteristics of an "obscure text;" as any study of the commentaries will demonstrate. Gordon Fee understands that the word "virgin" in this section (7:25-40) as one motif and the definition of "virgin" must be determined by this whole section. He then breaks this section down: (a) Singleness is preferable but not required (25-28); (b) Paul's reasons for singleness (29-35); (c) But marriage is no sin (36-40).[235] I believe this is the correct approach.

Singleness is preferable but not required: verses (25-28)

> Now concerning virgins I have no commandment of the Lord: yet I give my judgment, as one that hath obtained mercy of the Lord to be faithful.
> I suppose therefore that this is good for the present distress, I say, that it is good for a man so to be.
> Art thou bound unto a wife? seek not to be loosed. Art thou loosed from a wife? seek not a wife.
> But and if thou marry, thou hast not sinned; and if a virgin marry, she hath not sinned. Nevertheless, such shall have trouble in the flesh: but I spare you. *I Cor. 7:25-28*

Paul's reasons for singleness: verses (29-35)

> But this I say, brethren, the time is short: it remaineth, that both they that have wives be as though they had none;

---

[235] Ibid. p. 232

And they that weep, as though they wept not; and they that rejoice, as though they rejoiced not; and they that buy, as though they possessed not;

And they that use this world, as not abusing it: for the fashion of this world passeth away.

But I would have you without carefulness. He that is unmarried careth for the things that belong to the Lord, how he may please the Lord:

But he that is married careth for the things that are of the world, how he may please his wife.

There is difference also between a wife and a virgin. The unmarried woman careth for the things of the Lord, that she may be holy both in body and in spirit: but she that is married careth for the things of the world, how she may please her husband.

And this I speak for your own profit; not that I may cast a snare upon you, but for that which is comely, and that ye may attend upon the Lord without distraction. *I Cor. 7:29-35*

But marriage is no sin: verses (36-40)

But if any man think that he behaveth himself uncomely toward his virgin, if she pass the flower of her age, and need so require, let him do what he will, he sinneth not: let them marry.

Nevertheless, he that standeth stedfast in his heart, having no necessity, but hath power over his own will, and hath so decreed in his heart that he will keep his virgin, doeth well.

So then he that giveth her in marriage doeth well; but he that giveth her not in marriage doeth better.

The wife is bound by the law as long as her husband liveth; but if her husband be dead, she is at liberty to be married to whom she will; only in the Lord.

> But she is happier if she so abide, after my judg-
> ment: and I think also that I have the Spirit of God.
> *I Cor. 7:36-40*

Fee takes the position that the virgins here are betrothed women; which has the advantage of seeing both 27-28 and 36-38 as being addressed to the same man. (This is the crux interpretum of this section as far as this writer is concerned.) Paul's concept of the times in which he lived was that of "distress", and in this state it was better for a man to remain unmarried. Paul repeats his appeal for men to be content with their calling: Let every man, wherein, he is called, there abide with God. If you are bound in marriage to a wife, seek not to be loosed; if your loosed from a wife, seek not a wife. Paul is using common language to make a point. To be bound to a wife simply means to be married, and to be loosed from a wife means the person is single or a widow. It means this and nothing more. From this chapter we have shown that the unmarried are people who have never been married. An of course as Paul opened the chapter with his it is better to marry than to burn he now continues that theme with if a virgin marry, she hath not sinned. So Paul concludes this chapter with the teaching as Fee comments: "But Marriage Is No Sin."

Heth and Wenham note that the best interpretation of virgins in the context under discussion (v. 25-38) is that of J.K. Elliott.

> "He demonstrates that these virgins are engaged [betrothed] couples. In the rest of the NT 'virgin' is commonly used of a betrothed girl (Lk. 1:27, Matt. 1:18, 23; 25:1-13; II Cor. 11:2), and throughout verses 25-38 Paul addresses the men, and his special notations are to the women (cf. vv. 28b,34). The question these engaged couples ask Paul is whether or not to fulfill their promises of marriage in view of the present distress. So when Paul says in verse 28, 'But if you should marry, you have not sinned', he is not speaking to divorced individuals as a good number of

Erasmians suppose. He is speaking to those who are bound by a promise of marriage (= engaged) in verse 27. It is to this group that Paul says, 'But if you should marry, you have not sinned'(v28a).[236]

Nevertheless, he that standeth steadfast in his heart, having no necessity, but hath power over his own will, and hath so decreed in his heart that he will keep his virgin, doeth well. I Cor. 7:37

So then he that giveth her in marriage doeth well; but he that giveth her not in marriage doeth better. *I Cor. 7:38*

Paul's conclusion regarding the engaged: Yes, you can marry, but if you remain single it is "better." Paul now returns to the others who are loosed: widows:

The wife is bound by the law as long as her husband liveth; but if her husband be dead, she is at liberty to be married to whom she will; only in the Lord. *1 Cor. 7:39*

Paul repeats what he said in Romans 7:2. Augustine employed this verse 7:39 with as much energy in his defense of permanency marriage, as he did Romans 7:2-3. The point that is very interesting to this writer is that in both cases Paul does not even hint at any other event that could loose the marriage bond; absolutely no exceptions. Paul teaches a permanency doctrine which is equal to his Lord (7:10, 11). This fact reinforces the doctrine that states: "no-remarriage-this-side-of-death." Paul gives the approval of remarriage after the death of a partner. Here he appropriately chooses the death of the husband. It seems that antiquity even declares that women outlived the men. Consequently, the church as a social unit had to manage widows, to which the NT attests. Again the widows were admonished to remain single, and as a matter of fact they were looked upon

---

[236] Heth, Wenham; Jesus and Divorce; p. 137

as worldly if they did remarry: "But the younger widows refuse; for when they have begun to wax wanton against Christ, they will marry, having damnation, because they have cast off their first faith," (I Tim. 5:11, 12). Nevertheless, widows were permitted to marry, however this is to be "only in the Lord." This careful instruction compounded with the regulations of widows gives credence to the position that the NT does not make any remarriage provision for those who believe in divorce.

2 Cor. 6:14-18 The Unequal Yoke: and Marriage

Both the O.T. and the N.T. is filled with the idea of separation of believers and unbelievers in various texts. Their primary purpose is to separate Christ from Belial (Satan); that is to separate the truth of God, from the lies of Satan, or Light from Darkness. So here we have a broad range of applications for the exhortation: "Be ye not unequally yoked together with unbelievers". It's first real application to this rule to marriage was in the Law that forbid the men of Israel to intermarry with women of the nations of Canaan.

> Deut. 7:1 When the LORD thy God shall bring thee into the land whither thou goest to possess it, and hath cast out many nations before thee, the Hittites, and the Girgashites, and the Amorites, and the Canaanites, and the Perizzites, and the Hivites, and the Jebusites, seven nations greater and mightier than thou;
> Deut. 7:2 And when the LORD thy God shall deliver them before thee; thou shalt smite them, and utterly destroy them; thou shalt make no covenant with them, nor shew mercy unto them:
> Deut. 7:3 Neither shalt thou make marriages with them; thy daughter thou shalt not give unto his son, nor his daughter shalt thou take unto thy son.
> Deut. 7:4 For they will turn away thy son from following me, that they may serve other gods: so will

the anger of the LORD be kindled against you, and destroy thee suddenly.

Paul's application of this separation in 2Cor. 6 includes the use of Isa. 52:11 where Isaiah refers to the call for separation of the Nation of Israel, from their oppressor kingdoms of the world (Babylon) and Israel is nationally redeemed in the restored Millennial Kingdom

> Isa 52:11 Depart ye, depart ye, go ye out from thence, touch no unclean thing; go ye out of the midst of her; be ye clean, that bear the vessels of the LORD.
> Isa 52:12 For ye shall not go out with haste, nor go by flight: for the LORD will go before you; and the God of Israel will be your rereward.

This same text is used in the book of Revelation addressing the call to God's people to come out of the wicked city Babylon:

> Rev 18:4 And I heard another voice from heaven, saying, Come out of her, my people, that ye be not partakers of her sins, and that ye receive not of her plagues.

Here in 2 Cor. 6 we find Paul employing the Isa. 52:11-12 text to warn the Corinthian Church to separate from the false teachers who were infiltrating Paul's church at Corinth. This use of Isaiah is the basic idea of separation from false religions, idols, teachers, etc. This is the foundation of the "be ye not unequally yoke together." These false teachers in 2 Cor. 11:13-14 are called Satan's angels:

> 2Co 11:13 For such are false apostles, deceitful workers, transforming themselves into the apostles of Christ.
> 2Co 11:14 And no marvel; for Satan himself is transformed into an angel of light.

Here, Paul calls the believers in Corinth out of this darkness:

> 2Co 6:14 Be ye not unequally yoked together with unbelievers: for what fellowship hath righteousness with unrighteousness? and what communion hath light with darkness?
> 2Co 6:15 And what concord hath Christ with Belial? or what part hath he that believeth with an infidel?
> 2Co 6:16 And what agreement hath the temple of God with idols? for ye are the temple of the living God; as God hath said, I will dwell in them, and walk in them; and I will be their God, and they shall be my people.
> 2Co 6:17 Wherefore come out from among them, and be ye separate, saith the Lord, and touch not the unclean thing; and I will receive you,

There are many applications for the doctrine of being not unequally yoked together with unbelievers. It certainly has it application to marriage. However, the strongest textual application to Christian marriage is 1 Cor.7:39:

> I Cor. 7:39 The wife is bound by the law as long as her husband liveth; but if her husband be dead, she is at liberty to be married to whom she will; only in the Lord.

Here it is a definite command: The widow could remarry but ONLY in the Lord. It certainly should be the rule for Christian marriage. However, this is the strongest language we have textually. So the question is: Does the Lord unite "any" believers with unbelievers. The Scripture does lend itself to an answer with I Cor.7:13-14:

1Co 7:13 And the woman which hath an husband that believeth not, and if he be pleased to dwell with her, let her not leave him.

1Co 7:14 For the unbelieving husband is sanctified by the wife, and the unbelieving wife is sanctified by the husband: else were your children unclean; but now are they holy.

Here God defines these two as married and even goes on to say that the children are holy. I believe that sets the tone for a possible mixed marriage of a believer and an unbeliever. It is not the best arrangement, but it appears the order of creation-marriage applies here. It certainly applies with two unbelievers. Marriage as an institution precedes the state, Israel, or the Church.

Another principal teaching in the marriage doctrine of the church is that marriage like other partnerships, i.e. business partnerships, is to be between two believers. A partnership between a believer and an unbeliever is unequal: Be ye not unequally yoked together with unbelievers; for what fellowship hath righteousness with unrighteousness? And what communion hath light with darkness (II Cor. 6:14).

Husband of One Wife; Wife of One Man 1 Tim 3:2; 5:9

1 Tim. 3:2 A bishop then must be blameless, the husband of one wife, vigilant, sober, of good behaviour, given to hospitality, apt to teach; ITim. 3:12 Let the deacons be the husbands of one wife, ruling their children and their own houses well.

1 Tim 5:9 Let not a widow be taken into the number under threescore years old, having been the wife of one man.

The divorce-remarriage advocates have pounced on these two verses in (1 Tim. 3:2 and 3:12) asserting that they permit remarriage after divorce for the saints in the church, but that remarriage after divorce is forbidden to the bishop (pastor) and deacon; and at times forbidden to the Sunday school teacher, and other leaders in the church. This is a fallacy for two reasons: (1) divorce is forbidden to all; (2) and that remarriage after divorce is also forbidden to all. Period! So: the interpretation of the divorce-remarriage camp is in error. Please remember that Paul is the writer here, and we have established that Paul never taught that divorce was permissible and much less remarriage.

Notice the heading to this section: I also mention the "wife of one man" (1 Tim. 5:9). Paul wrote those words, "wife of one man" and he knew well what he said. So: What is this doctrine of the wife of one man? Let's see: Paul was writing about widows. Yes, and he was writing the doctrine of widows, as he wrote the doctrine of the bishop-pastor and the deacons. Marriage was certainly an element of all three parties (bishop; deacon; widow). The pastor and deacon were required to be the husband of one wife; and now Paul states his primary command: "Let not the widow be taken into the number under threescore years old, *HAVING BEEN THE WIFE OF ONE MAN, BOTH THE PASTOR AND DEACON WERE REQUIRED TO BE THE HUSBAND OF ONE WIFE.* Therefore: Here Paul has the pastor, deacon, and the widow-indeed as only permitted one spouse, wife or husband, in their life time. Paul goes on to deride the younger widows who would not live up to this standard:

> 1 Tim 5:11 But the younger widows refuse: for when they have begun to wax wanton against Christ, they will marry;
> 1 Tim 5:12 Having damnation, because they have cast off their first faith.

As Paul admonishes the younger widows who remarry; should he not also require the pastors and deacons to be subject to the same standard as the women of the church; and have equal treatment by the hand of God. Therefore, it is only fitting that the pastors and deacons should be treated equally as the widows-indeed; and so they are, as we see in 1 Tim. 3:2; 3:12; and 5:9. Thus, the permanency-marriage camp sees the pastors and deacons having the exact same requirement, i.e. the husband of one wife in their lifetime; as the widows having been the wife of one husband in their lifetime.

Ephesians 5:21-32 the Mount Everest of Marriage

Yes, this is the mountain peak of the doctrine of creation-marriage; as the book of Ephesians is the mountain peak of all N.T. doctrine regarding the Gospel. Douglas B. MacCorkle has written a splendid commentary on Ephesians titled, God's Special Secret. This special secret is fully revealed in (Eph. 5:32), "This is a great mystery, but I speak concerning Christ and the church." God's love affair with man culminates in his special gift of grace, i.e. permission to enter into the life of the trinity through Christ and become one with the Godhead, in the body of Christ, His Church.[237]The beauty of this love affair is highlighted by the analogy of what we know about permanent-creation-marriage. God chose to explain the church by taking us pedagogically—from the known to the unknown—by first taking us to what we know, permanent-creation-marriage, then onto his new doctrine of the union of Christ and the believer, the Church; as a marriage, literally the twain becoming one, indivisible man in Christ Jesus: "Having abolished in his flesh the enmity, even the law of commandments contained in ordinances, to make in himself of twain one new man, so making peace; and that he might reconcile both unto God in one body by the cross" Eph 2:15ff. This analogy of the body of Christ is the grandest truth we will ever know about the Gospel and creation-marriage. Ephesians has been called the Alps of the New Testament, and its teaching elevates marriage to shine as from the world's highest peak. This truth is so fundamental to the teaching of Christ, and to our Salvation that it cannot but receive our adoration,

---

[237] MacCorkle, Douglas; God's Special Secret (MBM Books, Cocoa Beach, FL 1993

and deepest conviction to understand, document, protect, and propagate. Oh, the unsearchable riches of Christ.

In the first three chapters of Ephesians Paul labors to explain the position of the believer specifically using the terms "in" Christ; almost countless times—a dozen times in chapter one alone. I like to explain the preposition "in" by envisioning a box. The believer is in the box. Paul emphatically states that the believer is in the box forever, literally in heavenly places in Christ. Permanently. This is an extremely important theological truth. This is the doctrine of grace; Sola Gratia. To be one with Christ is to be in the box; "And gave Him to be the head over all things to the church, which is his body, the fullness of him that filleth all in all" (Eph. 1:22, 23). The believer joined in one (married) to Christ is the Church; His body.

> Submitting yourselves one to another in the fear
> of God. *Eph. 5:21*

MacCorkle notes that a strong debate has raged over whether this verse goes with what went before in 5:3-19 (especially 5:18, 19) or what comes after, i.e. the subject of marriage. His response is simple, i.e. "This is indeed a transitional verse looking both ways." I believe he is certainly correct. Therefore, the doctrine of permanent-heaven-marriage begins with some practical applications of permanent-creation-marriage. Perhaps to the chagrin of the chauvinist type, the admonition begins with: "submitting yourselves one to another in the fear of God." In marriage, husband and wife are to both submit to each other. Paul clearly establishes the authority, i.e. the common denominator, "in the fear of God." The omnipotent sovereign Everlasting God is a powerful force to reckon with, leaving no room for insubordination. I find this verse leveling to both the husband and the wife, and superior to whatever follows: as some wrongly believe the word "submit" only refers to the wife. Please note verse 21 precedes verse 22 which requires the husband to submit to his wife and the wife to submit to her husband.

> Wives, submit yourselves unto your own hus-
> bands, as unto the Lord. *Eph. 5:22*

Again, MacCorkle catches the spirit of the submission text with his English version of the original Greek text: "For example, the wives are to keep submitting themselves to their own husbands in the Lord." He also expounds Gen. 3:16, "thy desire shall be to thy husband, and he shall rule over thee;" stating that Paul is only applying the Genesis marriage doctrine to having the husband rule and administer the home. This is God's will for the wife. The level of subordination called for here is lower than the one previous. In a godly manner the wife is to submit to the husband as she submits to the Lord. Mac Corkle argues that this must be a voluntary submission; i.e. that as the Lord loves her and she submits to His care for her, the wife is commanded to submit to her husband who cares for her. Should her husband require her to perform an act outside of God's will, we must note here: that she is told to submit to her husband as she would submit to her benevolent Lord. Therefore, should her husband's command be without the Lord's benevolence, she is free to follow the Lord; whatever that will mean to her husband. This verse certainly requires the husband's command to be benevolent. MacCorkle makes an interesting comment: "To their own husbands," may seem an unnecessary statement, but only to the naive. The track record of worldlings in this regard is an open one—certainly some words to contemplate. The idea of the husband's benevolence will go without saying for the husband will be commanded by God to love his wife in benevolence to the very point of dying for her if necessary.

> For the husband is the head of the wife, even as
> Christ is the head of the church: and he is the saviour
> of the body. Therefore, as the church is subject unto
> Christ, so let the wives be to their own husbands in
> everything. *Eph. 5:23, 24*

The wife's subordination is further clarified. The husband is the head of the wife, even as Christ is the head of the church. This can be supported by I Cor. 11:3, "But I would have you know, that the head of every man is Christ; and the head of the woman is the man; and the head of Christ is God." Christ to the church is Savior. The church submits to its benevolent Savior. Likewise, the wife is to be subject to her own husband when he treats her as his church, because he is her savior-type here on the earth. Benevolence is written all over the definition of a husband that is to be obeyed. Certainly, if the husband's commands are driven from a benevolent heart as from the Lord, then of course she is expected to obey her husband in everything. MacCorkle makes another fitting comment: "No sane person would suggest that wives be as Jezebel (I Kings 21:15, 23) or Herodias" (Mk. 6:19ff).

Husbands, love your wives, even as Christ also
loved the church, and gave himself for it; *Eph. 5:25*

We now come to the clincher in the submission debate. Paul now rolls out his big gun of submission and fires a round squarely into the heart of every husband. Paul now defines the submission necessary of the husband. As Christ hung on a bloody cross and died, dying for his beloved wife, the church, every husband is commanded to submit to God and to love his wife as Christ loved the church and if need be, be ready to give himself in death for her. This is the matchless definition of love. Only God can define love for God is Love. The ramification of this kind of love on the marriage bond is infinite. MacCorkle states, "Godly loving of his wife is put in the imperative form, a direct commandment of the Lord." The point here is not that the husband should just take a bullet for his wife, but that he should wear himself to the point of death for his wife if necessary; that of course does not void the former, the bullet. Now dear reader it also means that the forsaken believing spouse must wear themselves out till death, if necessary, waiting for their departed love one to return. This is the biting and perhaps the real bullet of death for your beloved spouse. Oh, so great love as He loved us; this is the actual Matchless Grace of God. What a wonderful testimony of a believing spouse. What a sacrifice! But divorce with remarriage is death to the spouse, and this is the teaching of the Law. What a contrast to Matchless Grace, the Gospel we preach in creation-marriage.

This verse makes the analogy complete. Christ's work in establishing his wife the church contains the full definition of Salvation by Grace; Sola Gratia. His remarkable work of redemption was fully displayed in His love for his wife the church. The Scripture states: "For when we were yet without strength, in due time Christ died for the ungodly. For scarcely for a righteous man will one die: yet peradventure for a good man some would even dare to die. But God commendeth his love toward us, in that, while we were yet sinners, Christ died for us. Much more then, being now justified by his blood, we shall be saved from wrath through him. For if, when we were enemies, we were reconciled to God by the death of his Son, much more, being reconciled, we shall be saved by his life (Rom. 5:6-10)." The union of Christ with His church was sealed in blood; a permanent marriage. The believer is literally in Christ and Christ is in the believer. The believer is literally the body of Christ: "And hath put all things under his feet, and gave him to be the head over all things to the church, which is his body, the fullness of him that filleth all in all (Eph. 1:22, 23)."

Dear reader lean forward for a moment and listen. Salvation means the eternal deliverance from all evil, i.e. the power and penalty of sin, and to be one with Christ and God. The believer is delivered from death both temporal and eternal. The believer becomes the body of Christ, who rose from the dead and now lives forever. Christ's body will never die. He that hath the Son hath life. That means every believer has security for eternity—Eternal Security. Marriage is therefore a picture of eternal security. "What therefore God hath joined together, let not man put asunder." Marriage, like the salvation of the church, is permanent; the gates of Hell shall not prevail against it. The Doctrine of Eternal Security is identified with permanent-creation-marriage. Permanent-heaven-marriage is the doctrine of Christ and His Church; therefore, as we have taught all creation-marriages are inseparable, indissoluble, and permanent. Thus, there is no-remar-riage-this-side-of-death because once married the couple is bound until death due them part; they have become one flesh on this earth till the death of their flesh due them part. Divorce of a marriage is impossible. So then while both partners live on this earth there is no other marriage for them; remarriage during the lifetime of a married partner is adultery. The analogy that God makes between marriage and the church dictates that as salvation is permanent and sure, so too marriage is permanent and sure. Therefore, the preacher who pro-motes the doctrine of divorce is at the very same time teaching that a believer can lose his salvation; thus, teaching that Christ will divorce the believer if He so wishes. That is a false doctrine. The primary problem with the one who teaches that salvation can be lost is that at the same time he is confessing to the doctrine that a man can gain or work for his salvation.

But our salvation is sure: "He that hath the Son hath life", and "My sheep hear my voice, and I know them, and they follow me: And I give unto them eternal life; and they shall never perish, neither shall any man pluck them out of my hand." Does this sound like Jesus will divorce one of his sheep if He so wishes? Fear not Christian, Christ will not divorce me nor thee.

Therefore, marriage is binding even in the event of adultery. Remember that Jesus took on the church while we were yet sin-ners and reconciled us while we were enemies. Love is at the heart of the matter. The innocent partner must provide the way for the adulterer— or any other marriage breaking sin of the partner—and permit the door of repentance to remain open as the way for the departed spouse to return to full marital union. Thus, marriage is a picture of salvation. (I certainly am not advocating sacramentalism).

If one does not provide the way of return and repentance for the separated guilty spouse, then one certainly does not preach Christ and His Gospel of Grace. For the Gospel is always open to the sinner, and that offer is until death does us part. The only time that God's offer of salvation is removed from the spouse is when the spouse dies and leaves this world. Jesus by equating His marriage with His church to human marriage declares that marriage on the earth is life long—a measure of the time that one lives on the earth. And that since a man establishes his salvation by faith—without the deeds of the flesh—then the door and way of faith in the marriage of earthly wedded couples must be kept open for their guilty partner during their lifetime. If you have followed my argument I have said: To believe in divorce is to believe in works for salvation. By divorcing a spouse, you are saying that the failed spouse has lost their picture of salvation by Grace alone; and thus, is to be accursed. The concept of divorce terribly fails to meet the analogy of marriage that God teaches us in (Eph. 5).

I am not preaching sacramental marriage—the Roman Catholic doctrine of receiving grace through marriage—I am teaching that marriage is a type or a picture of salvation. Some do not seem to understand the complications caused by sin in a marriage. The guilty spouse who believes in non-permanency marriage may have found in their eyes a more attractive person, which led to adultery. That spouse may see their "salvation" in this situation as: divorce with remarriage to the person of adultery. But according to permanency marriage the only thing that spouse has accomplished is to make-believe that their adultery is holy. Their adultery is continuous adultery and the children of adultery are always bastard-children. If the spouse had any children by their first spouse, those children are holy, and that spouse is the true parent of those children forever. But the children of adultery are unholy—this is compounded for evil when their pastor teaches that divorce with remarriage is holy, even holy for the saint in the pew. This is permitting and blessing adulterous-marriage to take communion with the Church. Adulterous-marriage is all too common in our evil world today; as stated some people just don't understand the complications of divorce with remarriage; and some pastors endorse divorce and then a life of continuous-adultery in remarriage. Thus, mixing the Law with Grace; they together are insoluble, they do not mix. Period! And what does this mean to one's soteriology (doctrine of salvation)? This is the back breaker and the ultimate danger. The Bible clearly reveals that adulterers shall not inherit the Kingdom of God. We are not discussing some minor point here; we are literally talking about Heaven and Hell (I Cor. 5:19-21; Gal. 5:5; I Cor. 6:9-10).

The other side of the coin here is that when the innocent spouse sues for divorce, they deny the guilty partner the promise of full marital reconciliation upon repentance; then it's as if that person is denying salvation to the guilty; since marriage is a picture of salvation. The most degrading event occurs when the innocent partner sues by the false doctrine of divorce, and then the innocent partner remarries under the Law. The debauchery here is that the new marriage is adultery, and any children born to this marriage are unholy.

The greatest sin in the marriage discussion is actually caused by the false teachers who are leading millions into darkness and apostasy. Let me explain. When a pastor counsels a person away from permanency-marriage, and pontificates that their marriage can be put asunder, for what he decides is a so-called legitimate reason and approves remarriage he is leading that person into apostasy. Any act of sexual intercourse for a married person with someone other than their living spouse is adultery. Divorce in other words for a married couple is impossible. By advising toward divorce with remarriage the false teacher is leading his hearers into apostasy, the falling away from the truth. The Scriptures declare that the latter day apostasy will be marked by marriage divorcers (covenant breakers, trucebreakers): "This know also, that in the last days perilous times shall come. For men shall be lovers of their own selves, covetous, boasters, proud, blasphemers, disobedient to parents, unthankful, unholy, without natural affection, trucebreakers [given to marital divorce, my comment] II Tim. 3:3)."

So, these false teachers enter the world of apostates themselves. Notice what they have managed to pull off—a vernacular term meaning to deceive. They have taken a clean holy vessel—a spouse who never committed adultery—and have led that spouse directly into an adulterous union and have accomplished even a greater feat; they have called the unholy act of adultery, holy matrimony. It is as if they are saying to the spouse: Go, the church blesses your holy-adultery. The crime here is enlarged since now the spouse is trapped into the bonds of sin without the immediate opportunity to repent and be forgiven; because they believe they are holy; or to others, that they have no need to repent and get saved. They willfully sin without any knowledge of their sin. This is apostasy.

Salvation sola gratia assures sinners that by repentance and faith they are saved; "For by grace are ye saved through faith; and that not of yourselves: it is the gift of God: Not of works, lest any man should boast; and the goodness of God leadeth thee to repentance." The false teacher's doctrine slaps sola gratia in the face. By teaching holy-adultery they have created an act whereby the sinner is at liberty to willfully sin and live comfortably—especially in the church—in a state of mind whereby they believe they are righteous. This is an affront to the Gospel—excluding the sin of adulter- ous-remarriage from the act of repentance—now the sinner cannot be forgiven because they do not know they are living in sin; and therefore, they will never repent. It is the same as teaching any sinner: homosexual, thief, drug addict, murderer, etc. that they do not have to repent and depart from their sin to be forgiven; to be saved. This is debauchery and apostasy; for certain. "Woe unto them that call evil good, and good evil; that put darkness for light, and light for darkness" (Isa. 5:20a).

> That he might sanctify and cleanse it with the washing of water by the word, that he might present it to himself a glorious church, not having spot, or wrinkle, or any such thing; but that it should be holy and without blemish. *Eph. 5:26, 27*

The husband is also called upon not only to prepare to die for his spouse but to live for her. He is to labor with her to make her beautiful and glorious, i.e. without the blemish of any sin. He must be determined to teach her or assure that she is taught the truth of the Scriptures that she may be spiritually clean not having any spot or wrinkle of sin. She can only be glorious if she is steeped in the Word. The couple should have a living dialogue with the Scriptures.

> So ought men to love their wives as their own bodies. He that loveth his wife loveth himself. For no man ever yet hated his own flesh; but nourisheth and cherisheth it, even as the Lord the church: For we are members of his body, of his flesh, and of his bones. *Eph. 5:28-30*

The man is again commanded to love his wife. The Lord expects men to love their wives as they love themselves. Most men savor food, and consequently most men love to nourish themselves with good food. American men generally prefer beef to fish; so, the landscape is littered with burger and steak restaurants. One might say men love grilled steak and hate boiled fish. The man's appetite is addressed here as proof that he nourisheth himself, because he loveth himself. We might go one step further and say that because man loveth himself he cherisheth a grilled medium rare rib eye steak, and he hateth boiled fish. Men are very happy and with joy eat the steak. This is the joy he should have in loving his wife, cherishing his wife as Christ cherisheth His church. Then Paul expands his teaching on the doctrine of permanency-marriage, stating that believers are members of Christ's body. We, the believers, "are" one with Christ; as Adam said, "This is now bone of my bones, and flesh of my flesh."

> For this cause shall a man leave his father and mother, and shall be joined unto his wife, and they two shall be one flesh. This is a great mystery: but I speak concerning Christ and the church. *Eph. 5:31, 32*

Here we find creation-marriage glorified in the doctrine of the body of Christ, the church. This is marriage; "a man shall cleave unto his wife: and they shall be one flesh." This speaks of permanency, and the permanency of the church is spelled Eternal Security. Creation-Marriage is permanent, and Heaven-Marriage is permanent. Salvation, the blessing of the church, is a heavenly marriage with Christ, "Blessed be the God and Father of our Lord Jesus Christ, who hath blessed us with all spiritual blessings in heavenly places in Christ" (Eph. 1:3). As is heavenly-marriage, so is creation-marriage they are both permanent, as God's words declare. Paul concludes the matter,"This is a great mystery: but I speak concerning Christ and the church." What more can I say!

Problem: When the Church Endorses Remarriage After Divorce

In the introduction I stated that those who teach divorce-remarriage have insulted the Gospel: The Doctrine of Salvation by Grace. The real problem is that divorce-remarriage is a picture of the Law; a gospel of Works. Permanency-marriage is a picture of Faith a symbol of the Gospel of Grace, as pictured in Ephesians. The simple point is this: When preaching the Gospel, one cannot mix Law and Grace. They just don't mix; like water and oil. In chemistry this resistance to mix is stated: these two liquids are not soluble; incapable of mixing or blending together. The entire concept of divorce in marriage is based on legalism, i.e. someone has broken the Law of Adultery, and therefore they must be punished by the righteousness of the Law: they must be expelled. This particular idea of punishment was derived from the Mosaic Law which stated that when adultery occurs; the innocent party must exercise the Law and that the two guilty partners must suffer the punishment of the death penalty.

Historically the Protestant Church had difficulty finding a way to permit, divorce and remarriage, to be practiced in the Reformation Church—a church which believed in salvation Sola Gratia (by grace alone). In 1648 the Church promulgated the decree that permitted divorce and remarriage; this was done in the Westminster Confession. (This Church rule is with us to this day). The rule was very unusual because for divorce and remarriage to be justified the Church had to build their doctrine on a fantasy of the Law. Read here the fantasy:

> Adultery or fornication committed after a contract [engagement], being detected before marriage, giveth just occasion to the innocent party to dissolve that contract. In the case of adultery after marriage, it is lawful for the innocent party to sue out a divorce, and after the divorce to marry another, as if the offending party were dead.[238]

Now that is a nice fantasy, but the fact is the guilty spouse is still alive, and the adultery has not been interrupted; it has not ceased. So, what did the Church accomplish? Nothing! The guilty spouse was to be considered "dead." Considered dead; what does that mean?—That was the only condition that permitted the Westminster Confession of divorce and remarriage to be promulgated; because the Word of God had no other punishment for adultery but the death penalty. Therefore, since the only way for God to accept remarriage is on the basis of a death of the guilty partner; the Westminster Confession proposes this foolish fantasy-of-a-dead-man. That is a pure imaginative dream, a fantastic pipe dream. Remember the doctrine of creation-marriage is universal, and therefore, it involves every single man and woman who ever existed since Christ; and all those whoever will be born into this world. The world is drowning in the sin of divorce-remarriage; as it is drowning in the murder of our innocent children in the sea of Abortion.

The Church, therefore, cannot permit divorce and remarriage. To do so it must exercise the Law. The Law is not Grace; they are insoluble. Thus, all marriages which the Church permits, where one or both of the spouses have another living partner from a previous marriage, has the Church endorsing and permitting that couple to

---

[238] The Constitution of the Presbyterian Church, (1915) Ch. XXIV Sec. V

live in open and continuous adultery. Whether the couple are saved, or unsaved the union is the same: continuous adultery. The Gospel of Jesus Christ is also insoluble with certain things; one of those things is adultery. The Gospel does not mix with adultery. Period! Adultery is actually an adversary to the Gospel. When they truly meet only one of the two are left standing, and I will assure you that the one still standing is not: adultery.

Therefore, if the church is comfortably housing adulterous-marriages—as Augustine calls them—that church is not preaching the Gospel of Grace. The only way to permit adulterous-marriages is to preach the Law. As both John the Baptist, and Jesus have proved the preaching of the Gospel and adulterous-marriage do not mix.

When the Gospel is preached it convicts of sin, and the act of continuous-adultery in the light of the Gospel must cease. Cease through repentance, and then putting one's faith in the vicarious atonement of our Savior the Lord Jesus Christ. The only way to permit continuous-adulterous-remarriage in the Church is for that Church to silence the Gospel by preaching the works of the Law. That's impossible. The Law and the Gospel cannot stand together. To preach the Law is anathema; it is just another false gospel. One must ask: Does this fantasy of a dead spouse doctrine preach salvation by Grace? After all, Grace is the only Gospel we have. "Ye are saved by Grace through faith—it is the gift of God—Not of works, least any man should boast.

Again: Does this fantasy dead man doctrine preach Sola Gratia? Certainly not! If your doctrine of divorce puts the sinning partner outside the realm of God's Grace, i.e. that the marriage can never be saved, reconciled, restored, you are teaching a doctrine that is anathema to the Gospel of Christ. If you believe that divorce can end any creation-marriage, i.e. any-first-marriage-this-side-of-death, then you have a conflicting belief with the Gospel of Salvation taught by the Lord Jesus Christ. The Salvation of God is by grace through faith and not of works. Our marriage to Christ is a great mystery (Eph. 5); it is an analogy of our salvation by the grace of God and His Son Jesus Christ. Oh, so Great Salvation! The very meaning of the word Salvation teaches perfect safety. Should the child of God, commit some sin, and depart from the Lord and Savior Jesus Christ for a season, we can be assured that He will never leave us or forsake us. He will never divorce you or me. He will never divorce any believer and no man shall pluck us out of His hand. He will wait your return, or may let you sleep, i.e. He may permit your early death (the sin unto death). The Apostle Paul counseled the innocent partner to peacefully wait for the return of the sinning partner: "For what knowest thou, O wife, whether thou shalt save thy husband? or how knowest thou, O man, whether thou shalt save thy wife?" If any creation-marriage can be put asunder then the Salvation of God; Christ's marriage to the believer ("For we are members of his body") can be put asunder. The divorce doctrine teaches that the Salvation of God can be lost because of sinful works, and if that is the case, you are confessing to a doctrine that you obviously gained your Salvation—your marriage to Christ— by good works. If one believes they can loose Salvation by evil works, then you believe that you can gain Salvation by good works. You cannot have it both ways: "What therefore God hath joined together, let not man put asunder." Only Legalism teaches divorce. The foundation of divorce is the Law. The foundation of permanency-marriage is Grace; it completely contradicts the Law to the minutest degree—to the nth degree.

Conclusion

Well, after this lengthy discussion of divorce we have finally reached the end of the road. The immense volume of literature which this subject has generated raises a serious question: Why all this literature? The answer is simple: men refuse to believe that God created marriage as a permanent organic union; till death do us part. The weight of Scripture, conscience, and nature teach man that marriage is permanent, i.e. a literal band of God. The literature is the result of man's feeble attempt to break God's bands asunder (Psa. 2:3) "Let us break their bands asunder", and God said, "Let not man put asunder;" nevertheless man believes he has found an obscure exception clause to rend God's prohibition, His band. But as I have labored to reveal, the obscure exception clause in the hands of man has become a deception-clause. This single fact has created the massive volume of historical literature on the subject of divorce. I have applied the rule of Scripture; that in the presence of an obscure text one should permit: "Scripture to interpret Scripture." I believe Scripture teaches that divorce is not even a possibility; it is non-existent in the teaching of Christ regarding marriage. You can be assured dear believer, as God said, "I hate putting away" (Mal. 2:16), be assured that Christ will never divorce me, and he will never divorce you. Jesus just does not teach divorce; to Him it is a mere figment of man's imagination, a pipe dream, and the invention of the Prince of Darkness, the Devil. But Christ is the Prince of Light, and He has faithfully promised each believer an eternal union with God the Father through Him and this union is indissoluble and eternally permanent.

> These words spake Jesus, and lifted up his eyes to heaven, and said, Father, the hour is come; glorify thy Son, that thy Son also may glorify thee As thou hast given him power over all flesh, that he should give eternal life [He will never take it back, my comment] to as many as thou hast given him. And this is life eternal, that they might know thee the only true God, and Jesus Christ, whom thou hast sent. *(Jn. 17:1-3)*
> Neither pray I for these alone, but for them also which shall believe on me through their word; That they all may be one; as thou, Father, art in me, and I in thee, that they also may be one in us [as in marriage: they twain shall be one, my comment]: that the world may believe that thou hast sent me. And the glory which thou gavest me I have given them; that they may be one, even as we are one: I in them, and thou in me, that they may be made perfect in one [marriage a type of the believer in the body of Christ, my comment]; and that the world may know that thou hast sent me, and hast loved them, as thou hast loved me. Father, I will that they also, whom

thou hast given me, be with me where I am; that they may behold my glory, which thou hast given me: for thou lovedst me before the foundation of the world. *Jn. 17:20-24*

We have eternal life, eternal security, in Christ, "For God so loved the world that he gave his only begotten son, that whosoever believeth in him should not perish but have everlasting life; For he that believeth on the Son hath everlasting life; He that hath the Son hath life. My sheep hear my voice, and I know them, and they follow me: And I give unto them eternal life; and they shall never perish, neither shall any man pluck them out of my hand. My Father, which gave them me, is greater than all; and no man is able to pluck them out of my Father's hand. I and my Father are one. The great mystery of being one with Christ, is salvation. Oh, how great salvation! Our heavenly marriage to Christ is everlasting. And dear born-again reader, if you in some way believe that you have departed from Christ and his doctrine, be assured that if yo repent and return to Him, He will receive you with open arms for Jesus said, Come unto me, all ye that labor and are heavy laden, and I will give you rest. He is a faithful husband that is still waiting by home's door since the day you left him. He is ready to receive you back into his arms.

And dear reader if you have never found repentance and faith unto eternal life I invite you today to turn from sin to God, and come unto Jesus the only true God and Savior and believe in Him for your salvation which he purchased with His own precious blood on the old rugged cross. "I Jesus have sent mine angel to testify unto you these things in the churches. I am the root and the offspring of David, and the bright and morning star. And the Spirit and the bride say, Come. And let him that heareth say, Come. And let him that is athirst come. And whosoever will, let him take the water of life freely" (Rev. 22:16-17). Jesus promises you eternal life, that is absolute everlasting life, and Jesus is not a liar, His word is sure and everlasting; heaven and earth shall pass away, but His word endureth forever, and so will you if you trust in Him. He will never divorce you, for that I am sure.

The most important subject in the divorce debate is the subject of Salvation by Grace. The sinning partner must be offered salvation; the fornicator of (I Cor. 5) eventually repented and was received back into the church of Corinth (II Cor. 2). Creation Marriage is an illustration of Salvation. Salvation is permanent, and for that reason Marriage is permanent. Divorced from Christ cannot be; so divorce does not fit into the married person's life. Therefore, if divorce is forbidden then the ABOMINATION of (Deut. 24:1-4) cannot be committed today; because all other liaisons of a married spouse (including remarriage) are simply adulterous, and that is the ABOMINATION today. To break a so-called state legal second marriage (an adulterous-marriage) is not a divorce, it is just the breaking of a man-made legal contract; that is all. Keep that in mind if you should so seek reunion with a divorced creation-marriage spouse. Furthermore, the concept of the abomination has been over-ruled to the permanency believer since Jehovah God himself told His sinning wife Israel to return to Him (Jer.3:1). The reason God could justly take Israel back as His wife in purity was only because God never put her away; God never endorsed, and never will endorse divorce. The divorce that Israel experienced was only an illustration, a metaphor. Jehovah God hateth putting away; He hateth divorce. Creation-Marriage is a type or picture of Salvation it speaks of eternal life with eternal security; for by Grace are ye saved by faith.

Final Comment

Consider the possibility of the judgment of Western Civilization, likened to the Judgment of the Flood and Sodom; and the violence of measure today would be man's violent treatment of God's ordained command regarding creation-marriage; then as we look about our once Christian America—especially the Bible believing church—and the other Christian countries of the West, the state of creation-marriage is quickly collapsing, thus we can say the next Day of Judgment draweth swiftly nigh. Yes, as mentioned in the "Introduction" of this book, "The fate of marriage and perhaps the fate of mankind may depend on your interpretation of those five words: "except it be for fornication." As the second Psalm directs: Kiss the Son, least He be angry, and perish from the way, When His wrath is kindled but a little. Blessed are all they that put their trust in Him; and note that adulterers will not inherit the Kingdom of God.

> *"Grace be with all them that love our Lord*
> *Jesus Christ in sincerity. Amen."*

www.ingramcontent.com/pod-product-compliance
Lightning Source LLC
Chambersburg PA
CBHW051132120626
46547CB00012B/773